M
Connection Method

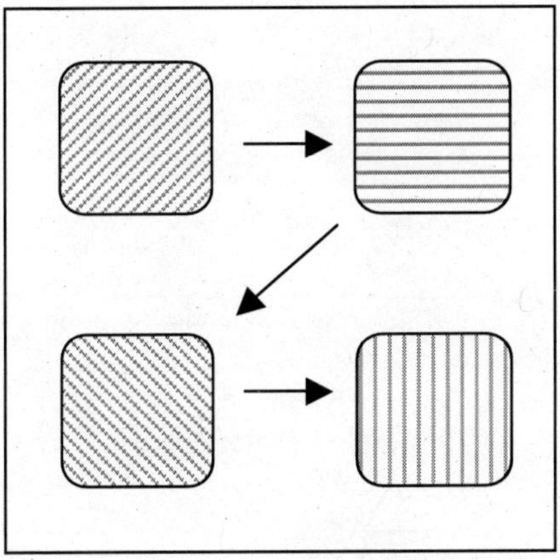

A Practical Guide Toward Cultivating Nurturing Relationships

o o o

Ivan Tucakov

KAMANALA PUBLISHING

Kamanala Publishing

First Edition, April 2010

Cover design: Ivan Tucakov
Photo: Michael Cound
Editing: Samantha Gray,
Tara Newstead, Owen Thomas, Nikola Tucakov
Interior design: Ivan Tucakov
Typography: Ivan Tucakov
Artwork and digital design: Ivan Tucakov

This publication may be purchased for
educational, business or sales promotional use.
This publication is also available online at
www.MindfulConnectionMethod.com
Contact:
info@mindfulconnectionmethod.com

Library and Archives Canada Cataloguing in Publication

Tucakov, Ivan, 1978-
Mindful connection method : a practical guide toward cultivating nurturing relationships / Ivan Tucakov.

Includes bibliographical references.
Also available in electronic format.
ISBN 978-0-9865199-0-1

1. Interpersonal relations. I. Title.

BF637.C45T834 2010 158.2 C2010-902074-X

Printed in Canada on FSC certified
100% post-consumer waste recycled paper

10 9 8 7 6 5 4 3 2 1

Mindful Connection Method

INTRODUCTION

The *Mindful Connection Method* presented in this book is a synthesis of multiple communication theories, diverse cultural experiences, education and personal research I gathered over many years. My aim is to strategically organize an effective method that is very practical and easy to implement and enables one to know where to focus when connecting to others, especially when emotionally overwhelmed or confused. I love connection. It inspires and grounds me. Seeing connection between people brings me joy and I write about it because I want to see more of it in the world and because I want to learn to communicate and connect well myself.

As a young boy, I observed adults go from heated arguments to joyfully sharing each other's company. I would marvel at the changes in these dynamics and wonder how the intense and harsh arguments would affect people's connection and how after times of discord they could cycle back to connection again. At times I would be scared and unsure whom to trust and other times people's kindness would leave me encouraged and assured. I was compelled to understand the different ways people relate and how the various approaches people took to reach out to others could create significantly different results.

Starting in early childhood I learned and used three different languages, one per decade, lived on three different continents and immersed myself in three unique cultures. This experience of being reared in culturally varying places with secure family values of my mother, father, grandmother and my brothers enabled me to see that, although cultural differences do exist in the way that people relate, there is a fundamental human need for nurturing connection; all human beings, no matter where they are from, long to be in authentic relationships. From this early experience, I realized that connection could be nurtured cross-culturally, despite dissimilarities.

In addition to having a culturally diverse upbringing, I have a twin brother. We have always had a world unto ourselves where we developed a deep sense of sharing and giving. When we were young we even created our own language. After years of this level of intimacy and deep understanding with my brother, reaching out to the world around me became a difficult undertaking as the response I received from others often significantly differed from what I was used to experiencing in my interactions with my brother. Naturally, I had many struggles and challenges in my attempts to connect to others throughout my life. These difficulties have in themselves supported and encouraged me to learn and grow. The resolution of these same difficulties has compelled me to share my discoveries.

Having had a thorough education in science, I've never grown tired of asking how and why something works (or doesn't) and this curiosity has largely influenced and led to the creation and shaping of this method. Throughout my education, I learned numerous computer-programming languages that influenced me to think in systematic ways. Algorithms used in computer science have led the flow of concepts used in the communication method presented here.

As a musician, I have played and explored the language of music through most of my life. I have come to realize that music can be appreciated both in an intellectual and emotional level. As we communicate with each other in this way as well, this notion has fundamentally contributed to the creation and structural shaping of this method.

While in university I created a self-directed student course on the topic of awareness. This experience provided me with further opportunity to research and study a variety of communication theories and was a turning point in starting to fully explore and put all these theories directly into practice. Close connections with friends who had similar interests and with whom I could explore these theories in length have also been pivotal. As a leader of a world music act, which in itself combines various cultural influences, I have had the role of a booking agent, employer, supervisor, road manager and promoter for more than five years, where I've systematically implemented and tested all my ideas and acquired many connection skills.

The result of all these endeavors is the *Mindful Connection Method.* As the title suggests, it involves *Mindfulness*, which is the ability to focus and stay focused on a specific area in one's life. This *Method* is basically a form of a universal, "cross-cultural" language in itself, organized in a way where its main goal is to empathically *Connect* to oneself and others.

It *is* possible to connect with people you have had painful struggles with. It *is* possible to repair years of disconnection and still be loving and understanding despite difficult circumstances. This book aims to cast a light on those difficulties in life and show that it *is* possible to create nurturing connection in their place. I hold a strong dedication to give back after what has been so graciously given to me throughout the years. The process of writing this book has bestowed me with immeasurable growth and connections; I humbly offer it as a guide towards continuous learning and a life of even more connection and fulfillment.

Ivan Tucakov

HOW TO GET THE MOST OUT OF THIS BOOK

BE SYSTEMATIC

Mindful Connection Method is a collection of tools that you can learn and use strategically in a given moment, know how to go to the next step and at times take steps back. They are grouped and broken down in a way where you can use the broad and simple concepts in regular conversation or you can go deeper and more elaborate into each concept in times of bigger challenges. Some people naturally respond to methodical books, others might want to take this as an opportunity to try out a systematic way of learning. You can also think of it as learning a new language.

EXPLORE

The book won't tell you what exactly to do; you can use it as a "map" to find your way; it also gives examples to illustrate different skills and practices to do and learn from. You need to explore, look within, and find ways that work best for you to create connections in your life. Every connection is as unique as the people involved in creating it.

PRACTICE

Just like any skill requires months and years to master, the skill of connection is the same. This book is not a "quick fix" for problems. You need to accumulate many hours of practice before it becomes second nature. Think of someone you know who is extremely skilled with something and how long it took her to get to that level of expertise. Repetition is one of the best ways to absorb knowledge well and turn practice into "second nature" behavior. There are many tools and lots of information. Take time with it all and be patient. It is a good idea to revisit Chapters few times. Although skills take time to develop, progress from practice can usually be seen immediately. This is also intended to be a practical book rather than a philosophical one.

LEARN TO FALL!

And yes, please do challenge yourself and learn to cultivate courage; one can only learn to walk by falling, getting up and keep trying. You can find out what works by finding out what doesn't work. As educational leader Ken Robinson says, *"you need to take chances; if you don't know something, you just have a go at it, you build the courage to 'be wrong' and 'make mistakes'".*[1] Unless you nurture the creative capacity that you were innately born with, you can lose it. As long as the goal is to connect with others, every challenge you take gets you closer to understanding and creating that connection.

CHAPTER ONE

MINDFUL CONNECTION IN YOUR COMMUNITY

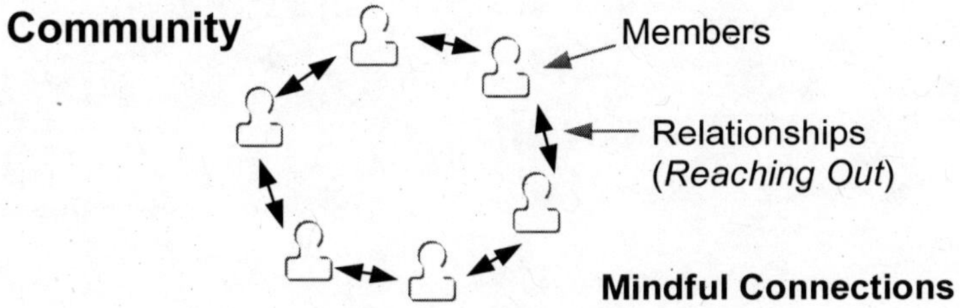

Consider a community that you live in. Community members are your immediate and extended family, spouses, partners, children, close friends, acquaintances, neighbors, society at large *and* yourself. Community members reach out to each other. *Reaching out* is any attempt a person makes to emotionally connect with another person and express a need of sorts. It could be a look a parent gives to a child, a smile from a stranger or gestures and interactions of any sort. *Reaching out* can even include unfriendly or hostile approaches, when people express their unmet needs and non-joyous feelings. *Reaching out* is a fundamental unit of emotional connection.[i] It is the building block for cultivating relationships between people.

Mindful Connection is when you aim to *connect* to a person that reaches out to you, while honoring and respecting yourself and also reaching out back in a way that makes it easy and inviting for her to connect back to you. The main aspect of this way of connecting is curiosity with the willingness and goal to listen and give empathy. This creates a balanced harmony amongst people in a community, a place where people focus on maintaining relationships and caringly attend to one another toward creating more nurturance. When your aim is to connect to another person, you can achieve remarkable connection even in challenging situations.

This *is* the goal of this book, to explore and acquire the tools to *Mindfully Connect* with other people and to make this a more consistent outcome in your everyday interactions. It is a nurturing way to cultivate possibilities toward getting your and other people's needs met.

---

[i] Note: Psychologist John Gottman defined this "unit emotional connection" as a "bid". I will use the expression "reaching out" when referring to "bidding" throughout the book.

TEACHER AND FOUR STUDENTS

Let's take a few community members as an example. Imagine a classroom with four students and a teacher.

THE TEACHER

The teacher loves to teach his students and while doing so, he tends to raise his tone of voice when he gets really excited about a concept or an idea.

During their class yesterday, all four students noticed the teacher's raised voice and all of them reacted very differently. Here is how it was for each one of them.

FREDDIE FEELS

Freddie Feels wears his heart on his sleeve. He is always takes the occasion to display how he feels and makes sure to take care of himself when things become too overwhelming.

When the teacher shouted while teaching, *Freddie Feels* got really scared and was too overwhelmed to do anything, especially continue the lesson. He asked to leave the class for a bit, where he could feel more at ease.

SADIE SOLVES

Sadie Solves is a girl that springs into action and solves any problem that comes her way. She stays very settled, un-triggered and is very keen to find out what's best to do in a given moment to meet her needs.

When the teacher raised his voice, she went and sat further away from the teacher so that his voice wouldn't be as loud and she continued paying attention to the lecture. If the problem were to persist, she would find alternative plans not to be affected by the teacher's loud voice: she would ask him to speak more quietly or decide to start bringing earplugs to class.

LISA LISTENS

Lisa Listens not only emotionally holds her ground but also can also easily attune to what others are going through. She likes to connect with people.

During the class, when she noticed that the teacher was talking loudly, she asked the teacher how he was doing and was very attentive to whatever he said. She was not overwhelmed and was interested in the lecture besides wanting to connect with what was going on for him.

ANDY ADVISES

Andy Advises enjoys offering other people to explore their problems together and support them in getting their needs met.

He offered to support the teacher in finding ways to resolve his struggle. They explored what the teacher could do around his tone of voice in order to have a constructive class. *Andy Advises* would even be interested advising *Freddie Feels* to successfully deal with the teacher's loud voice.

You might recognize yourself in some of these students. Some of their ways might seem very familiar and appealing yet some might look uninviting or even intimidating.

What all these students have in common is that each of their ways of acting and reacting complete the full picture toward building *Mindful Connections.* There is a time and place for each one.

I use members of this class throughout the book to explore various connection tools and methods toward creating *Mindful Connection* between them. I dedicate a Chapter to individually explore each of the character's ways of responding to the teacher including a Practice Section at the end of the book.

You have the opportunity to put yourself in each of these students' shoes, learn to face your fears and take on the adventure of building *Mindful Connection* with others and yourself.

Lets start the journey.

EMPATHY AND RESOLUTION FIELDS

In a nurturing community, all members have methods and ways of reaching out to cultivate *Mindful Connection* in relationships. They can be categorized into two fields: *Empathy Field* and *Resolution Field.*

EMPATHY FIELD

Empathy Field involves any action that you take toward creating empathy and focusing on what is emotionally going on for yourself or another person.

The basic purpose of the Empathy Field is to *identify met and unmet needs by attuning to all the feelings (both joyous and non-joyous).* Attuning is when one puts one's attention and is conscious, accepting and resonating with of one's bodily sensations and emotional states. You need to stay present to these until you or the person you are supporting feels at ease and grounded and in the process determine one's met and unmet needs. This will set grounds to building resilience and creating wellbeing.

Feelings ⟺ Needs

EMPATHY

Empathy, as the building block of the Empathy Field, is the capability to attend and be fully and unconditionally present to someone's internal state of being.

Buddhism has its own name for empathy. They call it Nying-je.[2] As The Buddhist spiritual teacher Dalai Lama explains, besides having a *regular emotional component* (affection, kindness, warm-heartedness, etc), empathy also has a more developed *cognitive emotional component* that involves rationality, such as acting out of concern for others based on reason.

Some great work on empathy comes from the psychologist Marshall Rosenberg.[3] He says that when you empathize, you are "not home"; you are "with the other person" and you are fully present and resonating with the feelings of that person. You "empty your mind" and listen to others or yourself with your whole being. Empathy happens during moments of silence in between talking and even thinking; it in itself has no words.

Biologist Frans de Waal demonstrates that empathy comes naturally to humans and that we are actually "preprogrammed to reach out."[4]

Psychiatrist Daniel Siegel describes empathy as a process of gathering insight about another person's feelings and imagining what's going for him through brain circuits called *mirror neurons.*[5] Mirror neurons help the development of empathy through the process of imitation.

Theory of Mind is a theory in which one has the ability to have an understanding that others have their own awareness and perceptions that are different form one's own[6]. It defines empathy as experiential recognition and understanding of different states of mind.

EMPATHIC CONNECTION

Empathic connection is a process where one attunes to one's own feelings and identifies one's needs.[7] *Empathizing* is when one empathically connects to another person's feelings and resonates with them. This is not just recognizing emotions but actively resonating with them and there are two ways of resonating: "identical" or "reactive". "Identical" resonance is when one feels exactly the same feelings, whereas "reactive" is when different feelings are aroused from the original feelings. These various reactive feelings can stimulate three different types of responses people can have.

The first response is the attempt to *connect* with the other person, which this book aims to cultivate. This response is instigated when concern, worry and related feelings are aroused. Other two ways of reacting are feelings like disgust and anger (which stimulates the person to attack and get aggressive with the other person) and feelings like indifference or fear (which can get the person to ignore and avoid the other person's emotional state). These three different ways of approaching (connecting, attacking and ignoring) are explored in more detail throughout the upcoming chapters.

You can empathically connect with yourself on your own or with someone who can offer you support. It is even possible to empathically connect by listening to or observing someone else receive empathy. If that person's story and situation is similar to yours, it could easily arouse feelings in you because of the presence of *mirror neurons.* The process of relieving one's own suffering by supporting another person creates interdependence.

RESOLUTION FIELD

Resolution Field is about any action that takes you toward focusing on rational thinking, logical inference and taking conscious, responsible and real action. It is about focusing on what can be done about a situation and acting on it.

The basic purpose of the Resolution Field is to maintain the met needs identified in the Empathy Field and to aim toward getting the identified unmet needs met. Doing this sustains the joyous feelings, resolves one's non-joyous feelings, builds resilience and creates wellbeing.

Needs ⇒ Wellbeing

Rational thinking, as the building block of the Resolution Field, is defined as mental clarity or sound judgment. As you find out in this book, attending to the Empathy Field facilitates this clarity by emotionally un-flooding and identifying one's own needs. Feelings once fully felt and attuned to, support rational judgment since they help the brain be focused on the critical information. Without them, the information would be incomplete or ambiguous when making real-life judgments.[8]

Being irrational would mean that one is thinking without having mental clarity and sound judgment, which is a result of just being overwhelmed with emotion, not properly having attuned to the feelings and unaware of the present needs. This can get the person into a "cognitive dissonance", [9] which is a state of tension that happens when one holds two psychologically inconsistent or contradictory beliefs or behaviors that get people to be irrational and succumb to self-justification.

For example, if someone makes an extremely important decision and realizes that the decision was a result of poor planning and got many needs unmet, the person might end up creating a belief that her decision was the best possible strategy and had the best possible outcome. Unless a person who's emotionally overwhelmed doesn't attend to the Empathy Field, she can continue to think irrationally and be in the state of "cognitive dissonance".

Logical inference is a result of rational thinking. It comes from making clear observations and then further making deductions and conclusions based on those observations. By attending to the Resolution Field with the support of the Empathy Field, you develop rational thinking and logical inference.

One easy way to understand the Empathy and Resolution Fields concept is to imagine yourself in a challenging conversation. You have the possibility to choose to either focus your attention on one's emotions or one's thoughts. The "Empathy Field" would represent emotions that "come from the heart" and the "Resolution Field" is about thoughts that "come from the head". Emotions are about attuning to feelings and determining one's met and unmet needs while thoughts help find strategies to maintain and get those needs met.

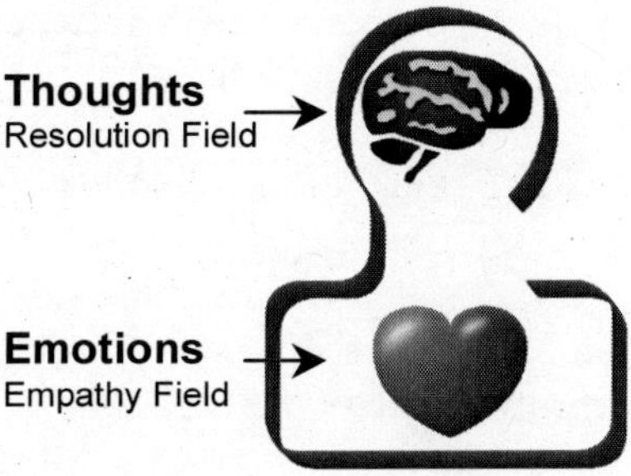

More descriptions of Empathy and Resolution Fields in various doctrines that involve topics of communication and connection

 Empathy Field	 Resolution Field	Mindful Connection Method
Empathy	Reason	Buddhism – Nying-je[10]
Emotional/Empathic	Cognitive	Neuroscience
Empathy	Strategy	Dr. Marshall Rosenberg[11]
Consideration - Angel of Comfort – Home Base	Agent of Futility – Compass Point	Dr. Gordon Neufeld[12]
Empathy	Responsibility	Dr. George Lakoff[13]
Experiencing Self	Remembering Self	Dr. Daniel Kahneman[14]
Listening	Assertion	Dr. Robert Bolton[15]
Feeling	Thinking	Dr. Carl Gustav Jung[16]
Unconditional Mother Love	Conditional Father Love	Dr. Erich Fromm[17]
Feminine Energy	Masculine Energy	
Yin	Yang	
React	Act	
Receiving	Giving	
Subjective	Objective	
Emotional	Rational	
Heart	Mind	
Left	Right	

Note that as much as this table makes a clear division between the two concepts, it in no way suggests that these terms are completely isolated and unrelated to one another. In fact, they are quite co-dependent and mutually sustaining of one-another. Recall that Empathy Field is sort of a barometer to let the Resolution Field know if needs need to get met by attuning to one's feelings. In a way, the Empathy Field guides Resolution Field, and the Resolution Field in turn fulfills the Empathy Field.

Neurologist Antonio R. Damasio[18] explores this inter-relation further in his book "Descartes' Error" by challenging the dualist separation worldview. He proposes that one's reason and behavior is shaped and guided by his emotions, and on the other hand, one needs to have "cognition" and senses to develop emotionally.

MINDFULNESS, LOVE AND COMPASSION

The concept of *Mindfulness* (or *Attunement*) plays a central role in this book and can be practiced in a few different ways. One is through the practice of meditation, which is practiced by becoming at ease and relaxed, focusing on breath and body sensations, sounds, images and accepting them as they are, without evaluating and judging. Mindfulness can also be practiced at any time in daily life by simply recognizing what is happening in the present moment. Any activity that you do mindfully is some form of meditation. Doing all this develops the part of the brain called pre-frontal cortex, which is largely responsible for your ability to maintain awareness and attention in specific areas in your life.[19].

As this book deals with practical and effective ways of communicating and connecting with oneself and others, applying mindfulness onto the Empathy and Resolution Fields is of great and essential value. Through mindfulness, you can focus on your emotional states and the body sensations (in the Empathy Field) and your thoughts and actions (in the Resolution Field) without identifying with and getting randomly caught up in them. The goal is to practice being present, attuned to and simply aware of these two Fields. This helps with attuning to feelings, problem solving, planning complex cognitive behaviors, decision making, moderating correct social behavior and intending to get your needs and those of others met.

Although the basic aim is to transform non-joyous feelings into joyous ones, it is the process that is more important than the destination. By attuning and going through the non-joyous feelings you grow and this is a life-long process. The reality is that you will always have non-joyous feelings in your life accompanied with unmet needs. It is not possible to have a life filled with constant joy and constantly met needs. At the same time, it is unhealthy to have a life of chronic suffering with unmet needs. Feelings are transient yet needs are invariable and *Mindful Connection* assists you in identifying and getting needs met through attuning to current feelings.

From a practical stand view and by stepping away from being philosophical, I would describe the concept of Love and being loving as the act of meeting one's own needs *and* the needs of others. Compassion is in essence the process of *Mindful Connection* and going through the Empathy and Resolution Fields. By attuning to your own feelings and those of others and by identifying your *and* other people's needs with the aim of getting them met, you are being compassionate and actively creating more Love in the world. Mother Teresa referred to compassion as *"Love in action"*.

YOURSELF AND ANOTHER PERSON

Having overviewed the two Fields the community members can focus on toward creating *Mindful Connection*, let's have a look at the members themselves. You can focus either on *yourself* or *another person*.

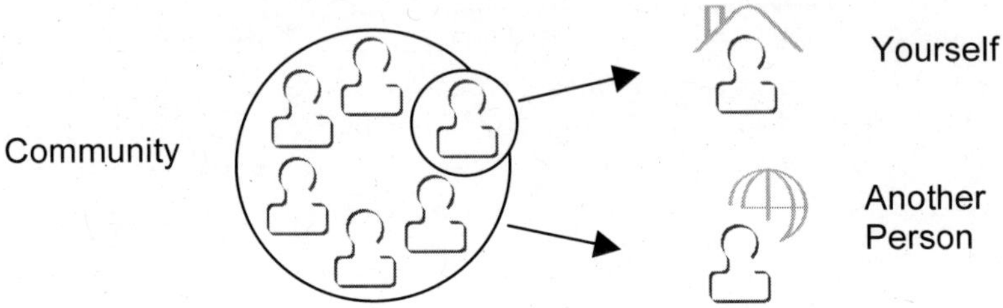

YOURSELF

Focusing on Yourself is when you give attention to the physical and emotional internal state you are experiencing in a certain moment; you identify your met and unmet needs and find resolutions and act towards getting those needs met.
Freddie Feels and *Sadie Solves* both focus on themselves.

ANOTHER PERSON

Focusing on another person is when you give attention to the physical and emotional internal state that *another person* is experiencing in a certain moment; you attune to that person's feelings in order to support her in identifying her met and unmet needs so that she can find resolutions and act towards getting those needs met. The important part is that the focus is not you.

Note that the concept of another person can imply one or more people or a whole society, all which are community members. If possible, you want to focus on one person at a time although it is possible to focus successfully onto groups as well. Note also that your interactions, connections and relationships are different with every person or a group of people that you interact with.
Lisa Listens and *Andy Advises* both focus on other people.

FOUR FIELDS OF MINDFUL CONNECTION

Each person that you connect to (including yourself) has Empathy and Resolution Field to focus on. This creates four different Fields one can Focus on at a given time: Empathy and Resolution Fields for oneself and Empathy and Resolution Fields for another person.

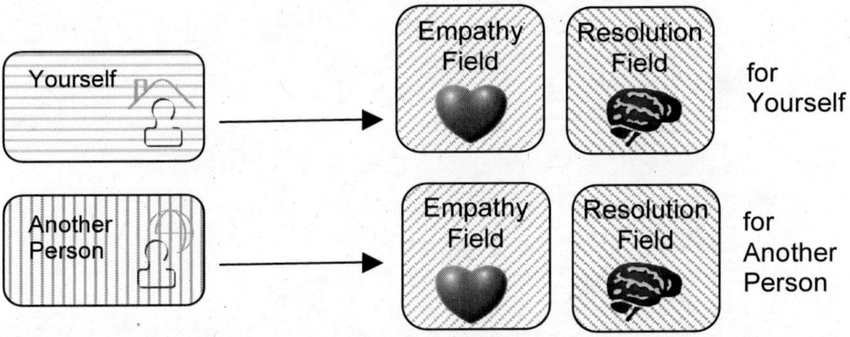

I call these Fields the **“Four Fields of Mindful Connection”**.
In our Example with the loud speaking teacher, each one of our students focused on one of these fields:

#1 - *Freddie Feels* focuses on the first Field:
“Empathy Field for Yourself“

#2 - *Sadie Solves* focuses on the second Field:
“Resolution Field for Yourself“

#3 - *Lisa Listens* focuses on the third Field:
“Empathy Field for Another Person“

#4 - *Andy Advises* focuses on the fourth Field:
“Resolution Field for Another Person“

FOCUSING ON THE FOUR FIELDS

Fields are "isolated" for simplicity sake and for ease of distinction from one another and to emphasize the importance of focusing on one at a time.

Field #1 (*Freddie Feels*)

Field #2 (*Sadie Solves*)

Field #2 (*Lisa Listens*)

Field #2 (*Andy Advises*)

Try the exercise "pat your head, rub your tummy". Initially, doing both motions is difficult and you might need to first individually focus on each. Once both actions are learned, you can do them both at the same time with ease as you have integrated both skills.

The same way, the skills you develop in each Field stay within you and get integrated. Once having internalized skills of all four Fields, you are able to function well within all of them, while quickly swapping back and forth between them and giving appropriate attention to each one, as circumstances require. You might choose to focus separately on each of the Fields or you could work with them all at the same time (like in the hand patting and rubbing exercise above). This way you build wholesome and nurturing *Mindful Connections* as a developed skill.

REQUIREMENTS FOR A MINDFUL CONNECTION

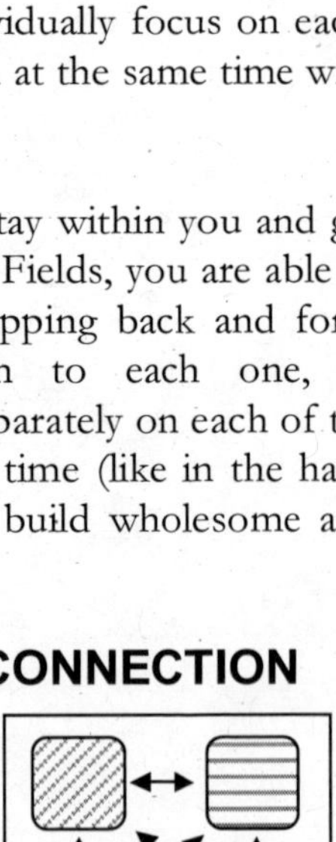

There are two important requirements when focusing on the Fields in order to maintain a Mindful Connection:

- *"Everyone Focuses on the Same Field at a time"*

and

- *"Balance the Focus between the Fields"*.

REQUIREMENT #1 – EVERYONE FOCUSES ON THE SAME FIELD AT A TIME

In a well-established nurturing *Mindful Connection*, a conversation naturally and spontaneously jumps from a Field to a Field at any time and everyone focuses on each of them together.

To nurture a *Mindful Connection* you want to make sure that everyone who is involved in the dynamic or a conversation is focused on the same Field at any given time. If people are focused on different Fields at the same time, connection is broken.
For example, *Freddie Feels* could be attempting to create conversation around emotional turmoil he has (Empathy Field), while if *Andy Advises,* who is listening would be attempting to give advice to solve his problems (Resolution Field). This creates disconnection because *Freddie Feels* needs empathy, not problem solving.

Everyone needs to not only be in the same Field but also in the appropriate Field for the situation or circumstance. When someone is in a certain Field, yet both people are focused on a different Field, disconnection happens.
For example, if *Sadie Solves* were emotionally disturbed (Empathy Field) and both her and *Andy Advises* were focusing on finding solutions around the problem (Resolution Field), it would create disconnection because *Sadie Solves* needs empathy, not problem solving, and frustration could come up for both of them.

Example: You and an another person are both focused on the "Empathy Field for Yourself" (Field #1)

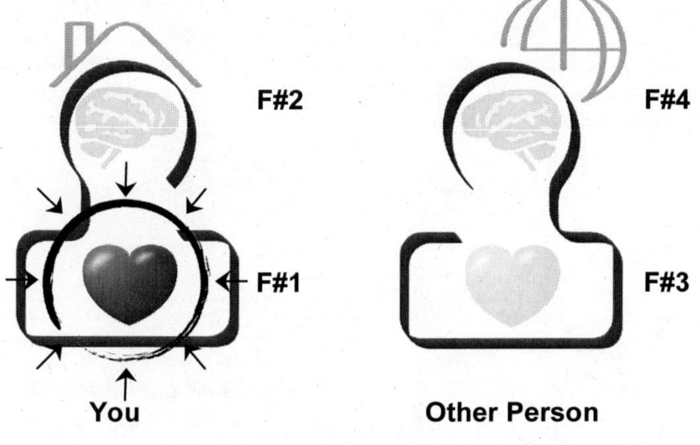

RESTORE CONNECTION USING REQUIREMENT #1 – "EMPATHY FIRST, RESOLUTION LATER" –

When the relationship gets disconnected, especially if the disconnection is strong, you need to reconnect with the other person by re-focusing on the *same* Field again. In order to do this, you need to "sweep through" and explore each Field in steps.
A good rule of thumb to use is: *"Empathy First, Resolution Later"*.
You would start at the "**Empathy Field for Yourself**" (F#1).

→F#1←

Once emotionally grounded, you can move to the "**Resolution Field for Yourself**" (F#2).

F#1 **√**, →**F#2**←

The other person might be there to support you in exploring these first two Fields. If that happens, you can already start creating connection by focusing on the same Fields. If the person is unable to do it, you can still focus on these two Fields either on your own or by seeking support elsewhere; although connection would not be happening with the other person yet, you are at least actively connecting with yourself.

After having gone through these two steps and connecting fully with yourself, you are be able to start focusing on and re-connecting with the other person by starting with the "**Empathy Field for Another Person**" (F#3). Again, use the rule of thumb: *"Empathy First, Resolution Later"*.

F#1 **√**, F#2 **√**, →**F#3**←

Finally, if both of you are grounded and not emotionally overwhelmed, you can choose to attend the "**Resolution Field for Another Person**" (F#4).

F#1 **√**, F#2 **√**, F#3 **√**, →**F#4**←

Going through all the four steps restores the unbalanced disconneciton and connection and creates *Mindful Connection*.

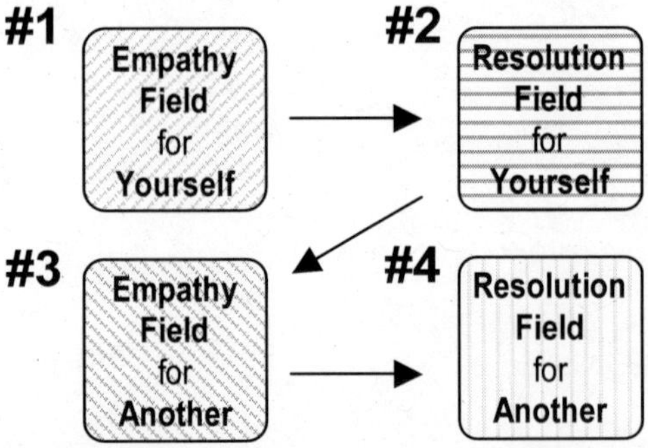

REQUIREMENT #2 – BALANCE THE FOCUS BETWEEN THE FIELDS

Even when people are focused on the same Field at the same time, it is very important that the amount of focus that is given to a Field is balanced in a way where it works for everyone.

This is different for everyone; some people might need to spend more time on a certain Field but are ok to spend less time on another one and for others, it could be opposite.
For example, *Freddie Feels* might not need a long time to successfully focus on his emotions (Empathy Field) but might not be very efficient with strategizing and carrying out tasks (Resolution Field). On the other hand *Sadie Solves* might need to focus on her emotions for a long time to connect properly (Empathy Field) while strategizing and carrying out tasks might come easy (Resolution Field).

If one person needs a lot of time to focus on a specific Field, and the other person wants to focus on other Fields, the first person can alternately seek support in that Field outside of the interaction in order to meet the required time that he needs.
For example, if *Freddy* Feels wanted to connect emotionally and was seeking support from *Sadie Solves*, he might not get enough empathy as *Sadie Solves* really likes to focus on Resolution Field. He could additionally seek support by finding *Lisa Listens* and focus on his Empathy Field until he feels better.

Example: Focuses on Fields between you and another person differ. The largest focus is on the *Resolution Field for the Other Person* (F#4); *Resolution Field for Yourself* (F#2) and *Empathy Field for Yourself* (F#1) have less attention and *Empathy Field for the Other Person* (F#3) has the least focus.

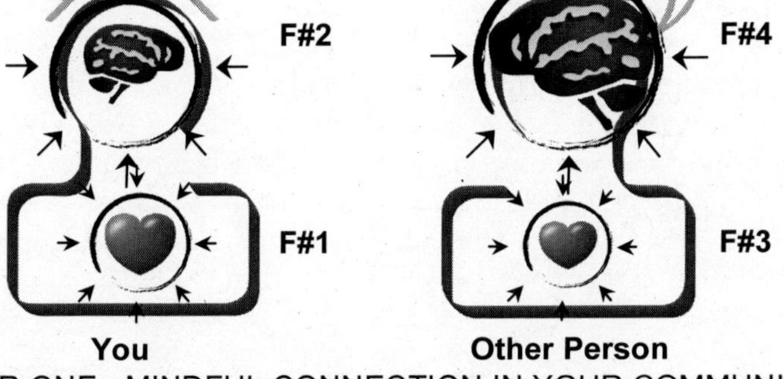

TWO WAYS TO KEEP THE FIELDS IN BALANCE USING REQUIREMENT #2

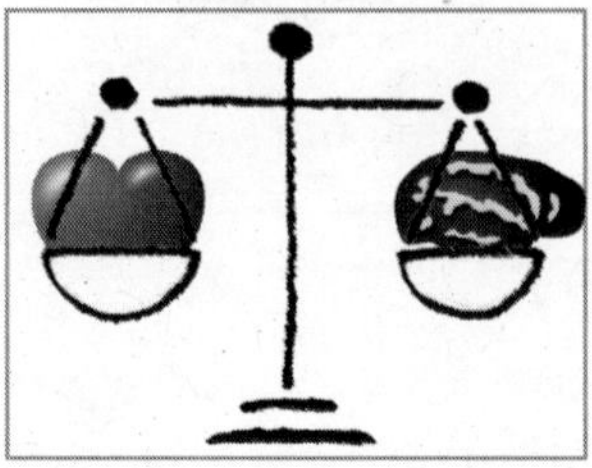

BALANCE THE FOCUS BETWEEN EMPATHY AND RESOLUTION FIELDS

Although everyone has his own capacity to sufficiently fulfill either of the two Fields, it is important to find one's own balance between the Empathy and Resolution Fields, and make sure not to over-emphasize one or completely neglect the other.

Once you start exploring both Fields when connecting with yourself or another person, you can stay present to and simultaneously build both, back and forth. In fact, connection can start anywhere within the four Fields and even outside of them, although it is always important to bring it back within the Fields, preferably starting at the Empathy Field.

Although partial, it *is* possible to communicate by exploring only the Resolution Field. This is what both *Sadie Solves* and *Andy Advises* are good at. This can leave the person operating mainly on a rational, resolution and calculated mode. He can come across uncaring, insensitive and emotion dismissing. Absence of going through the Empathy Field only has half of the picture in place and chances are that one's emotional state in the Empathy Field is different (if not opposite) to what is going on in the Resolution Field. After all, one needs the Empathy Field to identify the needs to meet in the Resolution Field and without it one's reason can merely make guesses to what's really going on for someone.

On the flipside, balancing things heavily on the Empathy Field (which is what *Freddie Feels* and *Lisa Listens* are good at) without relying on the Resolution Field can leave people acting potentially impulsively and on the whim, without necessarily being very conscious of and responsible for their actions. That's because the Empathy Field is about identifying needs, not strategically getting them met, which *is* the role of the Resolution Field.

BALANCE THE FOCUS BETWEEN YOURSELF AND ANOTHER PERSON

You need to create a balance between focusing on yourself and others. Some people tend to constantly focus on themselves and not attune much to what is going on for other people. Even when they listen to others, they regularly turn around the conversation back to themselves; doing this can create alienation from people.

Note however that sharing stories from personal experiences could be used to connect with others and it doesn't necessarily mean that one's only interested in focusing on one's own Field. In fact relating to one's own experiences can be a very powerful way to connect to those of others and find ways to resonate with what is going on for them.

Also note that it *is* possible to use the *Mindful Connection Method* to primarily work through your personal issues (bad habits, addictions, various distresses, etc.) by focusing specifically and only on your own Fields and not involving the Fields of other people.

In our Example *Freddie Feels* and *Sadie Solves* focus only on themselves.

It is also possible to consistently focus onto other people with aims to please or attend to their needs without ever connecting to one's own inner states and motivations. This state can create alienation with oneself and make it harder to truly *be* there for people.

In our Example *Lisa Listens* and *Andy Advises* focus only on others.

NOTE ON SELFISHNESS

Some people would comment that true connection and growth comes through sacrifice and through giving to others; and that focusing on yourself is a selfish act that gets you "nowhere", let alone to see it as a starting point in attempts to connect.

I'm an advocate of life of fulfillment. I believe that every being needs nurturance and care throughout her life; I am also an advocate of community, connection and giving. It is about creating a good balance between focusing on yourself and people around you; everyone needs to be included in the picture.

Giving can be a very fulfilling and joyful act that one does for oneself. I believe that when people connect to and know themselves they cultivate the need, motivation and the will to connect and give to people around them too; that's when giving becomes joyful. Or they might find themselves through the process of giving to others.

Connecting with oneself also supports a person to truly know herself and be less prone to identifying with things outside of herself. It builds individuality and uniqueness in every person.

Attempting to define behaviors and intentions and label or criticize them as selfish or non-selfish prevents people from connecting to others and also to themselves. As explained in the upcoming chapters, it's just another way to be disconnected and caught up in evaluative and alienating language.

NOTE ON MORALITY

The aim of this book is to work towards building *Mindful Connection* through nurturance. Morality here is whether there is presence of nurturance or lack of it. Humans do have "*an evolved moral sense, mechanisms for conflict resolution and cooperation within groups*".[20] Within our group we are naturally nurturing yet when it comes to "other" groups, humans can be very cruel and vicious and very non-nurturing, especially if we consider the group to be a threat to us. The goal here is to expand "our" group as much as we can so that we can be nurturing to *everyone*.

Cognitive linguist George Lakoff recommends thinking about morality based on how you're "better off". If you take care of your "group", your chances of surviving are higher so that would be considered morally "right". Not being nurturing towards "other groups" is usually also considered to be morally "right" because it implies taking care of your own "group". If you were not taking care of your group, it would be considered morally "wrong". The aim of this book is to create dynamics that take into consideration your and all the "other groups" with the aim to collectively work on getting everyone's needs met.

People often aim to reward or punish behaviors based on whether they think they were "right" or "wrong". The concepts of punishment and reward belong outside of the *Mindful Connection* framework because they create pretentious behaviors instead of nurturing behaviors. These behaviors fail to include true consideration of everyone's needs and getting them met. Considering that the aim of the *Mindful Connection Method* is to explore nurturance, it is inapplicable to use these concepts. Instead of asking *"is that 'right' or 'wrong"*, one would ask: *"are everyone's needs being met or not, and what are they?"*

Doing this helps you cultivate understanding and acceptance of others and learn to give appreciation. It supports you not only in connecting to others but you won't need to use extrinsic rewards when you like or are inspired by something someone did.

BELIEFS AND BEYOND

We all operate in both the Empathy and the Resolution Fields. People can draw conclusions and create principles in life in various different ways; and they can be driven by different needs too.

In order to draw conclusions, at times people trust themselves and other times they trust various authorities. When trusting themselves, sometimes people draw conclusions directly from their Resolution Field by relying on their reason and logic. Other times, they might make conclusions through the Empathy Field by relying on their "gut feelings" and "intuition". When the trust is relied on an external source or authority, it can also be based on rational thinking in the Resolution Field (when someone questions the authority and takes time to inquire into its validity) or on emotions from the Empathy Field (when one feels excited, confident or proud about it or has a "good feeling" about some person's judgments).

"Going with the feeling" could sometimes be more "rationally based" than one might think. On the flip-side, spending lots of time to learn about something might not be as "empirical' as you think. Malcolm Gladwell explores in detail the relations between making snap judgments and taking the time to thoroughly explore things.[21]

Most of the time when there is a simple, easily observable situation, it is easy to draw similar conclusions from both Fields. If there is a threatening person in front of you, you can conclude that that the person is dangerous because you feel scared (Empathy Field) *and* you can examine his behavior as you notice him staring at you dauntingly (Resolution Field).

Conclusions based on Resolution and Empathy Fields tend to start conflicting in circumstances when there are concepts that are not easily explainable, situations when there is not a lot of clarification and detail and even existential topics that can bring up lots of feelings of awe and wonder.

People who rely on their Resolution Field usually choose not to make conclusions based on these feelings and are ok not to make conclusions *at all* based on the lack of logical verification or pursue to methodically look for and examine more data that would support them in making rational conclusions. This is usually driven by the needs for clarity and truth. This can stimulate motivation to learn more, challenge and question, build and expand, update one's beliefs and create new strategies.

People who lean on their Empathy Fields to make conclusions might believe that rational thinking is limited and that it is acceptable not to draw conclusions through one's reason. They might trust the clarity that they have when they get good empathy and decide to use that clarity to make conclusions. These conclusions they make usually satisfy the need for understanding and meaning, which can easily be enough in themselves to accept the conclusions and bypass the needs for truth and clarity.

Debates between these two groups of people can usually be very charged, exhausting and non-productive. People who rely on logic would have a hard time accepting the other group's conclusions by saying that belief won't necessarily be a truthful observation just because someone feels good about it and they might fail to recognize that the other people get very important needs met in the process of drawing their conclusions. On the other hand, people who accept concluding through their Empathy Field can see the other group as being overly logical, closed-minded, emotion dismissing, insensitive and faithless and fail to understand that they inspire to meet some other important needs.

Furthermore, these groups of people usually do share same needs such as: peace, harmony, community, etc. Often, neither of these groups is able to connect to these needs, as their focus is so much on explaining their agenda and proving the other side "wrong" and their side "right". The conversations usually strictly end up in the Resolution Field where people spend *all* their time explaining and defending each other's strategies, instead of first touching up on and connecting with each other in the Empathy Field where they could acknowledge their values and identify their needs, which might just be very similar or even one and the same.

Despite the fact that the strategies we make to understand the world that we live in might differ, we inherently *all* still share the capacity to be nurturing and pursue getting our needs met and support others get theirs met too. Recognizing the importance of this and re-focusing our attention towards other people's feelings and needs is the stepping-stone to understanding and cultivating *Mindful Connection.* Once people start connecting this way, potential beliefs that they hold become less of an issue and concern when co-existing in a nurturing community.

PRACTICE

MINDFUL CONNECTION IN YOUR COMMUNITY

Turn to "*Mindful Connection in your Community*" in the Practice Section on page 187. It offers practices to observe the Fields and how balanced your focus is between them.

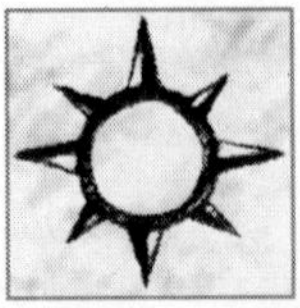

WHERE TO GO FROM HERE?

BREAKING MINDFUL CONNECTION DOWN

In the upcoming Chapters, I explore the Empathy and Resolution Fields in more depth.

As I noted before, when people are involved in a regular, emotionally uncharged conversation they spontaneously flow from one Field to another. When challenges arise, that's when Fields need to be explored in more detail.

I break down the Empathy Field into two steps:
Supportive Space and *Empathically Connect.*
You need to find suitable supportive space in order to properly empathically connect and identify your needs or support someone do the same.

Resolution Field has two steps too:
Explore Possibilities and *Carry Out Strategies.*
You rationally explore all the possibilities in order for them to be successfully carried out with the aim to increase the chances of getting your or someone else's needs met.

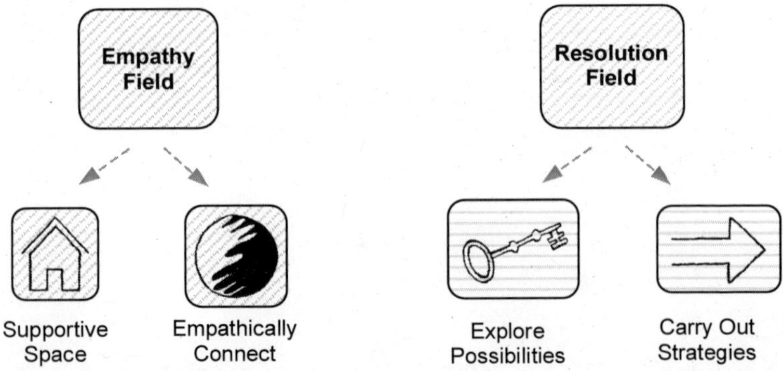

The more challenging an interaction or dynamic becomes, the more you need to explore the Fields. Each one of the four steps above is further broken into two more parts:

IN THE EMPATHY FIELD:

- *Create Supportive Space* consists of: *Initiate Supportive Space* and *Find Supportive Space.*
- *Empathically Connect* consists of: *Attune to Feelings* and *Identify Needs.*

IN THE RESOLUTION FIELD:

- *Explore Possibilities* consists of: *Observe Behaviors* and *Create Strategies.*
- *Carry Out Strategies* consists of: *Request new Behavior* and *Change own Behavior.*

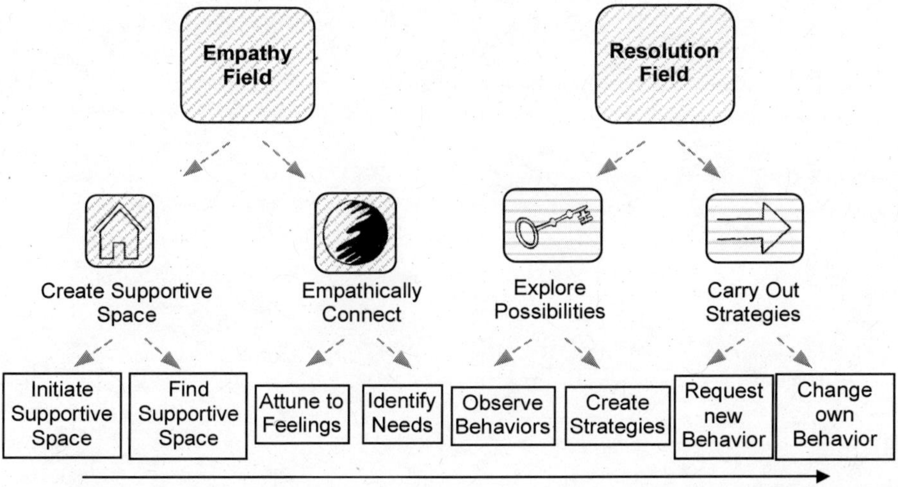

This makes for a total of eight steps that every person can explore within herself and that flow from one into another, starting from initiating and finding *Supportive Space* in order to *Empathically Connect* by attuning to feelings and identifying needs; then moving onto *Exploring Possibilities* by clearly observing behaviors and creating strategies and finally *Carrying Out Strategies* by requesting new behaviors from others and also changing own'es own behavior to find ways of getting needs met.

There are detailed methods that explore each of these eight steps of *Mindful Connection* in the upcoming Chapters. You will explore them with open-ended questions (the "Six Ws"), rather than questions that just stimulate "yes/no" answers in order to find your sense of exploration and curiosity.

You start your journey by focusing on Field #1 - "Empathy Field for Yourself" in the next Chapter.

CHAPTER TWO

EMPATHY FIELD FOR YOURSELF

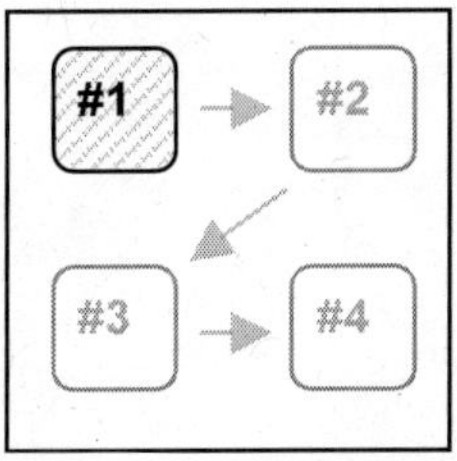

"Empathy Field For Yourself" (Field #1) is about focusing on creating empathy for yourself, just like *Freddie Feels* would.

Freddie Feels

Freddie Feels attends to his own Empathy Field in every situation he is in.

The purpose of focusing on the "Empathy Field for Yourself" is to identify your met and unmet needs by attuning to your feelings. This process is done through empathic connection with yourself which then helps you move on to focusing onto the Resolution Field where you can work on maintaining the identified met needs and finding ways to get your unmet needs met. Doing this sustains one's joyous feelings, resolves the non-joyous feelings, sets grounds for building resilience and creates wellbeing.

Cultivating the skill of identifying your met and unmet needs and attuning to your feelings is essential. Getting used to it and integrating it takes lots of patience. It's important not to underestimate the importance of taking enough time with it. There could be years of disconnection that needs healing.

FOUR STEPS IN THE "EMPATHY FIELD FOR YOURSELF"

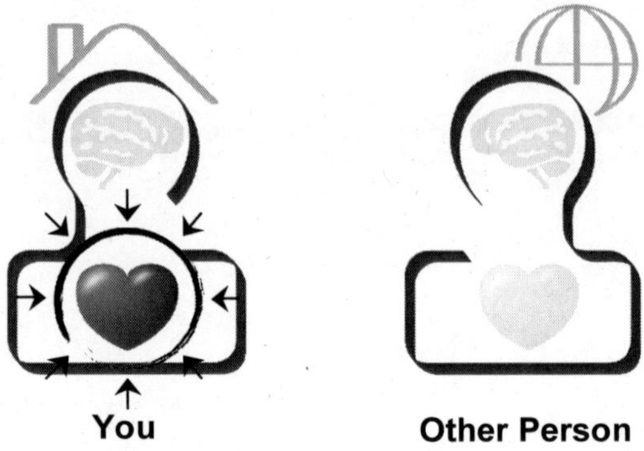

As introduced in Chapter 1, "Empathy Field for Yourself" consists of two parts: *"Create Supportive Space"*[i] and *"Empathically Connect"*[ii]

Both these parts consist of two steps that together make a total of four steps:

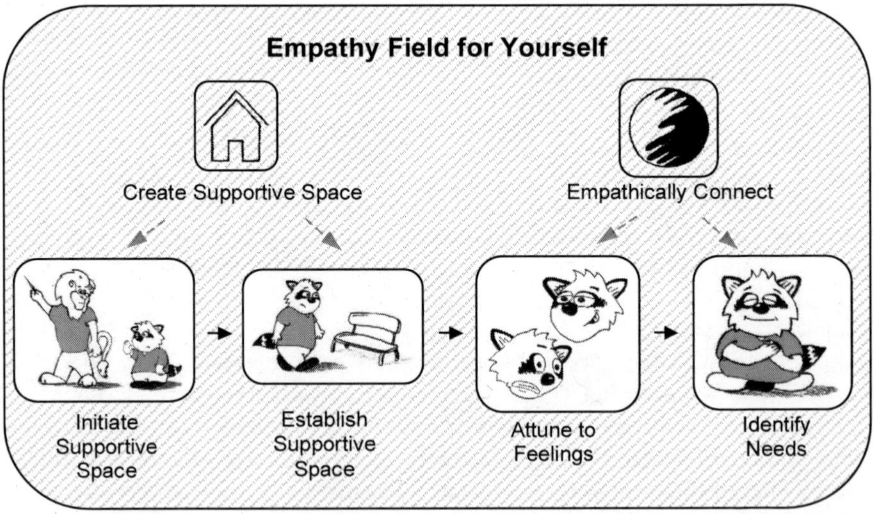

Each of these four steps has a collection of methods and you explore them all in this Chapter.

---

[i] One way to think of the process of creating supportive space is to associate it with the oldest part of your brain: the reptilian brain (or r-complex). It is responsible for basic survival responses, making sure that you are safe and protected.

[ii] One way to think of the process of empathically connecting is to associate it with the more recently developed part of your brain: the mammalian brain (or limbic system). It is mainly in charge of your emotional responses.

Freddie Feels
Create Supportive Space
When the teacher shouted while teaching, *Freddie Feels* got really uneasy and needed to find supportive space.

CREATE SUPPORTIVE SPACE

This first step of Field #1 is where you set off on a journey of self-exploration. When you find yourself emotionally overwhelmed, you first need to create supportive space in order to empathically connect, just like *Freddie Feels* would. It is about temporarily or permanently taking a break from communicating with someone in order to create a different, more supportive environment and "re-focus" and "re-connect" with yourself.

When you are fully focused on creating supportive space, it is harder to offer support to other people. Once you are in supportive space, you are unaffected by other people's feelings and behaviors and can fully focus on yourself. Supportive space is a place where one can empathically connect. It is not a place of grudge, resentment, bitterness or jadedness. You need to create supportive space when you get emotionally flooded in order to be able to un-flood.

Developmental psychologist Dr. Gordon Neufeld would call this place "home-base"; a place of safety where you can create *relationships*, *room* and *rest* in order to get the support that you need in order to empathically connect to your emotions.

Taking supportive space can even involve self-protection and self-defense, at times when your wellbeing is threatened or you find yourself in any kind of a violent or abusive situation.

A simple way of knowing if it's time to focus on this step is to take a deep breath, attune within yourself and check in to see if you are emotionally flooded and need supportive space.

It is also a good idea to create supportive space regardless of whether there are specific challenges emerging. Supportive space doesn't need to be sought only as a reaction to challenges. If you regularly create it, supportive space gives you resilience to successfully work with challenges when they do come.

You can create supportive space in a situation with the aim *not* to get triggered and have a respectful interaction with someone.

Note that although taking one's space and time does not involve active connection yet, it is still within the context of *Mindful Connection.* It is just in the initial stages of connecting with yourself, which is also necessary before connecting with other people. Supportive space is also a place where practicing *mindfulness* starts and can be developed.

You need to learn to recognize when you need supportive space and then make sure to take steps to get it. This could happen at any time or place; at certain times it could come up quite frequently and at other times occasionally. You might find yourself getting emotionally flooded and needing to instantaneously look for supportive space. It could come up during an occasion when you don't want it to happen, like an important meeting, an anniversary party or some other celebration you had waited for and wanted to be attentive and present for. As inconvenient as the timing might be, if possible, it is best to create supportive space and take care of yourself as soon as possible.

It is extremely hard and sometimes impossible to re-focus and be sensible when you are in a middle of a conflict or a challenging situation and you get emotionally flooded. It is very difficult to know what to do, not to mention understand another person's perspective or offer empathy back. You need to emotionally un-flood first.

It is invaluable to have a place or a person to go to when things get rough - a place where you can empathically connect. It is very valuable to create this for yourself if you don't already have it in your life. Having someone to hear your pain through empathy or a place where you can expressing your pain can really help you open up and start feeling and healing, especially if you have suppressed your feelings for a long time.

Certain behaviors and substances of various sorts can be very damaging to successful connection. Alcohol and drugs, unhealthy diet, certain personalities, "toxic habits" can significantly inhibit you from creating supportive space. A place of supportive space can on the other hand help you set a foundation for detoxification and to work with these kinds of challenges.

If you are creating space *only temporarily*, you are just making short-term arrangements to meet some of your core needs for support with the *goal* to attune to your feelings and identify all your needs. In that case this action makes this process belong in the Empathy Field. You would then attempt to get *all* the identified needs met in the Resolution Field in Chapter 3 when you request others to change their behavior and change your own behavior.

If however, your goal is to create *permanent* supportive space, this action would belong to the Resolution Field as the aim is not just to empathically connect but also to lastingly get important needs you decided on met, which is the function of a Resolution Field and is discussed more In Chapter 3.

The upcoming sections explore two steps in creating supportive space: initiating it and then finding it. The example of what *Freddie Feels* did after he emotionally reacted to his teacher's loud voice demonstrates these two steps.

Freddie Feels
Create Supportive Space
- Initiate Supportive Space -

Freddie Feels raised his hand, interrupted the class and asked if he could go outside. He said he needed some time out and would be back soon.

INITIATE SUPPORTIVE SPACE

This step is about interrupting and refocusing a specific dynamic or conversation to create grounds to find supportive space.

Questions to ask yourself in order to initiate supportive space: *"How do I initiate supportive space?" "In what way do I lovingly interrupt this dynamic?"*

Remember to keep asking open-ended questions (the "Six Ws").

Lets explore a collection of methods that can help *you* initiate supportive space. *Freddie Feels* chose some of these to initiate supportive space for himself.

INITIATE IT ONESELF

The "Empathy Field for Yourself" is about *you* making sure you take care of yourself. If you were to get overwhelmed in a situation, you need to aim towards initiating supportive space for yourself instead of expecting or waiting for another person to create it for you, or for her to take space for herself. You would avoid sentences like: *"Can you leave me alone", "Stop talking to me"* or *"She just never stops behaving like that", "Can't she be more sensitive to people"*.

It is especially impractical to assume that people will "read your mind" while you are giving subtle cues that they might be completely oblivious to or not giving clues at all.

If you want to initiate space but are not communicating it well to others and maybe just complaining about the situation, it can create frustration for them and you might even get people asking you *"What do you want me to do?"* Or if you want to be left alone or not be bothered, you might give untrue excuses like *"I'm busy"* or *"maybe another time"* because you feel uncomfortable, expecting in vain that people will "realize" that you don't want to really further engage in the conversation.

When you don't initiate supportive space for yourself in order to empathically connect, things can lead to resentment, grudge, vengeance and assigning blame to others for your suffering. In the long run, these ways of being do create more harm no matter what the outcome. You want to let these thoughts of blame and criticisms go by doing your best to focus onto getting support and empathy around your hardship. You might be holding onto just one event that was hurtful to you and spend years building self-justifications to villainize the person who performed an act you didn't like. The person might have been emotionally flooded at the time, not in the right head-space, maybe she didn't mean to do it, and what's more might have not even been aware of how her actions affected you. If possible, it is very important to clear up these kinds of unresolved pending resentments, and how to do this gets explored in details throughout the book.

The best way to avoid getting into a situation where you could build up a grudge is to act in the moment when a hurtful situation happens. Being able to do this positively reinforces everyone's actions. If not in the moment, it is still possible to remedy things at any time after the event.

It is important to put yourself on the front lines and speak up, just like *Freddie Feels* raised his hand to speak up in our example.

INTERRUPT

Interrupting is a way to initiate supportive space for yourself. If a conversation is not going very well it is essential to interrupt it and reconnect as soon as possible.

Interrupting can be very hard for people to do as it suggests that they are causing some sort of a disconnection and it is usually considered rude. The reality is: the disconnection happened way before. What you are really doing when stopping the other person from talking is wanting to reconnect. Interrupting while having in mind that you want to reconnect can usually make it easier for you to pause the other person while maintaining respect for everyone. Even more so, it is part of honoring the Requirement #1 for a Mindful Connection, which requires everyone to be focused on the same Field at the same time, and by interrupting, you are merely having the other person be aware that you are about to start focusing onto yourself and your own Empathy Field, because you are emotionally overwhelmed.

At times, the interruption can be the supportive space in itself. Once reconnected the conversation would keep flowing. Interrupting can be very subtle or almost unnoticeable and at other times more outspoken. In extreme cases when communication is unachievable, two people might need to literally physically separate in a conflict or an argument.

You can interrupt other people's interruptions as well. If you are explaining something and the other person is constantly interrupting, you can ask if she would be willing to listen to you until you have finished your train of thought. Especially if the person is already aiming to give you support, you can just reaffirm your wish to focus on your emotions (your Empathy Field) and that you'd been noticing the person address other things like giving you advice (your Resolution Field), relating your story to how she would feel in that situation (her Empathy Field) or telling you and exploring what she could do to never find herself in that situation (her Resolution Field). This tends to really surprise people, as many times they are not aware that they are doing it. Interrupting can create many great possibilities for connection. It is important to be mindful when making statements along these lines; next Chapter explores various ways of effectively reaching out to others.

Suppose *Freddie Feels* had not been overly triggered by the teacher's loud voice. He could have paused him in order to work out the challenge right on the spot by saying: *"Would you mind reducing your tone of voice?"* If he suspected that the teacher might be sensitive, he could have been less forward and asked something like: *"Can we pause? I would like to bring up something that's on my mind?"* This usually happens when one is already attuned to one's feelings and has identified one's needs. This is explored in detail later in this Chapter. In our example *Freddie Feels* did get very triggered and really needed to take a break from talking and have some physical separation. He told the teacher: *"I really need to take a break from this class, I am noticing that I am feeling triggered and seem to need some space"*.

If he'd been triggered to a point where he couldn't even get himself to communicate, he could have said a simple sentence like *"I really need to leave"*, without much explanation and leave the conversation until he was ready to reconnect again. He could explain later why he left the conversation.

Interrupting

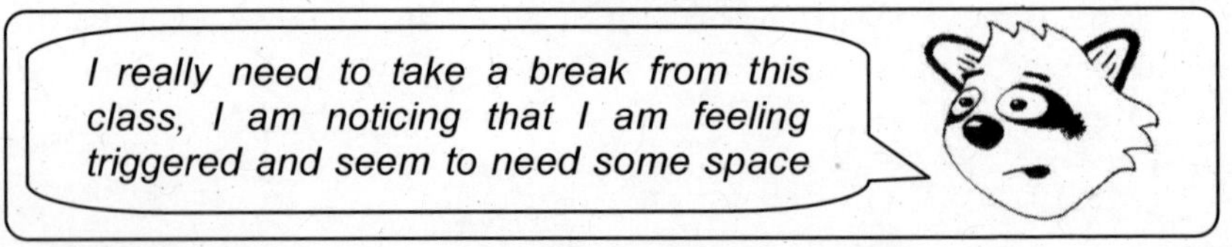

"BRIDGE"

Taking a break to be in a supportive space will pause the current dynamic or conversation. Usually people intend to continue the conversation at a later time. You can communicate explicitly that you intend to carry on the interaction at another occasion especially if the interruption is around a touchy subject.

Neufeld calls this process *bridging*, as if you're "bridging over time" until you see the other person again. Having the other person know that you do care to continue the conversation makes it much easier to reconnect later.

You can say something like: *"I would love to continue this conversation at another time"* or *"I really care for what you have to say and would love to hear about it later"*.

In our example, *Freddie Feels* expressed that he would come back to the class soon.

Bridging

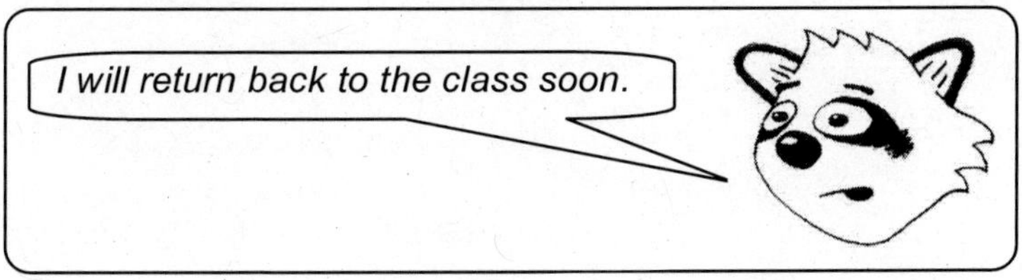

Freddie Feels
Create Supportive Space
- Find Supportive Space -

Freddie Feels found a secluded bench to sit on by himself where he could have some time on his own.

FIND SUPPORTIVE SPACE

This step is about finding a place within yourself or in an external space, where you can empathically connect with yourself. There are two different ways to find supportive space for yourself: **Alone** or with **Another Person**.

Questions to ask yourself in order to find supportive space: *"What kind of space/support do I need?" "How can I take time away?"*

Remember to keep asking open-ended questions (the "Six Ws").

Lets explore a collection of methods that can help *you* find supportive space. *Freddie Feels* chose one of these to find supportive space for himself.

FIND SUPPORTIVE SPACE - ALONE

- **Time Out – Short Break** – Even just getting a little bit of space and time on your own can be very beneficial. You can go for a quick walk or rest in a place where you can easily find peace. Some people like to perform various errands like cleaning up the house. *Freddie Feels* took a short break when he reacted to the teacher's loud voice and he sat on a bench to relax.

- **Time Out – Long Break** – Sometimes people get so overwhelmed that they just need to cut communication completely for a longer time. This break can last a little while and at times it can end up being indefinite. You can choose to remain in supportive space as much as you need until you get enough support, strength and courage to take it to the next steps.

- **Exercise** – Go for a run or bike ride, sign up for yoga, gym, and social games. Having a 20-minute walk 3 times a week is enough to have a healthy working brain and improve your thinking. (Medina)[22]

- **Fun** – There are times to let go of worries, relax and have fun; listen to music, watch a movie, go dancing or do recreational activities of any sorts.

- **Sleep/Rest** – The expression "let's sleep on this" exists for a reason. Sleep helps gain attention, memory function, mood, quantitative skills, logical reasoning and motor dexterity (Medina).[23] Trying to connect when sleep deprived can not only be ineffective but also potentially very damaging; whenever possible, arrange times to have important conversations with people when everyone has gotten good rest. It's also important to take care of oneself in times when hungry or thirsty.

- **Meditation** – Meditation permanently rewires your brain to be more mindful. Psychiatrist Daniel Siegel explains that this happens through nine different functions: your body becomes balance regulated, you're more attuned in communication, have emotional balance, ability to pause before acting, have better insight, capacity for empathy, fear modulation, intuition and moral behavior.[24] Meditation is also one of the best ways to cultivate patience.

- **Journal** – Writing a journal or that "letter that will never be sent" can be a great way to emotionally un-flood, let loose or relax, sort one's thoughts out and get clarity.

- **Creativity** – Some people like to dig deep into their creativity when working around challenges in their lives, this can involve any creative process. Some examples are painting, writing poetry, making pottery, playing music, and building things.

- **Deep Breath** – Sometimes you can truly be in a position where it is extremely hard to leave a challenging situation easily. Taking a nice deep breath can work wonders to set you in a place where you can get some peace of mind.

- **Protection** – This happens at times when your personal wellbeing is directly threatened and you need to find ways to find safe space and protect yourself from harm.

Note that some of these activities *can* be used as a "distraction" from upsets you may feel. Distraction can be helpful only from a context of allowing yourself time to un-flood from emotional turmoil but it is important to not use it as a tool to avoid dealing with what's going on for you completely. These supportive spaces are for the purpose of allowing yourself to empathically connect and successfully attune to your feelings.

FIND SUPPORTIVE SPACE - WITH ANOTHER PERSON

This is about getting in touch with someone in your life who you trust would be there for you and offer you support and "hold that supportive space" for you; a place where you can express yourself and feel.

It is important to make a distinction between people who you know are there for you and know how to offer you supportive space, from people who you would really *like* if they could offer you support while they may not really be able, interested, willing or skilled to do it. You can do this by paying attention to the ways someone is being attentive and listening to you when you want to connect and express something. Expecting someone to hear you out and be there for you when she cannot or is not, could only add more frustration to your already upset state of mind.

It is also essential to recognize the difference between getting constructive supportive space with others and just having an outlet for complaints. As much as it is important to vent and get things out, it is easy to get stuck in a vicious circle of complaining and having a hard time getting to the bottom of what's really going on for you once you've emotionally un-flooded.

Seeking support and asking for help is not an easy task at all. It takes lots of courage to do it. Sometimes you might need to take some time on your own to be able to ask for it. Other times it can happen more naturally and it definitively helps to know how to request support (I cover making clear requests in Chapter 3).

Freddie Feels could have also sought support from others, rather than just leaving the classroom and sit alone by himself. At that time, that's what he chose to do and what seemed to work for him.

SUPPORTIVE PERSON

This could be a family member, a good friend, a counselor or psychiatrist or even a complete stranger. Getting support with someone is the stepping-stone to building strong relationships. These supportive people are your "home base" in times of need and one of the main contributors and creators of nurturing, *Mindful Connections.*

You can even aim to find supportive space directly with the person you have the challenge with by asking that person to offer you support. This becomes more easy as you develop your ability to focus on more thank one Fields within the same conversation. Being able to connect with people by working things out directly can create very strong bonds and relationships, especially if it is a person that you care for and want to have in your life. In our example, *Freddie Feels* could have asked the teacher to take time to support and listen to him.

SUPPORTIVE COMMUNITY

Support groups, communities of people with similar beliefs and values and close or extended family are all potential sources of support. You can become an active part of a community like that to find your supportive space. In our example, *Freddie Feels* could have the class with the teacher and all the students be there for him to find supportive space with.

Sometimes, people who are in a negative vortex of emotions and overwhelmed with depression can really benefit by just seeking this change in environment and being around people. These need not be specific support groups; they could be social or recreational gatherings of any sort.

PRACTICE

CREATE SUPPORTIVE SPACE

Turn to "*Create Supportive Space for Yourself*" in the Practice Section on page 189. It offers different practices for creating supportive space for yourself.

Freddie Feels
Empathically Connect

Once *Freddie Feels* found supportive space on a secluded bench, he started empathically connecting.

EMPATHICALLY CONNECT

This second step of Field #1 is a journey of reaching the innermost places within yourself. Having created supportive space, you can now focus on empathically connecting with yourself, just like *Freddie Feels* would.

Imagine creating supportive space and wanting to empathically connect. You might not know how exactly to deal with everything that's coming up. A simple way of knowing if it's time to focus on this step is to take a deep breath, attune within yourself and check in to see if you are emotionally flooded and also if you *are* in a supportive space and receptive and ready to feel and empathically connect.

The upcoming sections explore two steps in empathically connecting to yourself: attuning to your feelings and identifying your needs. The example of what *Freddie Feels* did once he created supportive space for himself demonstrates these two steps.

Freddie Feels
Empathically Connect
- Attune to Feelings -

Freddie Feels attuned to his **non-joyous feelings** of being scared and very nervous. He sat with those feelings until he felt at ease and grounded. After that, he also attuned to his **joyous feelings** of being glad and empowered to have a teacher from whom he can learn so much.

ATTUNE TO FEELINGS

Attuning to feelings is when you consciously put your attention on and accept bodily sensations, emotional states and experiences that come up. It is different from when you are emotionally flooded and you let yourself get carried away with emotion without being present to it, or when you are thinking and rationalizing about what is going on.

Questions to ask yourself in order to attune to your feelings: *"How am I doing?" "How am I feeling?"*
Remember to keep asking open-ended questions (the "Six Ws").

There are seven primary emotions: sadness, anger, fear, surprise, contempt, disgust and enjoyment. You can explore each one of these in detail in the "Recognizing Emotions and Micro-Expressions" section in the APPENDIX (pg. 220). Secondary, or social emotions are more complex and come from inter-personal relations. Some examples are embarrassment, guilt, jealousy, shame, pride, etc.[25]

You can consciously choose to attune to feelings and not just get randomly emotional. Your capacity to connect to yourself and others, carry out tasks and grow loving relationships is compromised when you are not attuning to your feelings. Feelings help you connect with yourself, which is probably the most important step in all the Fields. Fully attuning to your feelings creates ease and a path to more consciousness and clarity in thought.

Feelings can be categorized into two groups: *joyous* and *non-joyous.* It is important to attune to both joyous *and* non-joyous feelings in a certain situation.

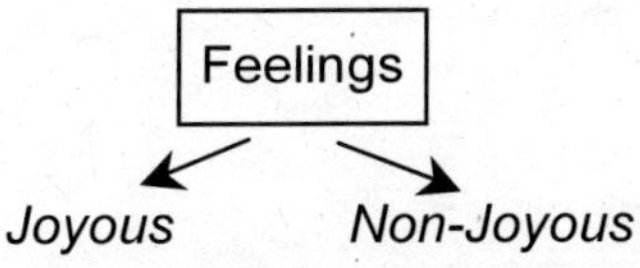

Mixed Feelings

The process of empathic connection involves developing the ability to attune to both joyous and non-joyous feelings and in the process identify both met and unmet needs. Developmental psychologist Dr. Gordon Neufeld calls this process "integrative functioning"[26]; the ability to have a variety of perceptions all at the same time and be able to still process and integrate it all.

This ability of being of "two minds" or having "mixed feelings" is essential to emotionally grow and gain maturity. It helps a person become independent and still be able to connect with others without the sense of losing one's own identity. It is healthy to feel many different feelings all at the same time when one has the ability to create emotional balance. Emotional balance is also one of the key functions that get generated through the practice of mindfulness and meditation. Processing "mixed feelings" can produce some very important and useful new feelings. For example, annoyance and caring creates patience, fear and caring generates courage, and so on.

When someone is overwhelmed with non-joyous feelings, these feelings can temporarily mask any joyous feelings a person might have. *Freddie Feels* for example, couldn't attune to his joyous feelings right away (the glad feelings resulting from him learning so much from this teacher) because he was overwhelmed with a feeling of being scared. Similarly, this can also happen when one is overwhelmed with joyous feelings, and these can mask certain non-joyous feelings that are present. A good example of this is when one is infatuated with another person.

Emotional flooding is when you become overwhelmed with feelings and emotional conflict triggers things like inability to think rationally, confusion, adrenaline and stress-related hormone release, high heartbeat rate, a break down of communication abilities and paralysis in action.[27] Although usually people tend to get flooded as a result of mixed non-joyous feelings, it is also possible to be overwhelmed with joyous feelings. Emotions can become extreme and prolonged too. Sadness can lead to depression, pleasure to addiction, fear to phobia, worry to anxiety, etc.

Lets explore a collection of methods that can help *you* attune to your feelings. *Freddie Feels* chose some of these to attune to his feelings.

#1 – USE CLUES/HINTS

Sometimes your bodily sensations, emotional states and experiences might be hidden, evaded, buried and hard to identify and attune to, especially around very sensitive and pending challenges. By using some of the clues/hints described below, you can get closer to feeling them.

THOUGHTS (AS CLUES/HINTS)

Verbally explore and give detailed history around what happened. You can let yourself talk for a bit. Talking and attempting to rationally explore things when emotionally overwhelmed is a very common way people tend to attempt to reconnect and can be used as a good starting point. The need for expressing oneself in itself can be enough to bring up a feeling. Based on what you say, you can start getting a sense of the sensations in you by using what you say as clues or hints. The way you think and rationally process certain challenges can shape your feelings. Once the feelings come up and especially when flooded with emotions, people tend to easily stay in "the head". They get swamped with more thoughts, interpretations, criticism rational thinking and in more extreme cases accusations and deceitful words. These thoughts usually just take people further away from being able to focus on getting present to their current sensations. This is because the focus is on rational thoughts. These thoughts can even stir up other different feelings that are unrelated to the dynamic at hand. Use these thoughts as a resource and link to attune to your current feelings.

For example, when people act out of jealousy, most of the time they are not even aware that they are jealous and instead mainly resort to blame and resentment towards others and very often gossip to get relief. It is important that you first acknowledge it when you find yourself in a jealous frame of mind. In itself, jealousy (just like aggression and anger) is a mere "umbrella word" that "hides" other feelings. Jealousy can show itself in the form of anger, hatred or rage. The feelings "hidden" behind jealousy are usually deeply rooted and hard to attune to due to the strength of the effect of jealousy. These could be deep insecurities, hurts and confusions.

On the flip side, same thing can happen when you get overwhelmed with joyous feelings. You can praise someone, use evaluative, rational talk to explain how that person is amazing and how "good" what she is doing is, instead of focusing what is going on for you, how you feel about the way that person inspired you and get present to all the sensations in yourself.

In our example with the loud teacher, *Freddie Feels* found himself saying things like: *"He is an aggressive idiot"*, *"I want to hit him"*, *"What's wrong with him to shout like that?"* or *"He is a loud buffoon".* All these statements can reveal the potential underlying feeling of fear. Suppose *Freddie Feels* were getting support from a friend. He could ask the person to support him in exploring what feelings she thinks *Freddie Feels* might be going through. She could find out through listening to *Freddie Feels's* words and observing his behavior that he is probably scared (amongst other feelings).

Once *Freddie Feels* un-flooded form his non-joyous feelings, he also aimed to attune to his joyous feelings. He still needed to pay attention to potential thoughts that he had and use them as clues/hints toward attuning to the joyous feelings like: *"He is a really good teacher" or "He is not always mean".* The joyous feelings him being glad and empowered to have a teacher from whom he can learn so much.

THOUGHTS - CLUES/HINTS

BEHAVIORS (AS CLUES/HINTS)

Physical behavioral patterns, if present, can also be good indicators to help you attune to your feelings. Sometimes these behaviors can happen very quickly, especially when they are suppressed.

When Freddie Feel's got scared from the teacher's voice, his body behavior changed; he stepped back, raised and pulled together his eyebrows and stretch your lips horizontally back toward the ears; his heart started to race, his mouth became dry, his skin turned pale and muscles contracted. These are all signs of fear and feeling scared.

Feeling glad and empowered can also be followed by bodily responses. When feeling glad, *Freddie Feels's* body relaxed and he had a genuine expression of smile on his face.

For more detail on behavioral responses for different feelings, refer to the "Recognizing Emotions and Micro-Expressions" and "Non-verbal behavior" in the APPENDIX (pg. 220 and 223).

EXPRESSING FEELINGS (AS CLUES/HINTS)

Expressing and verbalizing feelings (emotion labeling) keep getting you closer to attuning to feelings. This process of emotional recognition is a prerequisite to be able to resonate with the feeling itself. Sometimes expressing a feeling might hint toward and evoke the right emotional sensation, around the right sensation or it could at times take you away from it. If you or someone who is supporting you verbalizes the present feeling that you are having, it can really help you attune to the feeling instantaneously; other times, the emotions could be so obscured that it might take a some time to explore and narrow it down.

Even when someone is offering you support and you say *"I feel scared"*, you might get a response like: *"you don't have to feel scared"*. You can explain that you would like her to support you by listening to you express them and that your aim is not to deny your feelings. People can even get uncomfortable and dismissing around people who are feeling *joyous*. This can prime everyone in the dynamic to deny and ignore what one is feeling.

Feeling is not about getting relief either. It's quite the opposite; it's about getting present to some potentially very painful experiences. Relief can and usually does come if you really take the time to go through the feeling process fully. So when you sense that things are "coming up", you need to feel them instead of finding different distractions to create false relief and divert you from feeling.

One such distraction is when you "sugar-coat" any non-joyous feeling that might come up. We live in a very emotion dismissing society. People encourage "happy feelings", yet when someone is sad or irritated, they usually want to "cheer" the person up or find ways to get "happy thoughts into their minds". Another distraction is trying to "fix" feelings by finding solutions and strategies for circumstances that stimulated them. Emotions cannot be "cheered up" or "fixed", they need to be felt; there is no "positive" or "negative" way to approach emotions; you either attune to them or you don't.

Refer to the APPENDIX for detailed listing of joyous and non-joyous feelings (pg. 217 and 221). The more time you spend exploring different feelings, the easier it is for you to recognize them.

In the example with the loud teacher, when *Freddie Feels* asked himself, *"Am I bored?"* and *"Am I disgusted?"* it didn't quite match what was going on for him internally around the teacher's voice. However, when he said, *"I am scared"*, it aroused the appropriate emotional sensation and he identified the feeling that is really going on for him.

When he asked himself, *"Am I amazed?"* and *"Am I surprised?"* to identify his joyous feelings, it didn't match the actual emotional sensations that go with being glad and empowered and it side-tracked him from attuning to the right feeling, until he said *"I am glad"*.

EXPRESSING FEELINGS - CLUES/HINTS

When wanting to offer you support, some people can get very distracted and taken back by hearing about feelings and even hearing the word "feel" excessively; it can take away from them being able to focus on or even care for the actual feelings that are going on for you. This is important to have in mind especially if you live in communities where expressing feelings is a touchy subject, for you and for others. Find different variations to verbally express feelings, for example: *"I feel scared"* or *"I am scared", "this is scary", "I got goose bumps"* etc. At times it could be more effective to keep things non-verbal or maybe request from others to just give you some space and quiet instead of explaining to them what your feelings are.

It can be very helpful if a supportive person gives you her perspective about what she thinks might be going on for you. It is important for this person to know how to listen well and be able to recognize feelings underneath your words if you get caught up in evaluative and criticizing language.

When people see you in distress and want to support you, many times a common expression they use is *"I am sorry to hear that"*. This expression can be taken in two different ways. The word *"sorry"* can mean being apologetic and it can also mean that someone is sad. What the person wants truly wants to express is more important than the wording. Often, the person simply wants to support you and if you keep the focus on your Empathy Field and the fact that the other person is "feeling with you", it can help stay attuned to what is going on for you, instead of analyzing whether the person "shouldn't be feeling sorry/apologetic" or that it "isn't that person's fault". Even the word sympathy seems to carry two different meanings: honest kindheartedness/empathy vs. feeling pity and sorry for someone. It would be useful if this expression were just rephrased to *"I'm sad to hear that"* as the word *sad* has a much clearer meaning.

NEEDS[i] (AS CLUES/HINTS)

If you explore met and unmet needs, feelings can easily arise and you can attune to them. Feelings, as opposed to needs are transient and different feelings are aroused depending on whether certain needs are met or not.

Feelings can also change depending on whether you identify certain needs. They are shaped and modified by our awareness and connection to our needs versus just having evaluative and partial ideas about what happened and what we think people's intentions are. This process is called reappraisal.[28] It is a more lasting way of regulating one's emotions than the process of distraction, which is about turning one's attention away from certain emotions onto other experiences and sensations.

For example, when *Freddie Feels* identified that his unmet need around the teacher's loud voice is safety, this activated his emotions around that need and he felt scared. Determining other unmet needs like consideration, acceptance and appreciation also brought up same and similar feelings. When he identified more needs, other feelings came up too, like: tense, anxious, worried, angry, shy and more. If he hadn't identified these extra needs, he wouldn't have necessarily ended up attuning to these feelings. He was also able to predict how he would feel if these needs were met: safe, calm, content, composed, etc.

---

[i] The "Need" concept is introduced and fully explored in the next section

CONNECTING THE UNMET NEEDS TO FEELINGS

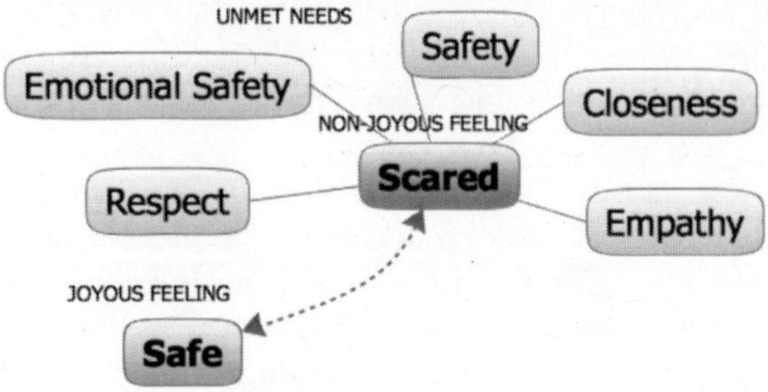

Freddie Feels recognized his met need to be one of *learning,* because the teacher offered great quality of teaching to him. This aroused feelings of gladness and empowerment.

CONNECTING THE MET NEEDS TO FEELINGS

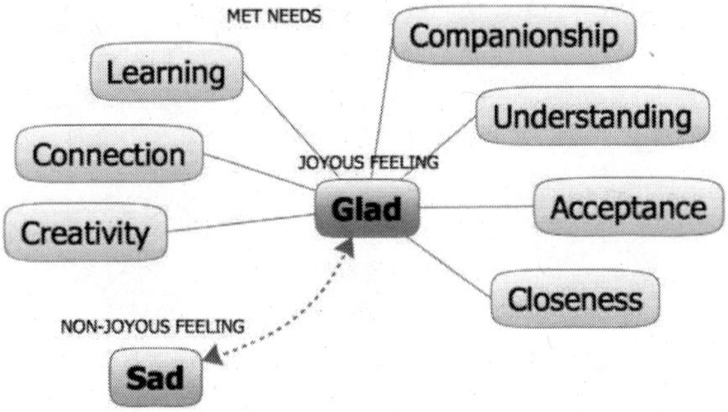

CLUES/HINTS - NEEDS

#2 – WELCOME THE FEELING

OWN THE FEELINGS

One of the surest ways to easily connect to your feelings is to recognize that it is your way of thinking and acting that arouses your feelings in a certain way. Taking responsibility for your thoughts and actions is empowering. If you learn to be responsible for yourself and your actions, you directly change how you feel day to day. Assigning this power to another person is basically allowing that person to control the way things happen in your life and how you feel as a result. It is a very disempowering place to be, especially if you believe that it's always someone else's fault any time you experience a non-joyous feeling.

I find that the word responsibility often gets mixed up with blame, fault, accountability and the context of "carrying burden". I understand and describe this word through expressions such as: "being conscious of", "accepting your role", "owning your part" "creating opportunities" etc. The word responsibility is very powerful when used and understood through these empowering contexts.

You need to own your feelings. Doing this is acknowledging that your feelings are based on your own ways of thinking and not on something someone else "did to you". *"You cannot control how people interpret your behavior; therefore you are not responsible for their interpretations or feelings that follow their interpretations".*[29] And vice-versa: nor are they responsible for your interpretations and feelings based on your own interpretations. You are responsible for your thoughts, interpretations and your behavior.

Note that responsibility can only be taken for thoughts and actions, not your feelings. Feelings themselves don't involve any action, they are just there for you to attune to them or not. In our example with the loud teacher, *Freddie Feels* can be responsible for what stimulated his emotions of him being scared (he put himself into that situation) or take responsibility around attuning to that feeling (he made efforts to create supportive space to empathically connect) rather than take responsibility for the feeling itself.

It is very important to accept your feelings for what they are and feel them instead of negating, fighting or criticizing them by saying things like: *"I shouldn't feel this way…"* or *"I am stronger than this…"* These sentences can also be preceded with the good old word that we all know: *"but"*. For example: *"but I thought I wouldn't have to go through all this again"*. As de Mello would say: *"when you fight something, you give it as much power as you are using to fight it. When you fight it, you empower it."* Attuning to feelings diffuses potential destructive power that could come out when they are suppressed, as in the case of anger, jealousy, rage and other related feelings.

BE IN THE PRESENT

Being present to what is coming up is another important step towards attuning to your feelings. You can really only attune to what you are feeling in the moment, not how you might have felt during a conversation that happened in the past. Long lasting upsets are created by feelings that happened in the past and those are still very alive in you in the present. And that's where you want to focus your attention.

Imagine an interaction that scared you a week ago. In the mean time, this feeling could have transformed into anxiousness or insecurity

PAUSE

When feelings come up, people tend to react right away in many different non-mindful ways rather than pausing and attempting to attune and get present to them and welcome the rising sensations and experiences.

Practice developing your ability to pause before reacting rationally or dismissively; you can develop this ability by meditating and building mindfulness (Daniel Siegel M.D.[30]). It can make a world of difference if you can pause for at least a short moment when things come up. This in essence is creating supportive space for yourself, even it is for a few seconds.

Research in neuroscience has even identified a specific "magic quarter second", which is the length of time one can use to catch the thought before it became an emotional sensation. This could be used to regulate one's emotions by predicting what they are before they even happen.[31]

ACCEPT FUTILITY[32]

A common thing that can deter people from welcoming and accepting their feelings is getting frustrated and aggravated when things don't go their way. As psychologist Gordon Neufeld explains, futility is the experience of something that you have no control over. People can get furious and hold grudges for very long times when they struggle to accept futilities of their circumstances. The more intense the emotional response to the wall of futility, the greater the likelihood that that reaction is one strong negative emotion, like anger for example. When a person develops the ability to hold and deal with mixed-feeling (through practicing mindfulness and focusing on the Empathy Field), more moderate reactions can happen when it can become easier to face the futility of a situation.

Facing things in life that are out of your control creates the opportunity to fully attune to all your feelings and learn to adapt in life; you learn to accept and become resilient. If you know there are things in life that you can't change and are bothering you, you can face and acknowledge them. This includes acknowledging any challenges you are struggling with or might have struggled with in the past, decisions you made that were not as fruitful as you hoped for and certain circumstances that you simply cannot control. Note that these moments of futility relate mainly to specific strategies that aim to get needs met rather than directly to the needs themselves.

When you find yourself getting angry or aggressive, it is important to recognize that you are most probably disconnected from what's really going on for you. Aggression is commonly a result of frustration that comes out of an inability to face things you have no control over. You might find yourself criticizing the situation or other people involved in it. A very important emotional process happens when you accept the futility of this kind of a situation. This process creates adaptation, a deep change that happens within you when you are faced with something you cannot currently change. Essential feelings that come up with futility are sadness, disappointment and a sense of release, often accompanied with tears and crying; it is important to have solid supportive space during this time.

For example, *Freddie Feels* found himself getting wrapped in being annoyed with and consistently complain about the teacher "being loud". It came from an unmet need for self-esteem and strength. This masked his feelings of being scared and made it hard for him to attune to that feeling. Once he accepted that the teacher's loud voice was affecting him and that he had no control over it in the moment, he got sad and disappointed.

Accepting futility clears the path toward fully attuning to other pending feelings in one's current challenge. Once having accepted his futility, *Freddie Feels* successfully welcomed and attuned to all his feelings in an even deeper and connected level: being scared when he would find himself around people who talk loudly and feelings of gladness when in class that he values.

#3 – FEEL

Up to now, all the steps have been to reveal the feeling itself. While still fully focused on your Empathy Field, once the feeling surfaces, you need to take as much time with it as you need to fully integrate what is coming up. You would do this by staying present to all the bodily sensations and emotional states and experiences. Avoid judging or identifying with the feeling; now is the time to simply focus on it and consciously feel.

If you are in a supportive space on your own, be very patient and caring with yourself. If you are in a supportive space where you have support from another person, make sure that he is present with you and holds that supportive space until you fully go through your feelings. It is helpful to have the person be there and listen with attentiveness, keep eye contact and even offer physical contact.

If you have fully accepted the futility of your situation, very often just briefly connecting to a feeling can be sufficient and would give you enough empathy to move on. Other times it might take more time and patience to allow deeply rooted and buried feelings to surface.

Make sure to attune to both joyous and non-joyous feelings. Non-joyous feelings can be harder to attune to but very important, as your essential goal is to transform those feelings into joyous ones.

Feelings can be accompanied with physical reactions too. People tend to also feel their bodies more. Sadness can come with chest pain and crying, anger and surprise can speed up your heart rate and breath, fear can make you shiver, etc. Very often physical discomfort in one's body and even sickness can be indicators of suppressed emotions.

Once the feelings are fully felt, calmness is what usually follows. The result is clarity in thought, which can now help you identify your met and unmet needs (unless you've already done it in the process of attuning to feelings).

In our example, *Freddie Feels* felt very scared and nervous.

Once he fully attuned to that feeling, he also connected to his feelings of gladness, joy and empowerment and smiled.

Freddie Feels
Empathically Connect
- Identify Needs -

Freddie Feels identified his needs:
Met needs:
Learning, connection, creativity and companionship.
Unmet needs:
Safety, understanding and respect.

IDENTIFY NEEDS

A *need* is a "state of being" that is at the core of one's existence and is necessary for survival, wellbeing and building resilience. Your identified needs are the fundamental means that assist you in finding connection with yourself and others. This connection happens in the process of identifying and getting the identified needs met. If a person can identify her core needs, they will also shape her feelings accordingly. Unmet needs will arouse non-joyous feelings and met needs will arouse joyous feelings. In this context, needs and feelings go hand in hand and can be recognized as mutual indicators and even stimulators of one another.

Needs are universal and we all share the same needs, although we all have different priorities around different needs. Needs, as opposed to feelings are invariable, what varies is whether they are met or not. For example, the need for thirst is ever present in all of us, you are thirsty when your need for thirst is not met, or not thirsty when your need for thirst *is* met. Needs are met through creating strategies, which you explore in the next Chapter. To satisfy the need for thirst, one strategy would be to drink water.

Questions to ask yourself in order to identify your needs: *"What do I need?" "What are my needs?" "What am I looking for?"*
Remember to keep asking open-ended questions (the "Six Ws").

When identified, needs can be in two different states: *met* and *unmet.* It is important to identify all the needs, both met and unmet. Met needs are what inspires and drives you to find ways to get the unmet needs met too. Unmet needs are used to re-establish a connection with yourself and others.

Needs

Met *Unmet*

Note that needs are essential for one's survival and wellbeing. This does not suggest that all needs are always granted to be easily met. A need that is met today might not be met tomorrow. Essential core needs can however, get met in pretty simple and straightforward ways and not always in the way you would like them to get met.

It is also important to recognize the significance of the *process* of recognizing one's needs and pursuing getting them met, which lasts a lifetime, rather than to want to just have all one's needs get simply and quickly met.

Lets explore a collection of methods that can help *you* identify your needs. *Freddie Feels* chose some of these to identify his needs.

#1 – VOCABULARY OF NEEDS

You need to build a good vocabulary of needs. Many researchers (Maslow, Alderfer. Rosenberg, Max-Neem to name a few) explore this concept and define fundamental human needs.
Here is a list outlining some of the core needs everyone shares.

- Meaning/Significance
- Autonomy/Freedom
- Love/Affection
- Empathy/Clarity/Truth
- Fun/Celebration/Recreation
- Creativity/Change
- Community/Appreciation/Respect
- Safety and Sustenance.

Refer to the "Needs" section in the APPENDIX (pg. 219) for a detailed listing of needs.

Note that needs are expressed in form of a noun: *"I have a need for water"* or *"My need is sustenance"*.

You already create grounds to meet many of these core needs in the very first step when you create supportive space. Even supportive space in itself is a need that can be met. Once the basic core needs are met (direct survival needs like sustenance and safety), one can take further steps towards identifying and meeting more needs (needs for wellbeing – autonomy, acceptance, empathy, etc.).

#2 – USE CLUES/HINTS

A way to identify your needs is to observe yourself in every moment, things that you say, way that you behave and feel and use those as clues and hints to explore different needs that are met and unmet. You can also have someone else support you in identifying your needs.

VERBS

An expression is *not* a need when it is expressed in form of a *verb*. Verbs represent strategies, which can get needs met (or unmet) but are not in themselves needs and are also not necessarily essential for survival or wellbeing. Also, strategies are part of the Resolution, not Empathy Field. You can use these verbs as clues and hints to figure out the actual needs that the strategies that they represent would potentially get met or unmet.

Examples of such verbs are "wants" and "desires". One could say, *"I want to drink water"*, which doesn't represent a need but rather just one strategy that can get the need for *thirst* met. Or you might not be thirsty and still express the "want' to drink water for various different reasons (habit, curiosity etc.)

It's also important to keep the distinction between using the word "need" in form of a noun and using it in form of a verb. If you say, *"I need water"*, you are using the word need as a verb and you are merely describing a strategy to get the actual need for sustenance met.

In our example with the loud teacher, when thinking: *"I want him to talk more quietly" or "My need is for him to talk more quietly"*, *Freddie Feels* was referring to a behavior/strategy, not a need. Essentially what his thoughts translate to is: *"I'm lacking safety and am not at peace and would appreciate if he talked more quietly"*. Here, the needs are *safety* and *peace* and "him talking more quietly" is a strategy. In relation to his met need, which in this case is for quality learning that he gets from the teacher, he *Freddie Feel*'s thoughts were: *"He teaches so well"*.

CLUES/HINTS - VERBS

PEOPLE AND OBJECTS

Another misconception is when needs are referred to a person or an object. These can all be indirect *means* to get needs met (or get them unmet) and are not needs in themselves.

If you say, *"I need him"*, you are not referencing to a need, you are referencing to a person. You can say *"I want to stay in touch with him, since I value our connection"* in which case, "staying in touch with that person" is a strategy, whereas *connection* is the need.

In our example, *Freddie Feels* thought that he needed earplugs. This was an indicator that his need for safety was not met. He also expressed his met need by saying: *"I really need that teacher"*. Again, this would mean that he was getting his need for quality learning met with this teacher.

CLUES/HINTS – PEOPLE AND OBJECTS

ALIENATING LANGUAGE

Evaluative language you tend to use when your needs are not being met can give you clues as to what those unmet needs are. This language can be any form of criticism, interpretations, evaluations and random thoughts.

In our example with the loud teacher, *Freddie Feels* found himself thinking things like: *"He is an aggressive idiot"*, *"That interaction was too much"*, *"He is really mean"* and *"I wanted to hit him"*. By scrutinizing the content of these thoughts *Freddie Feels* made a guess that yet again, the unmet need was safety as well as many other needs like peace, trust, space, etc.

Similar situation can happen when expressing met needs, when one resolves to use of praise and complimenting positive actions. When *Freddie Feels* thought: *"He is an amazing teacher" or "That class is really good"*, this language merely explains what he thought of and how he judged the teacher or his way of teaching. These expressions don't express a need, which in this case is the need for learning, which happened to be met with this teacher.

CLUES/HINTS – ALIENATING LANGUAGE

FEELINGS

Observing any non-joyous feelings that come up when you explore needs can confirm the right unmet need was identified. Also, if you explored some needs that were *met*, they would trigger joyous feelings. If there were no feeling triggered, that would indicate that the need that you are currently exploring is not relevant to your existing challenge.

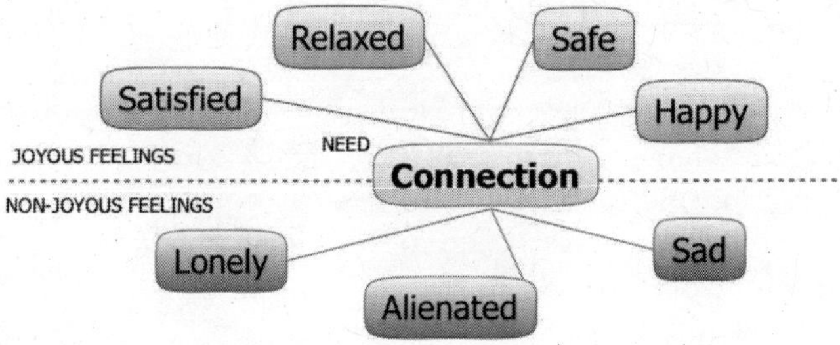

Refer to the "The Feelings and Needs Connection" section in the APPENDIX for a more detailed chart of the relationship between feelings and needs (pg. 219).

In our example, when *Freddie Feels* identified his need for safety, it triggered fear, anxiety, anger and other related feelings. This indicated that safety is the right unmet need (the anticipated joyous feelings if the need for safety were met would be: relaxed, composed, calm, etc.) Also, when he identified his need for learning, he felt glad, empowered, grateful or excited, which confirmed this need to be the one he wanted to identify.

If more than one feeling came up, a whole range of other needs could be discovered. Feelings of fear can bring up unmet needs like shelter, security and protection; feelings of anxiety can reveal unmet needs of stability and predictability; anger can bring up fairness and justice. Joyful feeling of gladness can indicate needs for comfort and belonging; feeling empowered can bring up clarity and independence. As a result, more feelings could come up through these newly identified needs, leaving one with a wide variety of feelings and needs to work with.

CLUES/HINTS – FEELINGS

Feelings can also be great ways of expressing a need without even necessarily directly referencing that need. Feelings are adjectives and as adjectives, they describe and quantify needs. For example, when you say, *"I am scared"* people can very easily associate to the need for safety even if you don't directly word the actual need.

By now you can see how feelings and needs can be direct mutual indicators of each other and work together toward cultivating successful empathic connection.

#3 – IDENTIFY ALL THE NEEDS

It is rare that there would be only one met or unmet need in a given challenge. One need might be a derivative of another more significant need. Furthermore, *that* need might be a result of yet another deeply rooted need. Do your best to identify as many needs as you can in a specific situation.

For example, imagine a teacher who invested years into training a young dancer. Suppose the young dancer decides to change her style of dancing and move to another potentially less noteworthy school. The teacher's reaction to this dancer's decision could have various unmet needs. Maybe she would be concerned for the young dancer's future training and progress in which case the need in question would be c*are*. Considering that the teacher invested time, energy and love into that person, a deeper need might one for a*ppreciation*, yet another even deeper need might be r*eassurance* if the teacher thought that she failed or *sustenance* if she were concerned that more students might start to leave her school too.

MET NEEDS

In our example, *Freddie Feels's* attending the class with the loud teacher got his need for *learning* met. Another deeper need was *connection, companionship and creativity*.

UNMET NEEDS

Not being able to follow the lecture as a result being scared got *Freddie Feels's* need for u*nderstanding* unmet. Another further unmet need was one for *respect* considering that teachers loud talking came across as if he didn't really value or care for the students. One of the deeper needs of course was *safety*.

Be mindful with how and how often you express your needs to others. Expressing needs using the same expression all the time in your daily interactions can come across overly mechanical, tiring and alienating for others; people can find it exasperating and even demanding because of such a common relation to the word 'want'. If not mindful with it, it could potentially create more disconnection.

Here are some different examples to express your needs: *"I have a need for safety", "My need for safety is not met", "I need safety", "I am unsafe", etc.*

PRACTICE

EMPATHICALY CONNECT

Turn to "*Empathically Connect*" in the Practice Section on page 191. It offers different practices for empathically connecting with yourself.

WHERE TO GO FROM HERE?

STAY HERE

As long as you are emotionally overwhelmed, make sure to stay focused on this Field. If you find yourself focusing on other Fields just bring your attention back and refocus on this one. Take extra care not to get overly caught in this Field either; doing this can set you into a "poor me", "victim" mentality where you could have a hard time stepping away from it and attending to the other Fields as well. To avoid this from happening, make sure to do your best to fully attend to this Field and honor your agreements around it.

GO BACK

If you are unable to successfully connect to your feelings, you need to find a more suitable place or arrangement to create supportive space. If this involves getting support from another person, you have to make sure you are both focusing on this field. If creating supportive space is not helping, go back to re-examining whether or not your goals are coming from a place of wanting to build nurturing *Mindful Connection.* In our example, if *Freddie Feels's* aim were to punish the teacher who was speaking loudly, or to blame himself for the situation (both ways of thinking focus away from connecting to his needs), he will probably continue to struggle without ever managing to find ways to meet his or the teacher's needs.

MOVE TO THE NEXT STEP

There is a grounding feeling that arises when you really connect to your feelings and feel all the things that come up. Once you've created supportive space, gotten the empathy that you need, and have fully attuned to feelings that came up, you are able to think more clearly and are aware of what your met and unmet needs are. Having identified your needs is where clarity starts. It is a very encouraging and empowering place to be. In the next Chapter, you move the "Resolution Field for Yourself" (Field #2) where you create strategies in order to take action toward getting these identified needs met and further build your resilience and create wellbeing for yourself. If there are other people involved in supporting you in this, make sure you all start directing your focus on this Field.

CHAPTER THREE

RESOLUTION FIELD FOR YOURSELF

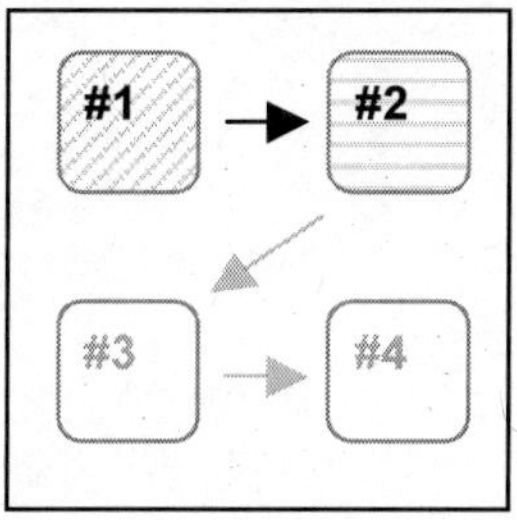

“Resolution Field For Yourself” (Field #2) is when you start focusing on your rational thinking, using logical inference, strategizing and carrying out actions, just like *Sadie Solves* would. This happens when you observe that you have emotionally de-flooded and are more grounded.

Sadie Solves

Sadie Solves focuses onto her Resolution Field in every situation she is in.
She is already grounded in her Empathy Field.

The purpose of the “Resolution Field for Yourself” is to maintain the met needs identified in your Empathy Field and pursue getting your identified unmet needs met. Doing this sustains one’s joyous feelings, resolves the non-joyous feelings, builds resilience and creates wellbeing.

It is very important to attend the Empathy Field before visiting this step. Finding ways to get your needs met will be very incomplete and weak without the deep learning and growth you get by attuning to your feelings and identifying your needs.

FOUR STEPS IN THE "EMPATHY FIELD FOR YOURSELF"

As introduced in Chapter 1, "Resolution Field for Yourself" consists of two parts: "Explore Possibilities"[i] and "*Carry out Strategies*"[ii]

Both these parts consist of two steps each that make a total of four steps:

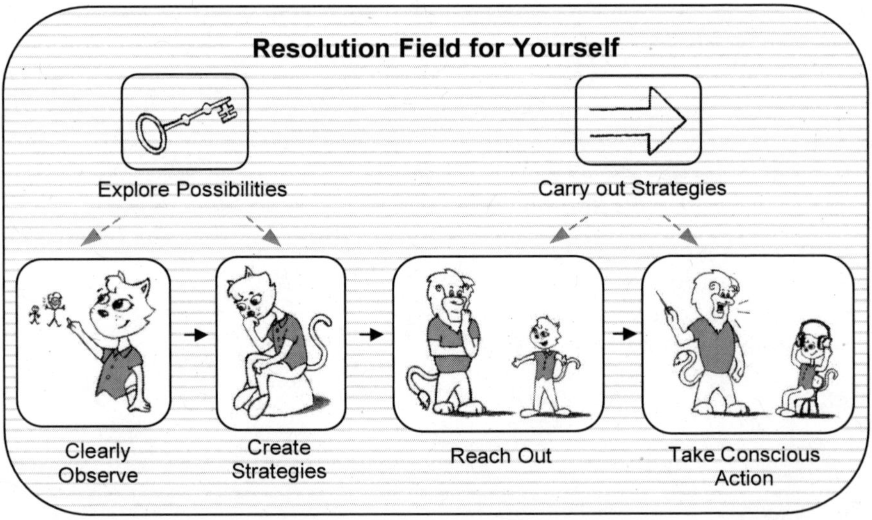

Each of these four steps has a collection of methods to carry out and you explore them all in this Chapter.

---

[i] One way to think of the process of exploring possibilities is to associate it with the newest part of your brain: the neo-cortex (or cerebral cortex). It is in charge of reason, thinking and planning.

[ii] Another way to think of the process of carrying out strategies is to also associate it with the newly developed neo-cortex (or cerebral cortex) as it is additionally in charge of speech and of control and execution of voluntary motor functions (motor cortex).

Sadie Solves
Explore Possibilities

When *Sadie Solves* heard the teacher's loud voice, she started exploring possibilities right away to get her needs met.

EXPLORE POSSIBILITIES

Exploring possibilities is the first step in Field #2 and is the part of the journey where you explore ways to get your needs met. It helps you develop strategies so that you can then carry them out in the second step of this Field.

Imagine successfully having gone through the Empathy Field, having the ease and clarity within, yet still unsure how to exactly get the needs that you identified met. It's a good time to explore possibilities, as you are more able and receptive to observe things clearly and create strategies.

A simple way of knowing if it's time to focus on this step is to take a deep breath, attune within yourself; check in to see if you got all the empathy you needed. If your feelings associated with this dynamic seem fairly or completely un-flooded, you are ready to use the clarity you have to start exploring possibilities towards getting your needs met.

The upcoming sections explore two steps in exploring possibilities: clearly observing behaviors in your current challenge first and then creating strategies around that observed challenge. The example of what *Sadie Solves* did around her reaction to the loud teacher demonstrates these two steps.

Sadie Solves

Explore Possibilities

- Observe Behaviors -

Sadie Solves observed both her and the teacher's behaviors around her met and unmet needs:

- Met needs behaviors: She attended the class that he taught where she learned a lot from him.

- Unmet needs behaviors: She made herself exposed to teacher's loud tone of voice and expected him to speak more quietly.

OBSERVE BEHAVIORS

Clearly observing behaviors is the ability to identify your behaviors in relation to another person's behaviors in a situation that is specific to time and circumstance. Observations are objective judgments that use rational thinking and logical inference with an ability to perceive external situations without involving one's own emotional reality and beliefs. By contrast, assumptions, evaluations and interpretations are subjective judgments of what you *think* or *feel* something or someone "is".

Questions to ask yourself in order to clearly observe behaviors:
"What did I/he/she do?" "What happened?" "When did it happen?" "Who was involved?" What was said?" "Do I have a specific example?"
Remember to keep asking open-ended questions (the "Six Ws").

Develop the skill of observing behaviors helps you avoid projecting your judgments onto others and taking things personally. Being objective can be difficult, especially when you are emotionally attached to people involved in the challenge. Once you empathically connect and fully attune to your emotions, observations become clearer and easier to do.

In order to use observed behaviors toward getting your needs met, stay focused on the actual behaviors rather than aim to figure out or presume potential intentions behind one's behaviors. There are two behaviors you can observe: *your* behaviors and *other person's* behaviors. Maintain your focus primarily on *your* behaviors and how they relate to the behaviors of others.

Behaviors

↙ ↘

Your Behaviors *Other Person's Behaviors*

Lets explore a collection of methods that can help *you* clearly observe behaviors. *Sadie Solves* chose some of these to observe behaviors herself.

#1 – OBSERVE THE OTHER PERSON'S BEHAVIOR FIRST

Describe the specific behaviors that the *other* person did in a certain situation in direct relation to your identified met and unmet needs. See if you can think of any specific examples that demonstrate that person's behavior. If the expression contains something else than a verb describing the behavior it is probably an evaluation of sorts.

You can start observing the other person's behavior by finding your existing "observation". An existing "observation" might or might not be a clear observation. It could be filled with conclusions, criticism and evaluations. It is important to notice it when you start thinking this way and refocus back toward your identified needs so you can find specific behaviors in relation to them.

Sadie Solves described the loud teacher's way of talking in our example in an evaluative and criticizing way: *"He's a loud buffoon"*. When she noticed herself do this, she first removed all the evaluations and criticisms. In this expression, the evaluation and criticism here are both the word *"buffoon"* and *"loud"*. *"Buffoon"* is not only an evaluation but also a straight up insult. These words describe what she *thinks* the other person is, and they are not observed behaviors.

Expressing evaluations and false conclusions can really decrease the likelihood that the other person hears your intended message. He will likely hear criticism and blame and this will probably cause him to become defensive. Additionally, this way of thinking and expressing one's thoughts is where assigning blame usually starts.

These kinds of expressions usually come about when someone is emotionally upset and is making conclusions and observations based on his current feeling rather than clear rational judgment. And when someone is emotionally flooded, it is very hard to be clear and objective. People tend to get very caught up in their heads instead of focusing back onto their Empathy Field to attune to their feelings and identify their needs. This can especially happen when feelings come up around circumstances that are not very concrete, such as various unspecified anxieties, worries and confusions, rather than concrete hardships where there is an obvious pain around a loss or something that happened.

Make sure to find just the behaviors that affect your currently met and unmet needs when making a clear observation, instead of wanting to figure out or predict the other person's intentions behind his behaviors. When observing behaviors, the goal is to find the behaviors that have been done first, before any potential intended behaviors that didn't come together.

Getting caught up in guessing the other person's intentions and motives will only sidetrack you from seeing the other person's behavior for what it is. Especially since at the core, people's "intentions" narrow down to them wanting to get their needs met. Some people might make themselves believe that they are very intuitive and can perfectly guess other people's intents and even create elaborate theories and "facts" around other people's "schemes" and motives. Meanwhile, they are really sidetracking themselves, because they are focusing away from being connected with themselves and their needs and then aiming to observe other people's behaviors with the aim to connect to them and their needs.

For example, *Freddie Feels's* need for safety got unmet and neither him nor the teacher intended this to happen. Being aware of this further helps *Freddie Feels* to see his needs for what they are, not mix them up with evaluations and intentions of any sort when identifying them and avoid taking things personally. It is of course possible that the teacher might have purposely scared *Freddie Feels.* Even in that context, teacher would have been attempting to get a need of his met. Needs stand on their own and it is very valuable to develop the ability to identify them as they are and how they are affected by specific behaviors.

Observing other people's behaviors also includes observing hurtful behaviors like lying, which can get those people's need for safety met and your need for trust unmet, being verbally or physically violent, which can get their need for self-esteem and validation met, and get your need for safety and respect unmet, etc. All of these are easily observable behaviors that connect to one's needs and have nothing to do with the other person's intentions behind these behaviors.

Avoid creating generalizations by using absolute exaggerations like "always", "too much", "never", "ever" or "rarely"; for example: *"He always shouts."* Some people tend to put so much meaning into someone's one-time unpleasant or hurtful behavior, that they create a permanent opinion of the person they had this interaction with. They use false reasoning like: "*if he talked to me like that once, that means that he always talks like that*".

From there on, they look for every sign to prove that what they think of that person is true and ignore all the other instances where the person is actually nice, or they use his niceness against him by saying that the person is being deceitful. They might even make completely false theories, for

example, that the teacher has some mental condition, that he has issues in his personal life and that he behaves like that with everyone and in order to take out his frustrations onto others. This way of thinking usually gets people in the vicious circle of resentment where they never truly get to know the other people around them.
Having a sense of skeptical thinking is a very important skill. There's a difference between skepticism and cynicism. Cynicism is an attitude of jaded negativity, filled with distrust of the integrity or professed motives of others that can be based on emotional upsets rather than clear thinking one has properly attuned to one's feelings. Skepticism is about carefully choosing where you put your trust and how. Make sure to nurture openness, curiosity and trust towards yourself and other people yet at the same time develop critical thinking and objectivity toward the realities of struggle and dishonesty life can offer. Clear observations of what happened can be obscured by misconceptions resulting from incorrect reasoning. These are called logical fallacies.

Consider these two claims: *"When people are emotionally upset, they don't think clearly"* and *"when people are emotionally upset, they tend to speak more loudly"*. Imagine making this conclusion: *"Because he talks loudly, he must not be thinking clearly and therefore doesn't know what he is talking about"*. Not every person who talks loudly is upset and therefore is not necessarily thinking unclearly.

Once having dropped the word *"buffoon"* and *"loud"*, *Sadie Solves* was left with a simple clearly observable behavior that the teacher did around her unmet need for safety and her met need for learning: he spoke with a raised voice at the class he taught.

Observing the other person's behavior

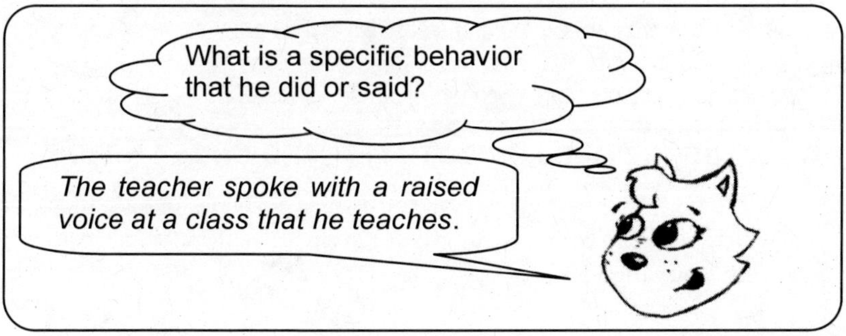

#2 – OBSERVE ONE'S OWN BEHAVIOR IN RELATION TO OTHER PERSON'S BEHAVIOR

Now let's observe why and how someone's *way* of behaving specifically influences and relates to *you*. You can do this by observing which of your *own* behaviors is getting your needs met or unmet in relation to the other person's behavior.

RECALL FEELINGS AND NEEDS

If you have successfully gone through the Empathy Field and attuned to your feelings, you wouldn't be emotionally charged when observing the feelings, you would simply be aware of what they were. As a result, the observation of the feelings would be mainly expressed in some form of a past tense, especially the non-joyous feelings. Expressing feelings in other tenses than the present also make it easier when expressing them to other listeners who might be easily triggered by your emotional states. This way, your present focus is obviously not on the feelings but rather on observing what has happened and further on creating strategies and carrying out actions, which is all part of the Resolution Field.

By going back to our example with the loud teacher, suppose *Sadie Solves* experienced similar feelings and needs as *Freddie Feels* attuned to and identified in the Empathy Field.

Recall Feelings and Needs

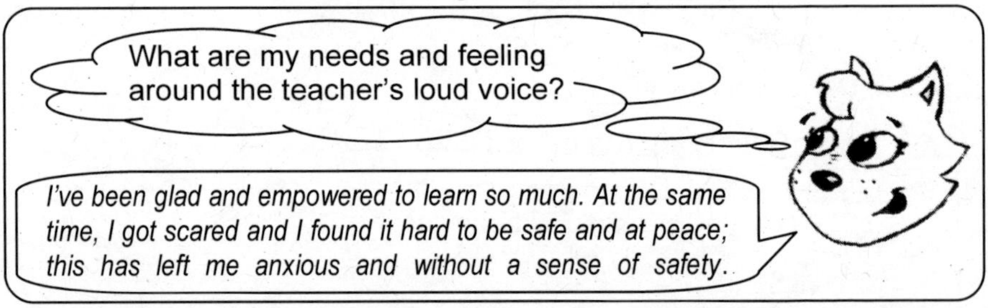

DISTINGUISH BEHAVIORS FOR BOTH MET AND UNMET NEEDS

Just like you created an observation of the other person's behavior at the beginning of this section, narrow down your own behaviors by scrutinizing your potentially evaluative language.

Find two sets of different behaviors:
- Ones that are keeping your met needs met and which have kept you in the dynamic that you are still in,
- And others that are keeping your unmet needs unmet, which is where the challenge arose.

Needs can get unmet through various sorts of behaviors like: involving or keeping oneself in a dynamic, expectations, such as the one of *Sadie Solves* expecting the teacher not to raise his voice; or assumptions such as assuming that the teacher would "know better" not to raise his voice in front of students; it could also be a lack of communication around what works for someone and what doesn't. In our example, one behavior that is meeting *Sadie Solve's* needs is *"attending the class"* and behaviors that are not meeting her needs are when she is *"exposing herself to the teacher's voice that she finds to be very loud" and "expecting him to talk more quietly"*.

It is very important to express the behaviors for what they are rather than for what they are not. Take the expression *"I don't have enough time"* for example. When rephrased into positive language, it reads" *"I do have time for other things that hold greater priority"*. Clear positive observations in some way expose the truth and are very hard to be used as excuses. What one gains through them is clarity and empowerment to create new strategies and possibilities because you work with something tangible and expressed, rather than something that is non-existing. For example, *Sadie Solves* would say: *"I attended his class"* instead of *"I didn't avoid going to his class"; "I made myself quite exposed to his voice that I found to be very loud when he spoke"* instead of *"I didn't find a way to not be affected by his voice"*; or *"I expected him to talk more quietly"* instead of *"I expected him to not talk as loudly"*.

Observing one's own behavior that's getting needs *met*

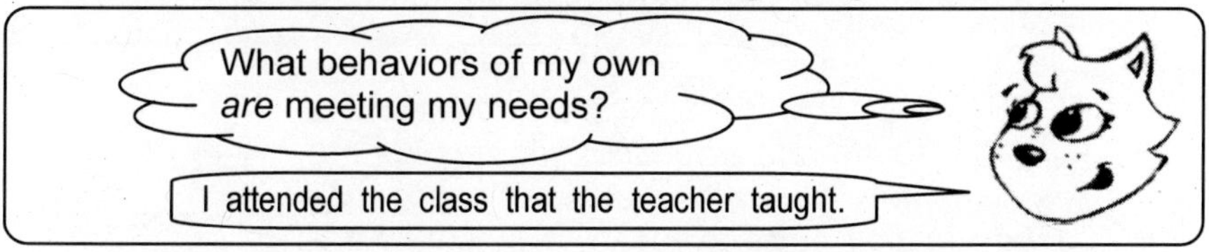

Observing one's own behavior that's getting needs *unmet*

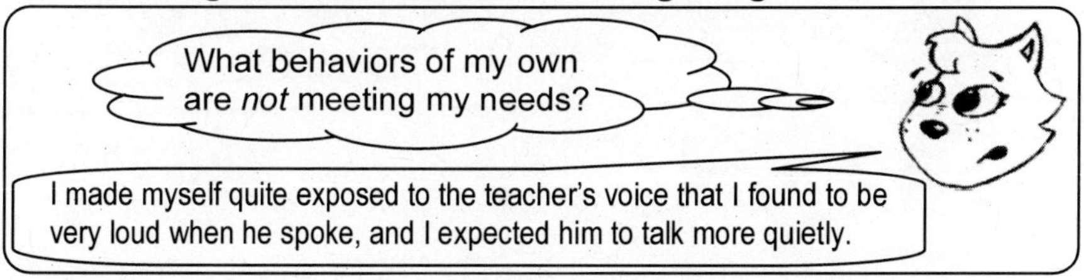

Note that when you explore your own behaviors, more feelings and needs could come up. For example, *Sadie Solves* fond out that she was feeling embarrassed to admit that someone's loud voice had aroused a scared feeling in her and she had less confidence as a result. She also found many more needs that were met, like companionship, creativity, etc.

#3 – CONNECT ALL THE BEHAVIORS

This is the point where you directly acknowledge that the feelings that you feel and your both met and unmet needs were brought about by the actions that *you* took in connection with the other person's behavior. You can do this by connecting the feelings and the needs to the behavior with the expression *"because I"*.[33] By doing this, you own your actions and take responsibility for what arose your feelings. Other person's behavior is still expressed; the focus however is on *your* behavior.

It is important to first view the behaviors that are around your *met* needs, because it helps you first connect to the essence of what's important for you in this dynamic.

Connecting all behaviors around the met needs

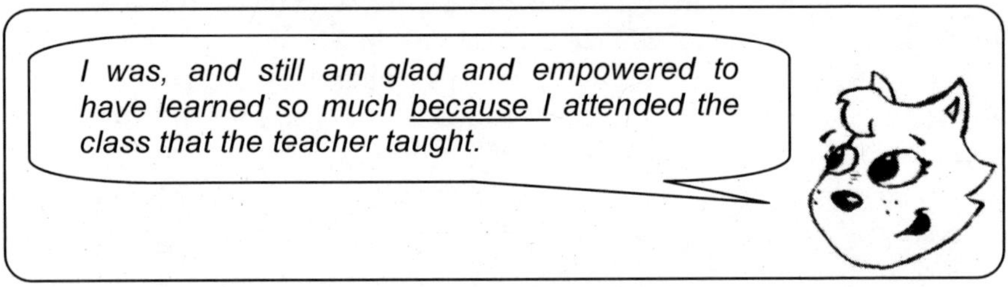

Connecting all behaviors around the unmet needs

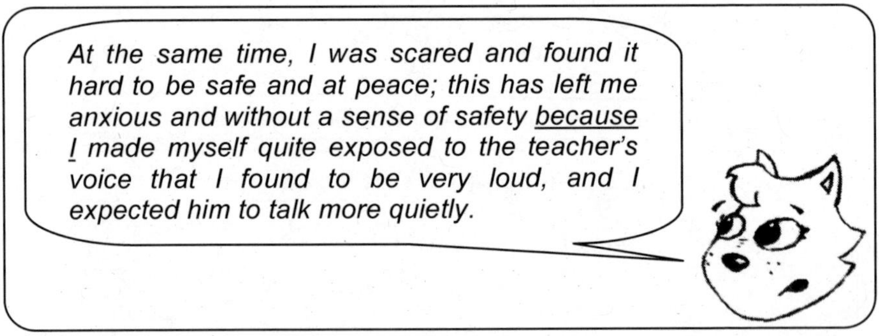

Sadie Solves
Explore Possibilities
- Create Strategies -

Sadie Solves created strategies toward getting her needs met with the teacher *and* elsewhere. Her needs for learning, companionship and creativity with this teacher were very important for her. She decided to keep attending the class. She would wear earplugs and also request the teacher to reduce his tone of voice in order to get her need for safety met.

CREATE STRATEGIES

Creating strategies is exploring ideas and making plans around the observed behaviors to get your unmet needs met and maintain your met needs. They are potential solutions to problems and challenges. Strategies are created using rational thinking to explore all the possibilities in a specific challenge and your needs around it.

One of the most important aspects of creating strategies with the aim of getting one's needs met is that they generate and increase the amount of joyous feelings, decrease the amount of non-joyous feelings and create wellbeing in one's life. Psychologist John Gottman shows that in order to maintain successful connected relationships, the overall ratio between joyous and non-joyous feelings in any given encounter needs to be five to one.[34]

Questions to ask yourself in order to create strategies: *"What can I do?" "What new strategies can I plan, and how?"*
Remember to keep asking open-ended questions (the "Six Ws").

When you are attuned to your feelings, have identified your met and unmet needs and have a clear observation of a situation, you can start creating strategies to get those unmet needs met. The goal is to find strategies that can aim toward getting all your needs met. A very important distinction to have in mind is that as much as you *can* facilitate getting and work toward getting *all* your needs met, you might not and probably won't be able to make all your desired *strategies* happen.

Note that different strategies can be and usually are in conflict. Needs on the other hand, don't conflict amongst themselves, they stand alone and are invariable. In our example, both the students and the teacher have the same need for connection and mutual exchange of learning. However, the teacher's strategy to get these needs met involves the strategy of raising his voice, whereas the students would rather get the same needs met using a strategy that involves a much more peaceful class. Strategies can be changed around to get these universal core needs met.

One's core needs can be met in a much simpler way than most people believe and like to strategize around. Creating new strategies does not guarantee that all your needs will easily get met. It can increase the chances of them getting met and support you in taking care of yourself and those around you, which in itself gets many core needs met.

Another very important thing to have in mind is that if you do decide to create new strategies, the process of letting go of the old strategies and adapting to the new ones can be fairly challenging and emotion arousing. You will need to face your "cognitive dissonances" and the futility that the old strategy hasn't seem to have worked for you. Support of the Empathy Field will be fundamental here.

Creating strategies is about taking the time and doing your best to plan and find resources to increase the chances of creating satisfying outcomes. It is not "wishful thinking", nor it is "hoping that the best will happen without worrying about it". Just passively hoping and believing that everything will work itself out doesn't quite cut it. It is important to have an optimistic and hopeful view towards everything in life. Optimism is about exploring what is possible. It's about cultivating courage to do something despite the fear of it. It is focusing on growing courage rather than growing fear.

Positive thinking is crucial to knowing what you want and to plan for it, which in turn increases the chances of getting your needs met. This doesn't mean that if things are working out well, it is *only* because you are having positive thoughts, or that things are not working out because you are thinking negatively or not thinking "positively enough" about it. There are many additional factors that contribute to strategies being successful, which is what all the tools in this book explore. It is very empowering to express things in terms of what they are rather than what they are not. Practicing seeing things through the positive lens can be life changing in itself and full of breakthroughs. So far, through the process of creating supportive space and empathy, you can build your awareness, confidence and courage to be in a place where you strategize and live through *"Yes, I can"* instead of *"No, I can't"*, or *"Yes, Things are"* instead of *"No, Things shouldn't be"*.

Make sure to find any oversights in your strategies and do your best to plan them out as well as you can. Merely working very hard to carry tasks out without a working and well-planned-out strategy in place doesn't mean that your attempts will bear fruit. Hoping that a poorly planned and weak strategy will be successful by simply "carrying it out very well" is a misguidance.

If you are seeking support from others, you need to make sure to have well-intended and constructive support. People give unsolicited advice all the time. Sometimes it could come from desires to help out; sometimes it could be a mere habit or even a belief that they need to guide others. If you find yourself taken back by other people's advice and advances, it is a good idea to check in with them about the reasons why they are giving you advice. You can be as straightforward as you want. If they are clear why they are giving advice it is easier for you to at least hear them out and create a bit more connection. Very often your question might confuse or embarrass them as it could expose that they actually don't have a clear idea why they are approaching you with advice. A similar situation can arise when people ask you about the strategies you are planning and have a habit of constantly scrutinizing and criticizing your strategies rather than being truly curious and interested in supporting you in your endeavors.

You need to find out whether you want to get your needs met with the person you are currently in a dynamic with or whether you would create alternative strategies to get them met elsewhere.

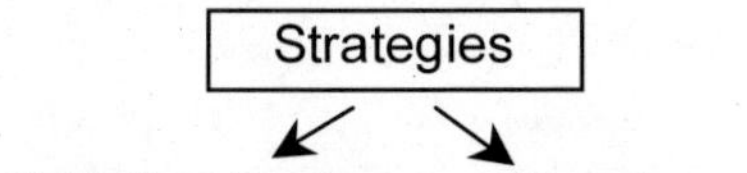

Lets explore a collection of methods that can help *you* create strategies toward getting your needs met. *Sadie Solves* chose some of these to create strategies herself.

#1 – EXPLORE WAYS TO MEET NEEDS

Exploring what significance and priority you have around meeting either of your needs with this person or elsewhere makes it easier to know how to create strategies. You can find this out by reflecting on the feelings that would come up if either of your needs were met or unmet depending on different explored strategies. Remember, the goal with creating new strategies is to create more joyous feelings in your life and consequently, more wellbeing. Different strategies evoke different feelings around *same* needs in people. Every person is unique in this way. That's why every person can find one's own unique and different way to meet same needs.

GETTING NEEDS MET WITH THIS PERSON

You might find that getting needs met with this person would overall, bring more joy than attempting to meet them elsewhere; at least in the current setting and dynamic. In this case, you could choose to strategize toward maintaining the met needs with this person and finding ways of getting the unmet needs around him met as well. With proper strategies and dedication, you can increase the chances in your aim of getting all your needs met in your dynamic with this person.

Sadie Solves recognized that getting the learning, companionship or creativity in her interaction with the teacher seems to be more important, valuable and bring more joy than the safety that she is not getting from the loud voice that he is using. This is because she knew how hard it was to get teaching of that quality and caliber. She also knew that if she chose this strategy, she would need to find ways to manage her fear around being in the class.

Sometimes empathically connecting around your unmet needs might reduce the severity of their effect on you. In our example, *Sadie Solves* might not even feel that scared around loud voices anymore if she got thorough empathy around it.

Getting needs met with this person

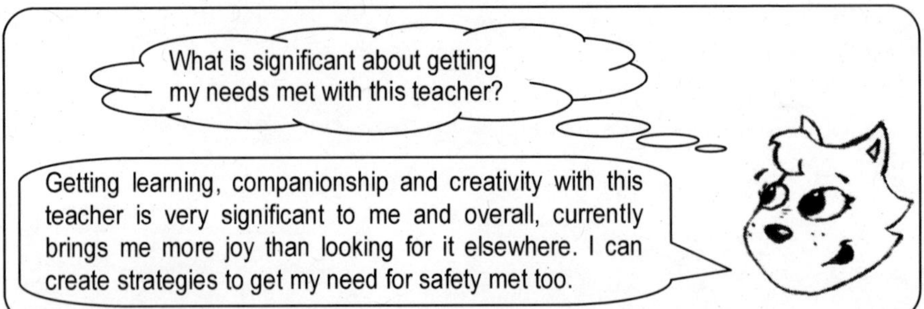

GETTING NEEDS MET ELSEWHERE

You might find that getting needs met elsewhere would overall, bring more joy than attempting to meet them with this person. In this case, you could choose to strategize getting your unmet needs met elsewhere where you might be able to have the currently met needs met as well.

In our example, *Sadie Solves* might have felt exceptionally scared as the teacher could not only be loud but threatening as well; or maybe his voice might have brought up way too much insecurity in her. In that case her need for safety could be stronger than the learning, companionship or creativity that she would get from the teacher. The excitement and motivation to have the needs for learning, companionship or creativity met with this specific teacher would not be as strong. These needs could instead be met by finding another teacher around whom she wouldn't feel as scared and would overall have more joy around.

Getting needs met elsewhere

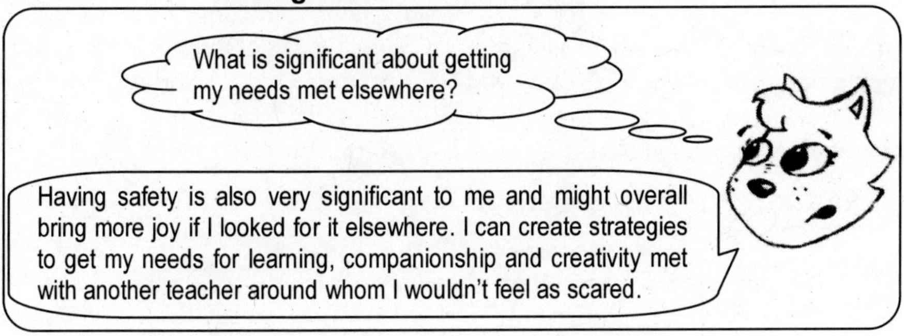

#2 – CREATE NEW STRATEGIES

Needs can get met in many different ways. Rather than having it be a specific scenario or idea on your mind, you can create many new different possibilities. Creating new strategies takes courage and can be a challenging step for many people if they have deeply rooted habits and attachments to certain relationships or dynamics. The old strategies that already get certain needs met can often be excuses and distractions from creating new strategies, which can meet certain very important *unmet* needs. Resisting working through this challenge usually leads to justifications, denials and various stories people tell themselves that keep them in the old dynamics and habits that they are attached and used to.

It is important to distinguish behaviors that you can realistically change from certain unchangeable circumstances. Sometimes you don't necessarily have a choice around the conditions you are in, for example the family, culture or nationality you were born into, painful circumstances in life, etc. Work on accepting these for what they are before moving on to strategize around them. You need to face the futility that certain strategies are simply not helping meet certain needs and learn to move on by letting them go. You would have already done this in Empathy Field and if more challenges come up, you will need to reconnect back to the Empathy Field again.

STRATEGIZE TO GET UNMET NEEDS MET WITH THIS PERSON

Explore how the other person could change or adjust his behavior and how *you* could do the same; both with the aim of meeting your needs met with this person. Note that you might have a hard time with the idea of having to plan what someone else needs to do. You might think that he should do this work, and not you. This step is about you getting *your* needs met. You are being proactive and taking responsibility for getting your needs met.

- "Request new behavior" - you can plan to reach out to the other person and request him to adjust or change his behavior. In our example, *Sadie Solves* could ask the teacher to reduce his tone of voice or adjust it in some other ways that his voice wouldn't impact her.

- "Change own behavior" - this is about reducing the other person's behavior's impact on you by changing your own behavior, without even necessarily interacting with him. In the example with the loud teacher, *Sadie Solves* could sit further away, get earplugs if she think that might help, go and ask for support from the principal of the school, etc.

Carrying out these two steps is explored in detail in the upcoming section.

Strategizing to get unmet needs met with this person

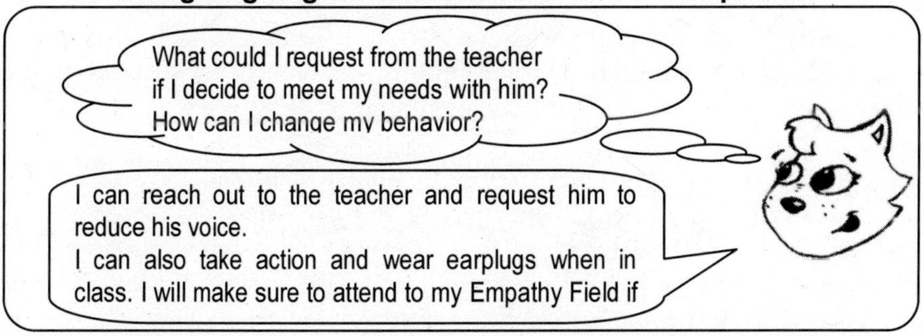

STRATEGIZE TO GET CURRENTLY MET NEEDS MET ELSEWHERE

This is about exploring how you could get your needs met by creating other new strategies and dynamics instead the one you are currently in. This step can be challenging due to many unforeseen feelings that might come up. You need to make sure you are ready to attend to your Empathy Field in this scenario as well. This would be around your *and* the other person's reaction to your attempts to get your needs met elsewhere.

- "Request new behavior" - you could reach out to the other person, and inquire about whether he knows someone with whom you could get your needs met in the way you did with him. In our example, *Sadie Solves* could request from the teacher to suggest another teacher that he knows of that teaches as well as he does. She could even go as far as requesting him to stop teaching the class, which of course could be a challenging undertaking with quite a sensitive topic to work with.

- "Change own behavior" - you could take your own action to get your needs met elsewhere. In our example, *Sadie Solves* could cease going to this teacher's classes and seek to find another place where she can get good quality of teaching, companionship and creativity.

Strategizing to get currently met needs elsewhere

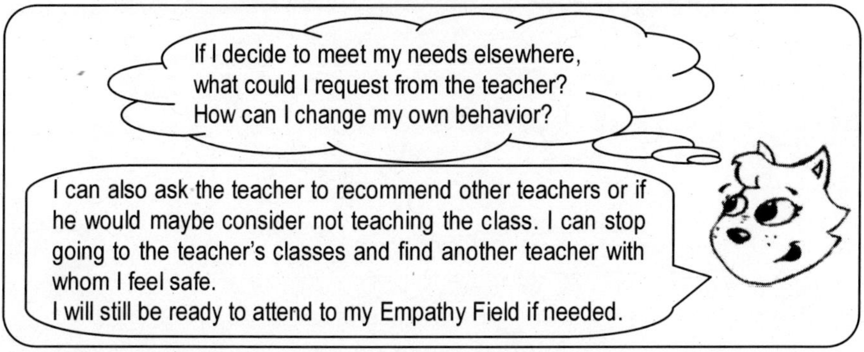

DECIDE ON ONE STRATEGY

Decision-making is very important in the strategies creation process. You need to decide on one strategy to commit to that you believe would be the best for you and would bring the most amount of wellbeing.

Make sure to spend some time thinking about which strategy would work best for you and then decide on one and put it to action; and remember, with all the clarity you can gain by going through all the previous steps, you have good grounds to make a choice that's best for you. And it's your choice to make, not someone else's to do it for you.

Note again that deciding to let a specific well-habituated strategy go can be a very emotional process that might require lots of empathy and healing.

In our example, *Sadie Solves's* needs for learning, companionship and creativity with this teacher were very important for her. She decided to stay in the class with this teacher and to request from him to reduce his voice. She would also bring earplugs to class and make sure she attended her Empathy Field whenever needed.

Deciding on one Strategy

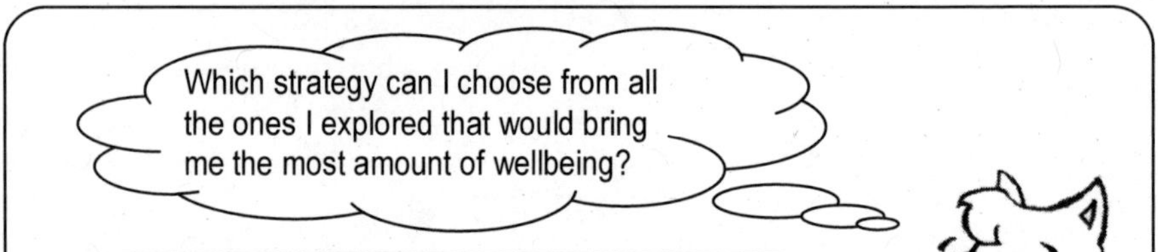

#3 – STRATEGIZE BASED ON THE OTHER PERSON'S RESPONSE

This step involves part of the strategy where you plan to make a request from the other person to do a specific behavior based on the strategy you decided to do. *Sadie Solves* decided to ask the teacher to reduce his tone of voice.

People can give out behavioral cues that can be very subtle yet observable and at other times these cues are much more obvious and direct. Refer to the APPENDIX for a list of "Non-Verbal Behavior" factors (pg. 223). These can help you recognize how people respond to your attempts to reach out. Different traces of emotions on people's faces are also described in the APPENDIX (pg. 220).

The way to plan around the other person's response is to be aware of the three different ways he might respond to your reaching out. Lets explore all three in detail.

1 - CONNECTING (TURNING TOWARD)

This way of responding is what you would essentially like to get and even inspire in the other person, by having a very connecting approach yourself, which is what *Mindful Connection* is all about. Even if the person might not be very happy with your reaching out, he still might be curious and willing to work things out.

Sadie Solves might find out when she reaches out to the teacher that he doesn't mind lowering his voice. In that case, she would have easily gotten all her needs met (learning, companionship, creativity and of course, safety).

Even if he didn't really want to reduce his voice, the teacher might still be interested in talking to her and working things out. For example, maybe he has a hard time expressing himself unless he talks loudly. Or maybe he is unsure about what he wants to do. This would open up a conversation to work together in the aims of getting everyone's needs met.

Other person connecting to the attempt to reach out

2 - ATTACKING (TURNING AGAINST)

The other person could get irritated by your request, refuse to change his behavior and even get aggressive and offensive. To get an idea what attacking looks like, imagine asking someone what time it is and the person responding with: *"leave me alone!"* or *"figure it out yourself!"* Gottman points out two more subtle ways one can recognize when someone is attacking one's attempt to reach out: by recognizing criticism and contempt.

This way of interacting with people creates so-called "sour relationships" where there is disconnection, frequent misunderstandings and lots of pain and hurt. This is one strategy (besides ignoring) that people use to avoid feeling pain and hurtful feelings. It is an attempt to protect themselves when they think their needs could get unmet. This strategy doesn't necessarily end relationships; it can easily maintain them, but in a discontented and "sour" state.

Although these kinds of responses are intimidating, they can be easier to work with than when someone ignores you. This is because you have something to work with and if you know how to listen "underneath" the other person's attacking words, it can help you find ways to still connect to him.

If staying in touch with this person and getting your needs met is important, you can choose to empathize with the person in order to build connection, which could increase your chances of the person starting to care for your wellbeing as well and potentially do something about it. Of course, you might need to create supportive space at times and set boundaries if the interaction is overbearing. If the interaction keeps being very overbearing, or you have tried offering empathy and attempted to connect unsuccessfully many times, you can choose to change your strategy and cease your interaction with this person and find ways of meeting your needs elsewhere.

Other person attacking the attempt to reach out

3 - IGNORING (TURNING AWAY)

When you attempt to connect, the other person might ignore you or completely change the topic of conversation. When responding this way, a person is usually attempting to avoid potential hurtful feelings to come up and get certain need met by being passive and evasive. Gottman points out two more ways one can respond in this way: defensiveness and stonewalling, which are usually responses to criticism and contempt when people attack their attempts to reach out. This can easily happen if the person is used to being attacked and criticized a lot and has developed this defense mechanism even in circumstances where people are not being attacking and aggressive.

These situations can usually be a bit harder to strategize around since there is limited amount of interaction to work with. It can be challenging when you are really wanting to and making eager attempts to connect and someone ignores you; there is usually little or nothing to work with. You can wait for any cues that can help establish a connection by giving that person some space; you can also try attempting to reach out a few times. This "wait" might delay taking care of your needs for a bit too. You would still be maintaining your goal to get your needs met with this person.

This response destroys relationships. If you are interested in having someone not be in your life, ignore his attempts to reach out to you. In turn, if someone is consistently not responding back to you, the relationship cannot sustain itself. Note also that although this response is very different and quite opposite in dynamics compared to when a person attacks, the hardship and consequences it can create can still be enormously hurtful.

If the ignoring continues or turns into attacking, you can also decide to change your strategy and temporarily take supportive space or permanently find ways to get your needs met elsewhere.

Other person ignoring the attempt to reach out

One of the surest ways to stop a dynamic is to stop "feeding it" in any way by staying away or not interacting at all if possible. You can do this with or without letting the person know that that's your goal. I would recommend taking time and consideration around deciding how and whether to communicate this decision to the person.

When it comes to changing strategies, one thing that people tend to be very sensitive to is a "change of heart"; if you change your mind about something or decide to commit to a new strategy, it could arouse lots of upset, pain and confusion in people who are closest to you and even in yourself. Change is an inevitable part of life and something that everyone comes across. When faced with people's reactions to your new strategies, you need to be able to take responsibility for your actions and also offer them empathy, which is explored in the next Chapter.

When having a hard time letting go a specific dynamic that is entirely not working for you, you need to ask yourself if you would rather keep a commitment around something that arouses pain in you and gets important needs unmet or if you would instead find new strategies and lovingly work towards changing any potential past promises you might have made and attempt to aim to be a part of the journey of finding ways of getting your, and ultimately everyone's needs met.

PRACTICE

EXPLORE POSSIBILITIES

Turn to "*Explore Possibilities*" in the Practice Section on page 195. It offers different practices for exploring possibilities for yourself.

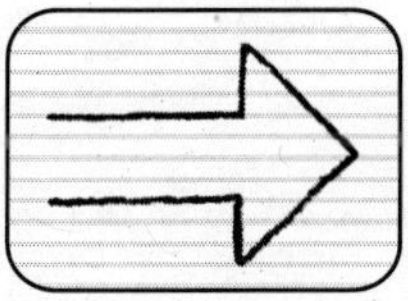

Sadie Solves
Carry out Strategies

Having explored all her possibilities and created strategies, *Sadie Solves* started carrying out the strategy she decided upon.

CARRY OUT STRATEGIES

This second step of Field #2 is the part of the journey where you set off toward getting your needs met. Having explored your possibilities, you can now start carrying out the chosen strategy, just like *Sadie Solves* would. Carrying out strategies is when you perform specific actions toward getting your needs met.

Going through the Empathy Field steps and also creating observations and strategies without following through with concrete action can leave you connected to yourself and aware of what's going on, yet it would only last temporarily unless you actually do something toward making your strategies happen. Doing this step completes the spectrum of what you need to do in order to get your needs met. A simple way of knowing if it's time to focus on this step is to take a deep breath, attune within yourself and check in to make sure you are emotionally un-flooded and grounded, have created solid strategies by using all the observed behaviors and are ready to start carrying it all out. This way, you can be proactive, avoid being passive and make sure you *responsibly* carry out the steps needed to get your needs met.

It is also this step where active communication with other people starts. Remember that you are still in the "Resolution Field for Yourself",[i] and even though the other person is to be actively involved in the conversation, you are still focusing on yourself and towards getting *your* needs met. You are inviting the other person to take the journey of supporting you in "getting your needs met" together with you.

The upcoming sections explore two steps in carrying out strategies: requesting new behavior from the other person and also changing one's own behavior. The example of what *Sadie Solves* did once she explored her possibilities and created strategies demonstrates these two steps.

---

[i] You also reach out to people when you interrupt to get supportive space in the "Empathy Field for Yourself", as discussed in Chapter 2.

Sadie Solves
Carry out Strategies
- Request new Behavior -

Sadie Solves made sure to have the teacher's attention. Then she expressed all her feelings and needs and asked him if he would consider reducing his tone of voice during class. She checked in if he heard the request properly.

REQUEST NEW BEHAVIOR

The process of requesting the new behavior involves approaching reaching out to the other person and requesting him to change or adjust his behavior which would support you get your needs met. You want to make your requests clear, non-blaming and non-demanding; and frame it so that "*it's a gift to people and so that it would make their life more wonderful for them*".[35]

Expecting others to do things for you because you extend the same behavior to them will regularly leave you disappointed. The expression "do unto others as you would have do unto you" unfortunately doesn't quite work the other way around. This especially applies if you expect others to "read your mind" and expect that people should "clue in" that the way *you* behave means that that's the way *they* should behave. Sometimes, this can happen naturally and people could be sensitive to your needs and respond. Most of the time, people are also concerned for and focused on their own needs and acting accordingly, you need to reach out and let others know what they could do to support you in getting your needs met.

Questions to ask yourself in order to request new behvior: *"How can I reach out" "How would I make a request?"*
Remember to keep asking open-ended questions (the "Six Ws").

Lets explore a collection of methods that can help *you* request new behavior from others. *Sadie Solves* chose some of these to request new behavior from the teacher.

#1 – PREPARE TO REACH OUT

ROLE-PLAY THE INTERACTION

Anticipating talking to someone with whom there's a fall-out or a difficult challenge can be intimidating and nerve wrecking. Role-playing the full interaction with a friend by exploring various possible outcomes can be of enormous help to build up the nerve to reach out and know what to say.

CREATE CONNECTION BY NURTURING THE RELATIONSHIP

In order for your reaching out to be meaningful and useful, you want to make sure to nurture the connection with the person prior to making your request. This is further explored when you start focusing on his Fields in the upcoming Chapters. Simply having an established nurturing connection with someone can make that person receptive to your request even if it is not worded perfectly. You want to make sure that the other person actually *cares* about what you want to say before you delve into making requests.

If the request revolves around something important that potentially holds a lot of pain, take it really easy at first by building some listening, patience and caring into the dynamic, accepting the other person for who he is and by focusing on his Empathy and the Resolution Field (upcoming Chapters). This involves starting conversations by inquiring about how the other person is doing and being ready to connect first before giving out requests.

If there is no relationship established, no mater how clearly or non-invasively you say something, there could be a lot of disinterest and resistance. Just imagine your receptiveness around a sensitive issue that might come up with your best friend versus a person you don't know very well. Sometimes you can even be very blunt with your best friend and it would be fine because he trusts and respects you.

Even in the counseling world, studies show that the best predictor for successful outcomes of counseling isn't what theory or model they use but rather if the client views the relationship with the counselor as a good one.[36]

BE EMOTIONALLY UN-FLOODED

If possible, it is important not to be emotionally charged when reaching out, especially when stating feelings. The person has to get a clear picture around what is going on for you rather than to presume he needs to give you support. If you are emotionally flooded, you need to focus on your Empathy Field and you probably won't be able to make clear requests. To give this a bit more context, think of how much harder it would be for you to hear about someone being angry with you by hearing it directly from the person in a heated moment or if a friend told you about it. Usually "second hand" information from someone else is easier to handle and connect to, since it is not emotionally charged.

HAVE THE PERSON'S ATTENTION

Just before you start talking and go into making a request, you want to make sure you have the person's attention and that he is present with you. By inviting the other person to focus on your Resolution Field, you are honoring the Requirement #1 for a Mindful Connection, which requires everyone to be focused on the same Field at the same time.

This is usually done by a simple act of eye-connection, you can look for a nod response and even a smile can be a good indicator that the person is "with you". You can also arrange a specific time to talk with the other person so that you can make sure that you would have the person's attention. This can also take certain amount of pressure off as it is clear that you have something to talk about and everyone has time to prepare for it.

ACKNOWLEDGE THE REASON FOR REACHING OUT

Remember that you are still focusing on yourself and that your reason for reaching out is to get your own needs met.

Supporting the other person to get his own needs met happens when you start focusing on *his* Fields. Requesting someone to do something because one believes that it is "good for him" can easily build resistance and disconnection. It needs to come from a place of being first connected to his needs and feelings, which will be explored in the upcoming Chapters. You can also let the person know that your aim is to make things work with *him*, despite various other options and strategies that are possible.

Connecting first when reaching out

#2 – STATE THE CURRENT BEHAVIORS

Before stating the request itself, express your observation of all the behaviors in the challenging situation to the person. Refer to "Observing Behaviors" section earlier in this Chapter.

Including your feelings and needs with the observed behaviors is crucial, because that's the part of the connecting where you put things more into context and the teacher can have better chances of connecting to your request. The observation also points out that it is *you* that is responsible for the behaviors that are both meeting and not meeting your needs. The aim of stating these is not to request the other person to offer you empathy because you've already gotten empathy. You are simply getting everything out into the light.

Stating the Behaviors

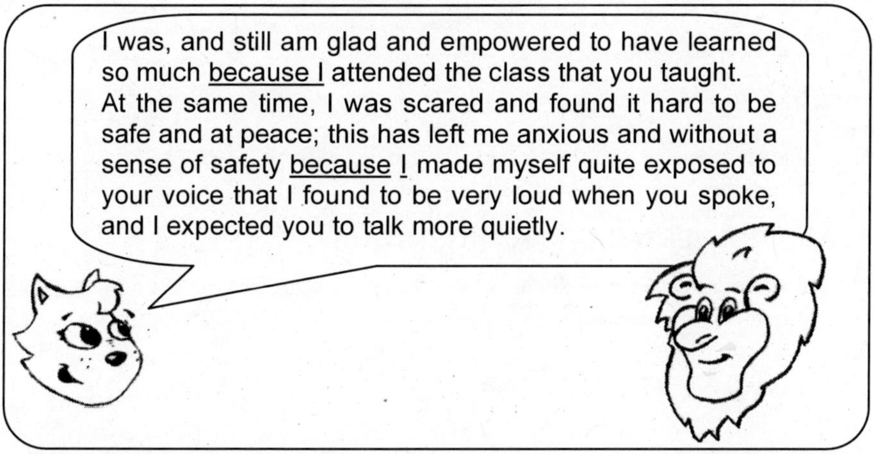

Giving such a detailed descriptions of behaviors might not be always necessary and is usually important when very challenging situations arise. More often, these sentences can be much shorter, concise and casual. It is also a good idea to express these behaviors in your own words rather than literally recite pre-made sentences.

Stating the Behaviors (Alternate Shorter Version)

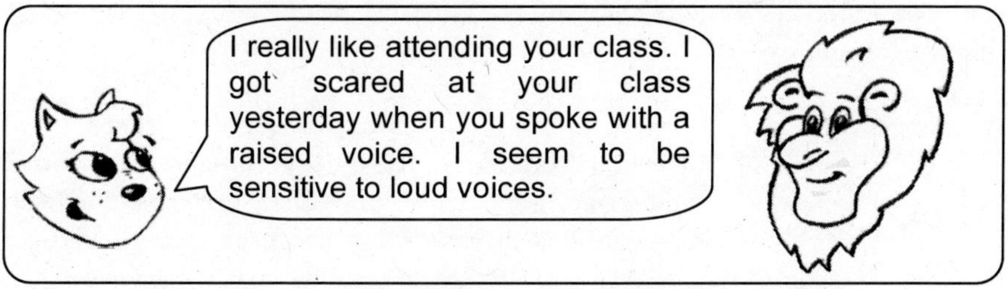

#3 – REQUEST THE NEW BEHAVIORS

SHAPE THE REQUEST POSITIVELY

When making requests, make sure to express what you "do want" the other person to do. If you know what you "don't want" the person to do, spend some time exploring and finding the positive behavior that you want to express in the request, that is related to the unwanted behavior.

For example, if *Sadie Solves* wanted the teacher "not to shout", she could rephrase that to wanting him to "speak more quietly".

EXPRESS SENTIMENTS AROUND THE REQUEST

When opening or closing requests, another step that is helpful is to express how much it would mean to you if the other person worked on supporting you in getting your needs met.

You can say things like:
"I would really appreciate it", "It would mean a lot", "It would really make it easier on me".
If you really care for the connection you have with that person, you can also express that in your own words.

START THE REQUEST AS AN INVITATION

When making requests, it always helps to give other people the opportunity to explore the matter with you, have a say, do things themselves or to be able to correct their errors. You can offer this if you state your requests in a form of a question or an offering.

Although *Sadie Solves* is requesting something of the teacher, her goal is not to make him do something, nor is it so that he would "change who he is"; her aim is to create a mutually beneficial arrangement where everyone's needs get met and find out if he would be willing to work on that together with her.

Dale Carnegie explores effectiveness of this approach towards developing leadership; he recommends giving people the opportunity to do things themselves and even learn from their own challenges.[37]

A request is always offered in form of a question unless there is an established understanding that you would be giving directions and that person has already offered to go along with your direct requests. This can happen in families, organizations, sports and other community oriented dynamics. Your aim is never to tell the other person what he should do. Even if you are giving guidance, it is ultimately up to the other person if he would comply with your request.

You can start with:
"What do you think about…?" "Do you think you could…?" "You might want to consider…" "Would you be interested in…?" "Would you be ok with…?"

SHAPE REQUEST THROUGH DIFFERENT SENSORY SYSTEMS

In order to help your request get heard even more effectively, you can shape it using sensory system that you consider matches your listener closest.

Sensory systems are specific and distinct ways that people's brains function and respond to outside stimuli. There are four of them: *Auditory*, *Visual*, *Kinesthetic* and *Cognitive*. If you observe how certain people interact and listen to the language they use, you can learn to notice which sensory system they tend to operate on more.

I remember once trying to explain a certain musical passage to a violinist that I worked with and as I was attempting to name the notes one by one, she was saying that she did not understand and that I needed just to "show her". She needed to get an *Auditory* or *Kinesthetic* presentation and I was offering it in a *Visual* and *Cognitive* way. Usually in these circumstances I would just keep "re-wording" things, which would just reinforce the confusion. Instead, I just played the notes and she easily learned it within seconds.

This step requires a bit of exploration and practice and once mastered, it can considerably enhance successful connection.

- If the person seems to be more ***Auditory***, you can word your request by using words like: *"How does it sound…" or "Would it resonate with you to…"*
- If the person seems to be more ***Visual***, you can word your request by using words like: *"Would you look into…" "Can you picture…"*
- If the person seems to be more ***Kinesthetic***, you can word your request by using words like: "How do you feel…" "Would it sit with you if…"
- If the person seems to be more ***Cognitive*** type, you can word your request by using words like: *"What do you think about…" "Can you figure out…"*

Pay attention to which expressions from above other person uses more often to determine what the prevailing sensory system for that person is.

Additionally, when making requests, explain which specific way of interaction works for you and what the best way is for you to understand their requests and observations.

Sadie Solves noticed that the teacher was very visual and would mindfully use language that she knew he could relate more to visually.

REQUEST THE SPECIFIC BEHAVIOR

Now you can ask the other person to do the specific action, a behavior that you identified in the "Observing Behaviors" section.
- If you've chosen to get your needs met with this person, you'd request the specific behavior that gets your needs met.
- If you've chosen to get your needs met elsewhere, a request might be unnecessary although sometimes it might be appropriate if the person could do a specific behavior that would clear the space for you to be able to get your needs met.

For example, *Sadie Solves* could have decided to ask the teacher about stopping teaching the class or recommending other teachers (the strategy to get her needs met elsewhere). In our example, she decided to go with the strategy of asking the teacher to reduce his voice because she valued the quality of learning she was getting with him and wanted to find ways of getting the need for safety around him met as well.

Requesting the Specific Behavior

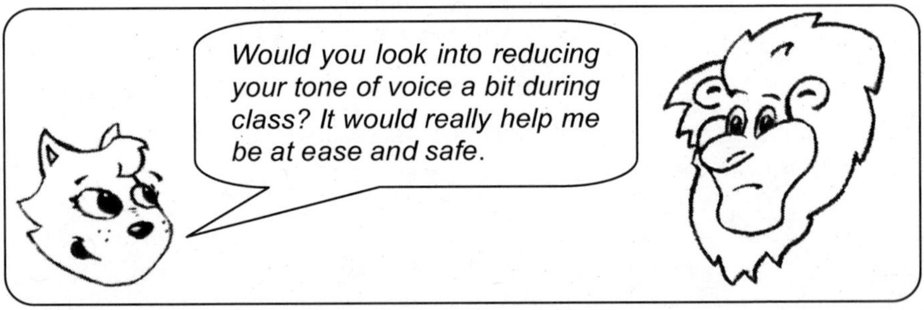

Recall that reaching out to someone can also be directed toward the Empathy Field (instead of the Resolution Field), when your aim is to create supportive space for yourself. The requested specific action would be for the other person to change the behavior that is making it hard for you to be able to have supportive space in order to empathically connect with yourself. For example, if the teacher was not allowing the students to leave class under any circumstances, the request could be for him to consider letting students out if they were to get emotionally overwhelmed.

#4 – CHECK IN IF THE REQUEST WAS PROPERLY HEARD

It is important that you make sure that your request was properly heard. You can inquire if the other person understood your request: *"How does that sound to you?" "How do you feel about this?" "What do you think about this?" "Did what I asked make sense?" "I'm curious to know how you heard what I requested?"*

Considering that your request directly relates to and involves other people's behaviors or beliefs, it is very probable that many times people will get emotionally triggered and reactive. You need to be accepting of any response you get from the person. That's what creates the distinction between a request and a demand. In a demand, you are attached to the outcome. In a request, you are willing to work with and adapt to different possible outcomes.

Someone who reacted emotionally to your clearly worded request might have understood it in a different way than you intended. You can recognize this by paying attention to their body language, or their direct response to you. If you are not getting triggered you need to focus on that person's Empathy Field (I cover this in detail in the upcoming Chapter). You need to be able to switch your focus back and forth between you and the other person during these times and create a good balance between offering him support and also making sure that he sees your standpoint.

When checking in with the person, he might connect, ignore or attack your attempt to reach out and this will further determine how you pursue with your strategies.

Sadie Solves noticed that the teacher's body language changed when she was making the request and she checked in with him to see how he took the request. Her request had emotionally flooded him and what he did was verbally attack her with a criticism: he called her a dictator. He also got defensive: he said that he didn't think that he talked loudly.

Clearly, the teacher was attacking *Sadie Solve's* attempt to reach out. Considering that she was emotionally quite grounded and didn't react to the teacher's aggressive response, she was able to focus on his Empathy Field (Field #3). This process is fully explored in the next chapter, with our character *Lisa Listens.*

As the teacher was being aggressive, another very important thing *Sadie Solves* did was to make sure to create supportive space for herself too, right after offering some empathy to the teacher. She requested if he could maintain the conversation calm and respectful which put the focus on her own Empathy Field (Field #1) (explored in detail in the previous chapter, with our character *Freddie Feels*). Then she brought it back to her initial request in her own Resolution Field (Field #2).

She was using the Requirement for *Mindful Connection* #2: balancing the focus between the Fields and also Requirement #1, making sure everyone focuses on the same Field at the same time. When interacting with others, there will be a constant dance between switching focuses between the Fields as the connection develops and grows.

Checking in about how the request was heard

Field #2 (*Sadie Solves's* Resolution Field)
Sadie Solves worked on getting her request heard.

How does this seem to you?

Field #3 (Teacher's Empathy Field)
The teacher reacted emotionally and attacked her attempt to reach out.

You are such a little dictator!
I don't think I talk loudly!
How dare you talk to me like this!

Field #3 (Teacher's Empathy Field)
Sadie Solves used the Requirement #1 to focus on the same Field as the teacher.
She empathized with the teacher.

My request seems to have upset you…

It sure has!

Field #1 (*Sadie Solves's* Empathy Field)
Sadie Solves used Requirement #2 and balanced the Focus between the Fields. Once she noticed that the teacher calmed a bit, she made sure to create supportive space for herself too as she was noticing that she was starting to get overwhelmed by the teacher's attacking approach.

Would you consider finding a way of keeping this interaction calm and respectful?

Ok, I can do that.

Field #2 (back to *Sadie Solves's* Resolution Field) She again explained and cleared up her intention and brought it back to the request.

My intention is to connect and find ways to work things out…

REPAIR IF ANY VERBAL HARM GETS CREATED

If you get emotionally triggered while expressing your request, it is quite possible and very common to slip into criticism, evaluative or even aggressive language. Maybe you were not very careful and said something that was inconsiderate toward the other person and it upset that person. If this has happens, it is important to recognize it, do your best to first create supportive space and empathically connect with yourself.

Different people can get triggered in different ways to other people's behaviors. Each one of us has our own set of trigger points that can elicit a reaction and cause distress around someone's behavior. It is different for everyone. A person can be very nice and polite, very passive and dismissive or aggressive and assertive. Any one of these could irritate you. The person whose behavior "pushes your buttons" is called a "petty tyrant"[38]. Whether a straight up bully, or a person totally unconscious of his effect on you, a petty tyrant is someone who can "bring out the worst in you". This can be an amazing opportunity for you to attune to what's emotionally coming up and identify what needs are getting unmet and aim to mindfully connect to yourself towards cultivating more growth in your life.

Psychologist John Gottman explains that depending on how people respond to each other, they create one of two emotional states in their relationship: *Positive Sentiment Override* (PSO) or *Negative Sentiment Override* (NSO). When you get involved into a dynamic with lots of attacking and ignoring between you and another person, you tend to create a *Negative Sentiment Override* state. This means that even small things can easily trigger you, interactions easily fill with criticisms, defensiveness and contempt. These harmful interactions increase while connecting behaviors happen less and less. The best way to change this is to first seek empathy and then start reaching out to other people. This helps turn the relationship back into a *Positive Sentiment Override* state, where there is mutual understanding and respect.

Priming is when certain thoughts influence and stimulate more thoughts and feelings of the same nature. Being in a state of a *Negative Sentiment Override* can be very priming for a person and for those who happen to be around that person. When you are primed, it is *very* hard to have a rational conversation with someone without consistently focusing on the issue you are primed around. If you believe that someone is malicious and mean, it would be hard for people to attempt to explain to you that that person's aim might not be to be mean and abusive, like the teacher, who just happens to talk loudly during the class. What you need is empathy.

Sadie Solves got scared from teacher's aggressive response to her request and got a bit attacking herself. She attended her Empathy Field right away (just like *Freddie Feels* did) in order to get back onto attending everyone's needs in the situation.

Once emotionally un-flooded, it is important to attempt to repair things with the person. You can do this by acknowledging what you had said and apologize for any hardhearted words that you might have said. This shows that your goal is to be authentic and nurturing and that just like everyone else, you are human too and susceptible to getting overwhelmed and sidetracked. The other person will need empathy too; the process of offering empathy is fully explored in the upcoming Chapter.

Repair if any verbal harm gets created

Field #1 (*Sadie Solves's* Empathy Field)
Sadie Solves reacted emotionally; she got scared and became aggressive too. She made sure to take a break from the conversation and empathically connect with herself.

You are such a buffoon!

Field #3 (*Teacher's* Empathy Field)
Once emotionally grounded, she reconnected with the teacher in order to repair the verbal harm she'd created (Requirement #2: Balance the focus between Fields).

My word must have been very hurtful.

Yes they were… I am quite hurt.

Field #2 (*Sadie Solves's* Resolution Field)
She explained and cleared up her intention and brought it back to the initial request.

I would like to apologize for my harsh language, my intention is to connect and I got overwhelmed without knowing what to do.

I appreciate you saying that.

IF NEEDED, CLARIFY THE REQUEST

After you've offered the other person empathy, have created a more supportive environment for yourself, the other person will probably get more clarity and ease. It is possible that due to having been emotionally flooded or having different way of thinking, he still might not understand your request or might even not completely remember it.

Considering that you are in the Resolution Field for yourself, your main goal when connecting with the other person is to get *your* needs met. Getting into a discussion about it being his fault for not hearing your request the first time will probably take you further away and make it harder to find arrangements with him to get your needs met.

The best thing is to recognize that no matter how clear you were initially, you *did* offer the request at a time when the other person wasn't very receptive to it. Even if you repeat the exact same request when the person is more emotionally receptive, your request would probably come across as being clearer. In that case, it is a good idea to acknowledge that you were not being clear enough initially and either repeat the exact same request or re-word it a bit.

You can say things like: *"Let me clarify…"* or *"I wasn't clear…"* and then state the request again.

Clarifying the Request

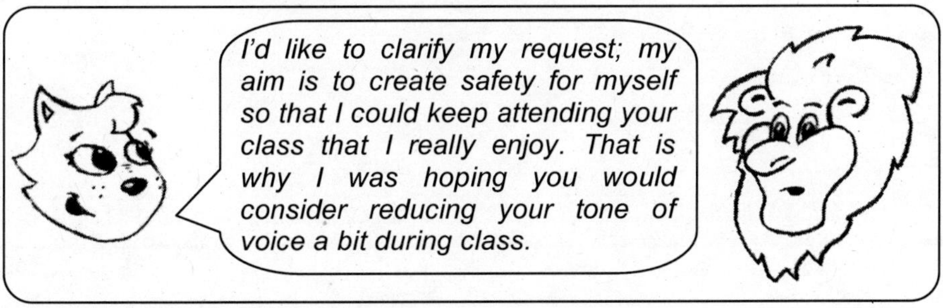

INQUIRE ABOUT PERSON'S INTENDED ACTIONS

Once you have gone through all of the steps above, you can probably manage to get enough interaction and responses from the other person to get an idea what his aims are around supporting you in getting your needs met. If you still haven't gotten a clear response or gotten a clear picture of his intended action, you can ask the person what he intends to do.

Remember that this chapter is still focusing around *your* needs. Conversations are rarely just 'one-sided' and there will be a constant balance between focusing on the other person's Fields and your own (Requirement for Mindful Connection #2). Strategies will change depending on how the other person's Empathy and Resolution Fields unfold and what strategies he creates. What is important is to make sure not to 'lose sight' of why you reached out to the other person for and what your request is about. Even if you have spent lots of time focusing on the other person, you still need to come back to your original request and see what the other person's intended actions are around it; and of course where you are at as well, since your strategies might have modified after having interacted more with the person.

So far, the teacher seems to be interested in considering reducing his voice around *Sadie Solves*. The upcoming Chapters explore connecting further with the teacher in order to support him in meeting his needs as well.

Sadie Solves
Carry out Strategies
- Change own Behavior -

Every time the teacher raised his voice in class, *Sadie Solves* sat further away from him and also used earplugs in order not to be affected by his loud voice.

CHANGE OWN BEHAVIOR

Changing one's own behavior is the part of carrying out your strategies when *you* adjust or change your behavior and take action. You can think of it as if you are requesting yourself to do behavior-changing actions, just like you did with the other person. Everything is planned out and in place; it just needs doing. This can involve anything from getting simple errands done, to doing huge life changing acts.

The reason I called it "conscious" is because the attunement that you have been working up to through previous steps would by now give you a clear picture of what you need to do and why you are doing it. It is a time to take full responsibility for your actions.

Questions to ask yourself in order to change your own behavior: *"How can I take action?" "How do I persevere?"*
Remember to keep asking open-ended questions (the "Six Ws").

Lets explore a collection of methods that can help *you* change your behavior. *Sadie Solves* chose some of these to adjust and change her own behavior.

#1 – PREPARE TO CHANGE BEHAVIOR

POSITIVELY REINFORCE ACTIONS

You can start by doing smaller independent tasks in your daily life that are straightforward, easy to pull off and rewarding. Accomplishing them successfully can build a solid collection of finalized actions, "positively reinforce" getting things done and make it easier to do it again in the future. Getting the gratifying feeling right in the moment when the task is done is what builds the incentive to keep getting more tasks done.[39]

Many people have resigned from doing specific types of actions as a result of consistent "negative reinforcement" due to their failed attempts. If someone has had many failed attempts, it could make it very challenging for him to successfully keep on carrying a planned action as it brings up emotional flooding. This could also get them into a state of chronic *Negative Sentiment Override.*

Another way of successfully reinforcing your actions is to create a self-governing system in your environment, a place where a person can exercise one's own opinions, organize oneself and take responsibility. One of the pioneers of using this idea in education was Alexander Neil who created a self-governing school in the beginning of the twentieth century called Summerhill[40]. Through this approach you create autonomy, mastery and purpose towards gaining motivation to carry out your actions[41].

Consistently carrying out strategies helps you build reliability and trust with others and within yourself. Whenever you commit to an action and don't follow through, people might have a hard time relying on you and trusting you and your confidence in yourself can diminish too.

BUILD CONFIDENCE

Confidence builds in the Resolution Field with the support of the Empathy Field. It goes hand in hand with courage, which you cultivate in yourself while doing all this work. It is about finding trust in yourself.

Author Don Miguel[42] advocates to "always do your best", even if it at times it might not mach your ideal goal. Dr. Neufeld would suggests that in times when you are uncertain, you just need to "be the answer".

Note that being confident is not the same as being a "know-it-all" and knowing exactly how things will unfold. Confidence includes making and admitting to having made misguided decisions and breaking long standing habits. In order to do this you need to face your "cognitive dissonance"[43]; reconnecting back to the Empathy Field will help expose and work through any established self-justifications.

People who get very far in carrying out tasks they set for themselves and create lots of connections in the world tend to get lots of credit for being "talented geniuses" or "determined individuals who made it on their own". Accomplishing this step of changing one's own behavior does take a lot of work and determination, trial and error and no person is alone in this journey. One needs to keep learning and growing, it comes from having a solid source of supportive space or network of family and friends, finding the courage to look within and attune to one's feelings, building willingness and courage to reach out to others and developing the determination and resilience to persist.

These are all part of the process that helps you build confidence and connect to your needs before you can set out on the journey of carrying out your strategies. A wonderful book by Malcolm Gladwell called Outliers covers specifically the topics of what it takes to grow and become masterful in one's own capabilities, in this case, the capability of cultivating nurturing *Mindful Connection.*[44]

#2 – DO IT!

So far, you have gone through the Empathy Field and fully attuned to your feelings and identified your needs. You've explored the Resolution Field and have thoroughly created strategies that will support you in pursuing getting your needs met toward creating wellbeing and building resilience. Now you need to adjust or change *your* behavior to achieve this goal.

Everything that you have worked on up until this point won't bear fruit unless you actively make sure you stick to your agreements with yourself to carry out the strategies you have and facilitate getting your unmet needs met. The only way to take change one's behavior is by doing it. It is not about figuring out how to do it, anticipating it and postponing it or talking about doing it; you simply need to take the action.

There are barriers that can make it hard to follow through with taking action, like being attached to a specific outcome or afraid of failing without a supportive space to hold. It can open up many "hidden wounds" and expose many new unmet needs that you might have not even been aware of. It can be very hard to cope with potentially getting some needs (that are currently met) unmet.

Relief and clarity that you can get from empathically connecting in the Empathy Field can also really hold you back from doing action, especially if you got empathy from another person, outside the challenging situation. Everything might seem just fine because you feel more at ease and content than before. Empathically connecting however is different from carrying out important strategies that get your needs met; because Empathy Field just resolves feelings temporarily (which are transient to start with); and it only supports you in identifying your needs, it doesn't help you get them met. Unless you take action, the old non-joyous feelings will probably come back again when you continue your interaction with the other person and you both carry on with the behaviors that are not getting your needs met.

You also need to keep the action consistent until you get your needs met or decide to change your strategy. Honor the decision you chose and follow through with the action. You need to watch yourself (or have someone help and support you with it) to see if you are stepping outside of the action you decided you would do. For example, *Sadie Solves* could keep unhappily going to the teacher's class instead of stopping her attendance or bringing earplugs to class. As a result she could self-justify her actions and find various reasons to keep doing it. This way she is not honoring herself and she would keep having important needs in her life unmet.

#3 – RE-VISIT THE EMPATHY FIELD

Changing and adjusting your behaviors can enormously trigger your feelings and bring up unmet needs because you face direct challenges and changes due to taking action.

When your old habits and ways take over, it is usually easy to say things like: *"I can't do this, this is just not who I am…"* You need to go to the Empathy Field and use the things that are coming up as clues and hints to explore your feelings and needs, some which will be same as before and some will be new.

And remember that your actions are not who *you* are. Your old behaviors, as conditioned and deep-rooted as they might be are all transformable and changeable. And the best way to do that is to start carrying out the newly strategized actions in the Resolution Field, with the help of the Empathy Field. Having a solid and consistent support and empathy is very important in order to follow through with your actions. Someone who is there in times of struggle with carrying actions out can be of tremendous value.

In our example, if *Sadie Solves* decided to stop the interaction with the teacher, it might turn out to be a big challenge. It might seem like noting else is as good as what she had with this teacher. By attuning back to the Empathy Field she might find out that she is losing her outlet for creativity and feels very bored and frustrated in her attempts to learn with any other teacher. Wearing earplugs to class, as a potential solution might feel uncomfortable and could be distracting her from getting these important needs met.

RETURN TO THE RESOLUTION FIELD

Once you've taken the action, attuned to any feelings that came up and identified any needs that got unmet, you can now go back to the Resolution Field and observe where you are at. From here you can either keep going with the strategy you initially set, tweak the strategy if necessary or maybe even find new strategies. Remember that changing strategies is not about running away from the ones that you struggle with carrying out; it is about finding the strategy that truly works best for you, and also for the other person, which is what upcoming Chapters explore.

You can probably slowly start seeing the balance and "dance" between the Empathy and Resolution Fields. You need to keep going back and forth between the two until you create a good balance between them and working dynamic toward getting all your needs met.

#4 – BEHAVING AROUND THE OTHER PERSON

SET BOUNDARIES

In many circumstances you need to set boundaries, assert your stand and not feed the old dynamic anymore. Often there are occasions when people in your life won't have the capacity or ability to understand or connect to what's going on for you and might pursue doing things that go against your needs. This can happen even if you have reached out, offered your request and done all you can to create a mutually beneficial situation.

It is important to stay authentic to your strategies and avoid succumbing to letting things slip or being polite if you find get intimidated in a situation. There is a complete difference between being authentic and being constantly polite to avoid uncomfortable situations. Authenticity can at times involve being polite and nice; at other times it involves being assertive, having disagreements, setting boundaries, "putting one's foot down" and most importantly it involves honesty – honesty about how you feel and what your stand is on something. Being able to be honest takes a lot of courage and requires lots of support. When honest, it is also important to be sensitive to others. It can make a world of difference to speak your truth *and* at the same time deliver it in a manner that takes other people's feelings and needs in mind. This way you are *connecting*, instead of attacking or ignoring the person you are interacting with. Honestly communicating and setting boundaries helps you get the respect you need in order to have nurturing *Mindful Connection.* Others respect you when they see that you genuinely respect yourself.

Being overly polite can lead into being consistently permissive. Permissiveness is on the opposite spectrum of being very authoritarian and strict. People who get themselves used to dealing with situations by being consistently polite and permissive can usually only resort to aggression when politeness doesn't seem to work. By not taking action around attending to their needs, they end up being passive aggressive.

Politeness and permissiveness brings me to another important concept: being afraid to say *"no"*. At times when, in order to honor your own authenticity, you will need to say *"no"* to other people's requests and demands. The act of saying *"no"* might confuse you if you are attempting to see and do things from a "positive perspective". You might find yourself asking: "If I'm focusing on the positive, then how can I say *'no'* to these people's requests and demands?" When you say *"no"* to something you don't want in your life or don't believe in, you *are* honoring and saying *"yes"* to what you *do* want in your life, to yourself and what *matters* to you. You are also saying *"yes"* to what you truly believe is the best you can offer to the other person. Sometimes it is very important to connect to what it is that you don't want to have in your life in order to find what it is that you do want.

In more extreme cases, you might need to do specific forceful physical actions to reduce someone's impact on you. The idea is not to "fight fire with fire" nor to punish the other person for what you think he has done, but rather to value and respect yourself and do your best to protect yourself from any harm that is or could be done to you. Your need for safety could also be so significant that you might need to stop interacting with the person altogether.

Note again that the only way to go about taking action is to actually do it. Making plans to take action, talking about doing it, reflecting on it's effectiveness or going back and forth with it is *not* changing one's own behavior, it is still merely strategizing to do it.

If the other person had been behaving harmfully and you had built up resentment toward him, it will be much easier to let go of your thoughts of resentment, blame and accusations now that you have gone through the Empathy Field and felt all the non-joyous feelings. This will go hand-in hand with setting your boundaries with that person in the Resolution Field. Finding forgiveness toward others is a very significant self-process of acknowledging the pain that you had gone through, finding the core needs that were not met and having found a place to work toward getting them met. The process will be even more significant once you've had the chance to empathically connect to the other person too. This process is explored in the upcoming Chapters.

Suppose that after the teacher were unresponsive to *Sadie Solve's* request to reduce his tone of voice and she decided to still stay in class. Every time he would start shouting, she would stand up and sit further away from him, or take the earplugs and put them in. This way she would respect herself and also authentically follow up with her own agreements with herself to take action. *Sadie Solves* would *only* do this when he starts shouting and not at all times. If the teacher noticed her doing this, it could emotionally affect him. This would give *Sadie Solves* the opportunity to focus on the teacher's Empathy Field again.

REPAIR IF ANY BEHAVIORAL HARM WAS CREATED

Note that as it was possible for you to say something harmful when making requests, the same could happen through your behavior when taking action. You might get aggressive and even abusive while wanting to set your own boundaries. Or you could get passive and dismissing, which could also create harmful dynamics.

If you have found yourself doing to that, you need to recognize it, create supportive space and empathically connect with what upset you. Then you can go back to the person, acknowledge what you'd done, apologize if needed, repair the harm your behavior might have created, create supportive space for him, offer empathy and recreate *Mindful Connection.*

PRACTICE

CARRY OUT STRATEGIES

Turn to "Carry Out Strategies" in the Practice Section on page 198. It offers different practices for carrying out your strategies for yourself.

WHERE TO GO FROM HERE?

STAY HERE

As long as you haven't found arrangements to start facilitating getting your needs met, make sure to stay focused on this Field. If you notice yourself focusing on other Fields just bring your attention back and refocus on this one. Take extra care not to get overly caught in this Field either. Doing this can set you into an "only thinking of yourself" mentality where you could have a hard time stepping away from it and attending to the other Fields as well. To avoid this from happening, make sure to do your best to fully attend this Field and honor your planned actions and agreements around it.

GO BACK

Carrying out actions can be ineffective if the strategies were poorly planned out. In this case you'll need to go back to making observations and creating strategies all over again. Carrying out actions can also be emotionally triggering, especially if you are attempting to change old strategies.

In that case you need to go back to the "Empathy Field for Yourself" (Field #1). Additionally taking action can and will arouse reactions in other people too in which case they will move their focus to their own Empathy Field (Field #3). If you are triggered, you won't be able to offer them empathy. If you are well practiced and skilled in attending all the Fields, you can attempt focusing on both your and the other person's Empathy Field at the same time.

MOVE TO THE NEXT STEP

If you successfully carry out all your intended actions and start the process off getting or do manage to get your needs met while still staying emotionally grounded, you will have created *Mindful Connection* within yourself. All this challenging and significant work of having gone through the Empathy and Resolution Fields successfully can bring up lots of joy.

With this grounded connection within yourself, you have a solid foundation to start supporting other people in building *Mindful Connection* and move to the next Field #3 ands start by focusing on their Empathy Fields as well and building loving and nurturing relationships.

CHAPTER FOUR

EMPATHY FIELD FOR ANOTHER PERSON

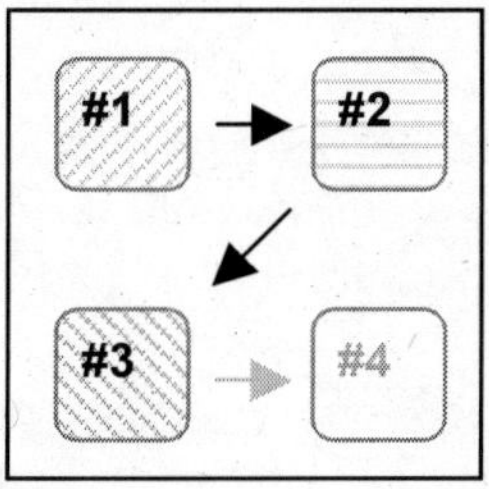

"Empathy Field for Another Person" (Field #3) is about focusing on supporting another person in empathically connecting, just like *Lisa Listens* would. It is where connection and relationships with others starts.

Lisa Listens

Lisa Listens attends to another person's Empathy Field in every situation she is in.

Once you've successfully finished exploring your Empathy and Resolution Fields, you probably got many of your basic needs met. It is important to understand that you haven't created full connection in your life unless you've also focused on other people's fields, *especially* of the people that are close to you and have directly supported you in your own Fields.

You are about to start the journey of focusing outside of yourself and give your time, attention and support to someone else in order to connect with her, which both our students *Lisa Listens* and *Andy Advises* are very good at. Focusing on another person's Empathy Field will in large include and develop the ability to attentively listen and be present with others.

The purpose of this Field is to listen, support and empathize with the other person toward getting connected to her feelings, regardless of whether these feelings are coming up through a challenge in interacting with you or someone else. By identifying her met and unmet needs in the process, she can move toward the Resolution Field with the aim of getting her needs met. Doing this sustains her joyous feelings, resolves the non-joyous feelings, creates grounds for building resilience and creates wellbeing.

An idea a friend once told me comes to mind: we have two ears and one mouth and we ought to use them proportionally. This would not only exercise our listening capacity yet it would result in a third of our interacting time with someone being in total silence.

It is *very* important to focus on another person *only* if your aim is to empathize by focusing on her Empathy Field. When people reach out towards you, they are attempting to create an emotional connection even if their attempt to reach out is charged with 'rationality' or negativity. The chances are that many times people will be either attacking or ignoring your attempts to connect with them; at times they will also aim to connect.

The only other two occasions when you would reach out to others are:
- Interrupting to find supportive space in the "Empathy Field for Yourself".
- Reaching out to connect and make behavior-changing requests toward getting your needs met with a clear strategy on how and why those needs are affected by that person's behavior in "Resolution Field for Yourself".

Focusing on this field will also dissolve any consistent destructive patterns that people might have built throughout the years that are present in day to day interactions; especially the patterns where people are used to criticizing, evaluating and not listening to others.

We've all also experienced listening to "the same story" for months or years while trying to support someone. You might have built up aggravation and resignation toward that person. If you really want to offer authentic and helpful support, here are a couple of questions to ask yourself:

Why do you want to support and contribute to this person's well being?
Get in touch with your feelings and needs. Explore specific ways you could support her next time you meet. It would be helpful for the person to connect to your incentive to reach out to her.
What kind of support does this person want from you?
If this person keeps coming for support, respectfully ask her this question and attentively listen to connect to her feelings and needs around the

matter. You can also ask the person in what way she would like you to be there for her. This is especially important if the person is "not happy about your way" of offering support. This could easily happen if people have a habit of being in a "complaining mode" and might feel estranged or even reluctant and afraid of looking "deeper inside" of themselves.

Unless that person *specifically* asks for your advice and thoughts related to her Resolution Field, it's best to keep focusing on her Empathy Field. Next time someone reaches out to you, ask yourself whether the person is expressing something that requires focusing on her Empathy Field or whether the person is particularly asking for support in exploring doing something related to the Resolution Field.

SUPPORTING MORE THAN ONE PERSON

There are times when others may come to you seeking support around finding ways of offering support to someone else who is in a difficulty. You need to first focus on the Empathy Field of the person who approached you as she is obviously struggling around supporting someone. Since there is another person involved, there is a whole other Empathy Field and Resolution Field in the picture. It is common to skip the Empathy Field for the person that you are supporting and jump straight to either:

- *Resolution Field of the person you are supporting* – when you find yourself telling the person what she could or should be doing to connect to the person she is wanting to support (F#4 in picture below).
- *Empathy Field of the person that's the topic of conversation* – this is when you attempt to help the person you are talking to understand and connect to what the other person that she's wanting to support is feeling and needing and how to do it (F#5 in picture below).
- *Resolution Field of the person that's the topic of conversation* – this is when you start giving the person you are talking to insight on what she could tell the other person that she wants to support to do (F#6 in picture below).

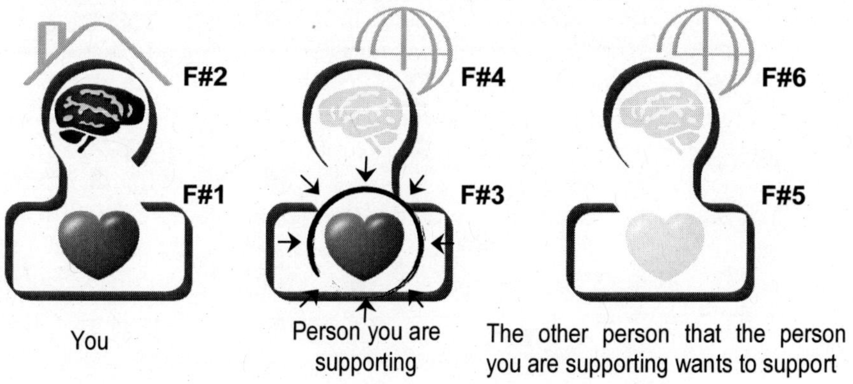

Instead, you need to first focus on the Empathy Field of the person you are supporting. This person is struggling in being there for the other person and unless she attunes to her feelings and identifies her needs, it can be challenging to move toward focusing on the other Fields and effectively support the other person.

It is also very important to know how to focus strategically when you attempt to support two people who are both involved in a same challenging situation. This could be two close friends, colleagues or family members who *both* came to you for support. Since you are focusing onto Fields of more than one person, when you find yourself talking to one of them, you have to make sure not to get tangled in for example, trying to get him to "connect" to what *she* is "going through" without first empathizing with *him*. Trying to get him to "see her perspective" and telling him what to do can only get him more frustrated and he might even think that you are "choosing sides" because you are taking the focus away from what he came to get support around. Just because you understand and are connected to what she is going through doesn't mean that he is ready to do the same. It is easy to slip into this when you care for both people involved and want to help everybody. You might even get emotionally triggered yourself. Sometimes it's easier to make sure that people get separate sources of supportive space. If however, you do choose to take on this task, be connected to yourself and clear of your motives so that you can give solid support separately to everyone.

You can use this method in bigger group settings as well. It's a good idea to have arranged agreements and rules around how everyone can contribute to supporting everyone else in the best way possible. You can have people agree that there will be respectful language used, that people will do their best to observe their own behavior and own their part in any challenges that come up in order for everyone to have proper supportive space. It is a good idea to have a designated person as a facilitator to be responsible for attending individually or in-group to people's concerns and to make sure that *everyone* is focused on a specific Field at a time. Attendance of everyone who is involved in a specific challenge is usually very important so that everyone who wants to speak can get a turn. If a group of people come with a collective concern, it is possible to hold the space for them, offer support and empathy where they would *all* be heard collectively and be able to move forward towards finding resolutions. Dominic Barter created the concept of "Restorative Circles" and has explored working in these environments in more detail.

Nurturing connection only happens in direct interaction with others. Mediums like email or phone do help get exact information across; written notes can be used as solid reference points too; they are usually safe emotionally, since you know you won't get flooded in the moment. If you strictly practice this way of relating, you won't really get a chance to learn the essential skill of reaching out to another person and directly connecting or holding your ground in difficult situations. It takes courage to interact with others in difficult dynamics and the benefits are immense.

Note that focusing on another person's Empathy Field can in extreme cases help you "create supportive space" for yourself. If the person is very confrontational and aggressive and directly threatens your wellbeing without the possibility of easily getting into a supportive space, your only option might be to listen to the person in hopes it will get her to emotionally un-flood. If you have developed the ability to empathize, it should be pretty straightforward to create supportive space for her and indirectly for yourself too. Right after offering supportive space and empathy and noticing a bit of a shift in the person, you can request if she would be willing to interact more calmly and less confrontationally.

The methods in this and the next Chapter mainly explore skills on knowing how to support people who struggle with connecting and effectively communicating. The process is much easier if another person already knows how to focus on and own her Empathy and Resolution fields. Both you and the other person could happen to be emotionally overwhelmed at the same time. In that case, you might either need to create supportive space and empathically connect first so you could be able to attend her Empathy Field, or you could both attempt to mindfully attend to both Fields together, while exchanging focus on them as you connect.

FOUR STEPS IN THE "EMPATHY FIELD FOR ANOTHER PERSON"

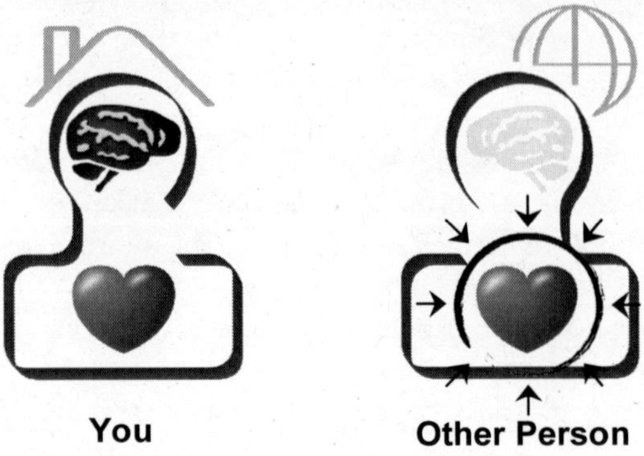

As introduced in Chapter 1, "Empathy Field for Another Person" consists of two parts:
"Support Another Person in creating Supportive Space" and *"Empathize"*.

Both these parts consist of two steps each that make a total of four steps:

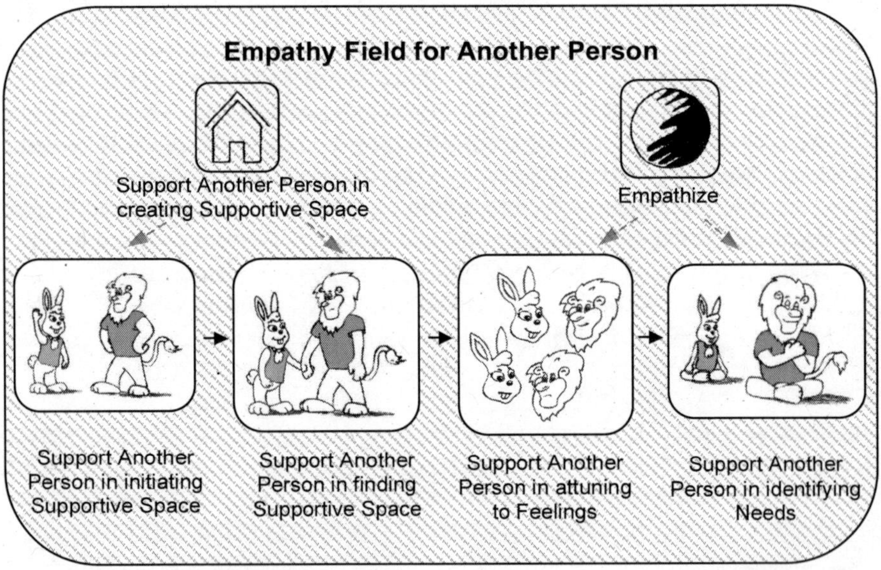

Each of these four steps has a collection of methods and you explore them all in this Chapter.

Lisa Listens

Support Another Person in creating Supportive Space

When the teacher reacted emotionally to *Sadie Solves's request* and also got unpleasant with the students, *Lisa Listens* offered to support him in creating supportive space.

SUPPORT ANOTHER PERSON IN CREATING SUPPORTIVE SPACE

This first step of Field #3 is the part of the journey where you set off to support another person in her self-exploration. When you recognize that the person is emotionally flooded and unable to deal with a certain situation, you need to make sure that she get supportive space, just like *Lisa Listens* would.

This will ensure that the person is unaffected by her surroundings (other people's behaviors and feelings) and can really put all her focus on herself. In this warm, caring and supportive environment, she can identify her needs by empathically connecting with herself.

Note that you can support the person in creating supportive space if the challenge is coming up directly in your interaction with this person; or you could support her in a difficult dynamic with someone else. *Lisa Listens* did both, she observed the teacher react emotionally to *Sadi Solves's* request and the teacher got unpleasant with her and the students while teaching class too.

The upcoming sections explore two steps in supporting someone in creating supportive space: supporting the person in initiating it and then finding it. The example of what *Lisa Listens* did with the teacher demonstrates these two steps.

Lisa Listens

Support Another Person in creating Supportive Space

- Support Another Person in initiating Supportive Space -

Lisa Listens requested to speak and told the teacher that she noticed that his mood had shifted and asked if he needed to take some space and talk about it before continuing the class.

SUPPORT ANOTHER PERSON IN INITIATING SUPPORTIVE SPACE

This step is about interrupting and refocusing a specific dynamic to create grounds to finding supportive space for the other person. Basically you are inviting the person and offering supportive space in order to empathize. When you support another person in creating supportive space, you are also simultaneously working on creating connection with her.

Questions to ask yourself to support a person initiate supportive space:
When *you* are initiating the supportive space: *"How do I initiate supportive space for this person?"*
When you are supporting the person initiate it herself: *"How do I support the other person in initiating supportive space?" "In what way do I support the other person lovingly interrupt a challenging dynamic?"*

Questions to ask the other person to support her in initiating it herself:
When *you* are initiating the supportive space: *"What kind of space do you need?" "How would you like to take time away?"*
When you are supporting the person initiate it herself: *"How would you initiate supportive space?" "In what way could you lovingly interrupt that challenging dynamic?"*

Remember to keep asking open-ended questions (the "Six Ws").

Lets go through a step-by-step method that can help you support another person in initiating supportive space.

INITIATE IT ONESELF

When people are upset, they usually either attack or ignore the people they are in a dynamic with, instead of facilitating supportive space and empathy for themselves. For this reason, waiting and expecting another person to initiate supportive space for herself can leave you very disappointed. That's why *Lisa Listens* attempted right away to reach out to the teacher in aims to create supportive space for him.

At other times, people will come to you to ask for support around initiating supportive space in a challenging dynamic they are in.

INTERRUPT

Interrupting honors Requirement #1 for a Mindful Connection, which requires everyone to be focused on the same Field at the same time. You are making sure to have the person you are supporting be aware that you are about to start focusing onto her Empathy Field. How you will proceed with interrupting the dynamic depends on whether she attacks, ignores or connects to your attempt to reach out and support her.

THE PERSON ATTACKS YOUR ATTEMPT TO REACH OUT

The person might start arguing with you and become criticizing and contemptuous. Doing a quick check through your own Emotional and Resolution Fields can give you a sense of your own emotional state and your unmet needs. As explained in previous chapter, it is always a good idea to first express the aspect of the dynamic that gets your needs met, for example if you value connecting with the person. You can say that you are observing a shift in the person's behavior and that it might be a good idea to take a small break. Remember that your strategy is to make sure the person gets supportive space.

Interrupting the person who is intimidating can be very challenging. If you get overwhelmed yourself, you might need to additionally interrupt the conversation and create supportive space for yourself.

Being aggressive and attacking is the way the teacher had reacted to *Sadie Solves*'s request, and he carried that onto *Lisa Listens* and the students too. He spoke aggressively to the students by saying *"Sadie Solves is such a little dictator! I don't think I talk loudly!" Lisa Listens* recognized this and started focusing on the teacher's Empathy Field in aims to initiate supportive space.

THE PERSON IGNORES YOUR ATTEMPT TO REACH OUT

Everyone can get tired or overwhelmed. Even people who put a lot of time into creating good connections with others can have moments of emotional flooding. When that happens, people need rest and support. When someone seems to be overwhelmed and is ignoring your attempt to reach out, even if you want to support the person and offer supportive space, you need to recognize it and give that person space. Expecting people to communicate when you want them to, without considering their state of mind means that *you* need to take a step back and check in with what's going on for you and then re-approach with the aim to empathize.

You can try to re-initiate the conversation. Avoid initiating supportive space by talking about yourself, making requests of any sort or telling the person what she should or shouldn't be doing. It might be tricky to connect if there's discord and little interaction.

You can start by checking in with something like: *"How have you been?" "I've had a hard time connecting to what's going on for you and I'd like to know"* or *"I care for you and am interested to hear about what bothered you last time we talked"*. If the person ignored your attempt to reach out by changing the topic of conversation, you can interrupt to reconnect with: *"I would like to hear what is going on for you around what we just talked about"*.

THE PERSON CONNECTS TO ATTEMPT TO REACH OUT

The other person might respectfully interrupt the conversation *herself* and want to take space alone; or might be interested in creating supportive space with you. It is important to recognize it and be ready to listen and not use the opportunity to keep talking to her about your needs and ignore her need to get supportive space where she can empathically connect.

"BRIDGE"

Make sure to remember to let her know that if she were to take space on her own, you would still want to connect at a later time. Or if you are to offer the person support and empathy that you would still be interested in coming back to the initial conversation, before she got upset.

Initiating Supportive Space

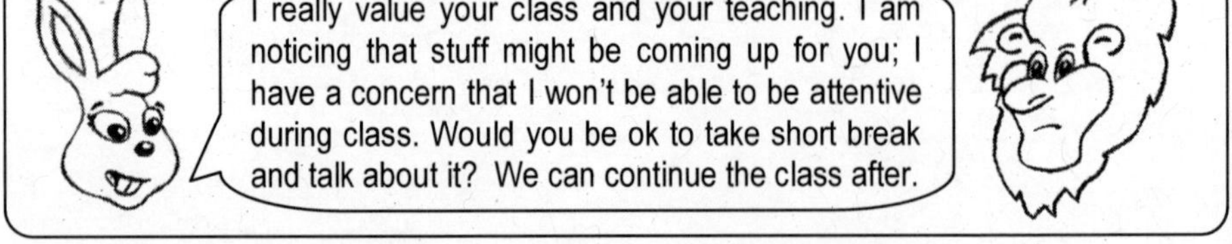

Lisa Listens

Support Another Person in creating Supportive Space
- Supporting Another Person in finding Supportive Space -

As the teacher decided to get support from *Lisa Listens,* she stayed in the classroom after the class to offer him support.

SUPPORT ANOTHER PERSON IN FINDING SUPPORTIVE SPACE

This step is about supporting another person that is in midst of emotional challenge in finding a place within herself or in an external space, where she can empathically connect with herself. You can do this either if the person has a challenge with you or with someone else.

Questions to ask yourself in order to help another person find supportive space: *"How do I support the other person in finding the kind of space/support she needs?" "How do I support the other person in finding ways to take time away?"*

Questions to ask the other person: *"What kind of space do you need?" "How would you like to take time away?"*

Remember to keep asking open-ended questions (the "Six Ws").

Lets go through a step-by-step method that can help you support another person in creating supportive space.

ALONE

If the person seems to need space on her own, you can offer to help her explore different kinds of ways of finding it. A number of options are explored in Chapter 2.

WITH ANOTHER PERSON

The other person might choose to go and find supportive space with someone else or with another community. She might decide to have you be a part of that space and ask you for support too. If that doesn't happen, it could trigger various feelings in you.

If both of you end up getting triggered, you need to find supportive space for yourselves. Trying to be there for the other person when you need support yourself can be very hard; usually things like upset or jealousy can easily come up; it can also create aggravation and resentment. Unless you have the resourcefulness and the practiced skills to be there for each other at the same time, the most loving thing at a time like this would be to request the other person to seek support elsewhere and make sure you do the same.

Otherwise, if the person accepts your offer to be there or requests it, you could be the person who would be there to hold the supportive space for her and have her transition to empathically connecting with herself.

In our example, the teacher decided to have *Lisa Listens* support him with what was coming up for him. They arranged to stay in the classroom after class and talk about it.

PRACTICE

SUPPORT ANOTHER PERSON IN CREATING SUPPORTIVE SPACE

Turn to "*Support Another Person in Creating Supportive Space*" in the Practice Section on page 201. It offers different practices for supporting another person in creating supportive space.

Lisa Listens

Empathize

Once *Lisa Listens* created supportive space for the teacher, she started empathizing with him.

EMPATHIZE

This second step of Field #3 is a journey where you are simply there for others as they reach into to the innermost places within themselves. Having supported the other person create supportive space, you can now focus on empathizing with the person, just like *Lisa Listens* would.

Empathizing is when you put all your focus towards attuning to another person's feelings and in the process help identify her needs. It is a place of care and active support for another.

Every time you empathically connect to another person, you strengthen and build the relationship with her. Psychologist John Gottman[45] calls this "putting money in the emotional bank account". You can deplete it by attacking or ignoring a person with whom you thrive to have connection with. When you do fulfill your "emotional bank account" with connections, it makes it that much easier to connect with that person in the future when more challenges arise.

Every time another person is talking to you, the first thing you need to do is aim to empathize. It would be great to start every interaction that you have with the aim to emotionally connect first. This is even embedded in language, people say, *"How are you?"* or *"How is it going?"* when starting conversations.

A simple way of knowing if it's time to focus on this step is to take a deep breath, attune within yourself and check in to see if you already have an abundance of supportive space and are emotionally un-flooded and able to offer empathy to another person that's reaching out to you.

Whenever a person reaches out to you, you can see it as an invitation and take the opportunity to connect with her. The possibility of deeply connecting with that person is so much greater if you first attune empathically to her. We inherently all want to connect to others. Being able to be attuned and connected to others in a profound way is a path towards building nurturing, compassionate and conscious communities and lifestyles.

Think about how often it happens in families, friendships, work and communities where people struggle with thoughts such as: *"No one understands me"*, *"Nobody is listening to me"* or *"Nobody cares"*. It can be very painful when people reach out and allow themselves to be vulnerable while needing connection and community, yet the world around them either scrutinizes or criticizes them or completely ignores them and their attempts to reach out.

There could be times when people get very resigned from what's going on for them and might even say something like: *"It doesn't matter…"* or *"I don't care"*. You can still keep supporting the person by saying: *"It seems to me that it does matter…"* or *"I think that you do care…"* This will not only validate the person's feelings but it will also show that *you* care and are interested to listen and understand what is going on for that person.

You might also have a person in your life that tends to regularly direct conversations towards herself and you may believe that giving that person attention would only maintain her tendency to keep doing that. This is true if the person never truly gets empathy. If you manage to fully empathize with her, the person will probably start wanting attention much less in the future and you will be able to truly connect with her. And if you stay in touch with your Empathy Field too, you avoid the pitfall of taking her "self-focus" personally and building resentment.

Empathy is about being present and attuned. It is very important to remember that empathizing is *not* about taking responsibility for the causes of another person's feelings or attempting to solve other person's problems and challenges; especially when the other person is highly overwhelmed and even potentially blaming you for the way that she feels.

The process of empathizing in itself is quite straightforward. You simply need to be fully present with the other person, listen attentively and non-judgingly, with the aim to attune to her feelings and identify his her needs. Even a small amount of empathy can make a world of difference.

Listening is another contribution to a person in need of empathy. You need to listen with attentiveness, keep eye contact, some people like to have physical contact too. A well-experienced listener is able to focus on objective aspects of what's being said in order to connect with what's "underneath" the words: "what might be emotionally going on for the person?"

I consider the act of empathizing with the aim of getting *only* your own needs met and *not* the needs of others to be manipulative behavior. Especially since empathizing creates connection and starts developing trust with the other person. Without the true goal to meet everyone's needs, this would be unloving action under false pretences. There is lots of opportunity and ways to use the tools in this book in this way, without authenticity and out of pretense of having admirable principles, intentions or feelings. As much as one can gain certain outcomes by doing that, getting a loving connection is just not applicable with that kind of a mind-frame and without the aim of working toward getting everyone's needs met.

On the flipside, your goals can be very honorable and honest and while you can still have moments where you can be overwhelmed, tired and unable to easily connect with others. You might need lots of supportive space and if unable to get it, you might get irritated and curt. It is not possible to force people to connect when they are not ready or momentarily able nor is it helpful to call them inauthentic or hypocritical.

The two distinctions above are important, as not every disconnection is necessarily a sign that a person doesn't care, neither is every sign of connection an indication that the person is being honest. You need to trust your judgment and even get support when wanting to determine if an interaction with a specific person involves hypocrisy (when pleasant) or temporary disconnection (when unpleasant).

The upcoming sections explore two steps in empathizing with someone: supporting the person in attuning to her feelings and identifying her needs. The example of how *Lisa Listens* empathized with the teacher once she supported him create supportive space for himself demonstrates these two steps.

Lisa Listens

Empathize

- Support Another Person in attuning to Feelings -

Lisa Listens supported the teacher in attuning to his **non-joyous feelings** of being upset, embarrassed and insecure. She held that space for him until he felt at ease and grounded. After that, she also stayed present while he felt his **joyous feelings** of being glad, encouraged and confident.

SUPPORT ANOTHER PERSON IN ATTUNING TO FEELINGS

You can support someone in attuning to her feelings by encouraging her to consciously put her attention on and accept bodily sensations, emotional states and experiences that come up. Once the person does that, you need to be present, attentive and ready to listen.

Questions to ask yourself in order to help another person attune to her feelings: *"How do I support another person around how she is doing?" "How do I support another person around how she is feeling?"*

Questions to ask the other person: *"How are you doing?" "How are you feeling?"* [i]

Remember to keep asking open-ended questions (the "Six Ws").

Note that empathy allows you to resonate with the other person's feelings. This means that you associate with and even feel the other person's current emotional state. Although you are having emotional reactions, the goal of this step is to support the other person in attuning to her feelings *herself.* When you are present and resonating with other people, it helps them attune to their feelings.

It is important to support another person attune to both joyous *and* non-joyous feelings in a certain situation. Lets explore a collection of methods that can help *you* support another person in attuning to her feelings. *Lisa Listens* chose some of these to support the teacher in attuning to his.

---

[i] Note again that some of these expressions are built into opening lines when starting conversations. This just shows how important it is to first aim to connect emotionally with others.

#1 – USE CLUES/HINTS

Sometimes the other person's bodily sensations, emotional states and experiences might be hidden, buried and hard to identify and attune to, especially around very sensitive and pending challenges. By finding ways of identifying clues/hints in the other person's behavior described below, you can get closer to supporting the person in feeling her feelings.

A good starting point to help the other person attune to her feelings is to ask her to verbally describe what happened or what is going on for her and let her talk in detail. Based on what the person says, especially if she resorts to evaluative and blaming talk, labels, criticism or acts of cruelty and aggression, you can start getting a sense what is going on for her by using these explanations and actions as clues/hints. The person could be so caught up in thoughts and beliefs that it could make it a challenge for her to get to the feeling. Rosenberg says: "Judgments, evaluations, diagnoses, criticism and blame are just alienated expressions of how people feel and what needs of theirs are not being met."[46] Understanding that the other person is merely unsuccessfully attempting to connect to her Empathy Field (Field #3) and probably not even thinking about either your Empathy or Resolution Fields usually makes it easy to not take her behavior personaly.

You may need to clarify some of the person's words first. You might even need to assert your boundaries (your own supportive space) in order to proceed toward focusing on the person's feelings. If you know you are sensitive to harsh language, you might want to be adamant about the person using more friendly language in order for you to be able to hear her out and support her in attuning to her feelings. That way you are making sure you are taking care of yourself too while supporting the other person.

THOUGHTS

You can use various thoughts that the other person expresses to identify feelings. Language and rational thinking is usually one of the first things people use when emotionally overwhelmed. Note that expressing oneself could in itself be enough to bring up a feeling. This language can be filled with evaluations, criticism, accusations and even deceitful words.

In our example, when the teacher said things like: "*She is such a little dictator*" "*She is so insensitive*" or "*How rude of her*", *Lisa Listens* used this as a hint that he is upset and embarrassed. She also noticed that he was insecure.

Once *Lisa Listens* listened and empathized for a while and supported the teacher in un-flooding form his non-joyous feelings, she also supported him in attuning to his joyous feelings. She still paid attention to potential thoughts teacher said like: *"She is an attentive student" or "It is a good class of students".* She used these as clues/hints to support him in attuning to his joyous feelings. She found that he was glad, encouraged and confident.

THOUGHTS - CLUES/HINTS

BEHAVIORS

You can watch the other person's behavior and body language to explore potential joyous and non-joyous feelings.

When *Lisa Listens* talked to the teacher while he was upset, he raised his voice and imposed his body forward; he pulled his eyebrows together and tightened his lips. Once he was glad and encouraged, his eyes brightened up and body relaxed.

For more detail, refer to "Recognizing Emotions and Micro-Expressions" and "Non-verbal behavior" in the APPENDIX (pg. 220 and 223).

EXPRESSING FEELINGS

It can be very helpful for the other person to get a sense of being understood if you ask to repeat back what you heard her say. If the person's words are filled with evaluations and interpretations, you can "re-frame" what she said by talking about her potential feelings. This can get the person closer to attuning to her feelings and also creating more direct connection between the two of you.

You can start by inquiring about how the person is feeling and if she responds with an evaluation of sorts, then you can check in back and attempt to guess the feeling based on what the person said. Many times when people are overwhelmed it might be harder for them to verbalize their emotions and it might be easier for them to stay present to their bodily sensations and emotional states wile you support them in exploring their feelings with them. This kind of verbal responding gives the other person a sense of being understood and can get her one step closer to her feelings.

Offering feedback or rephrasing however is *not* empathy! It is merely emotional recognition and a very helpful tool to *get you* to being present to another person's emotional state and emotionally resonate with her. Even if you are very good in re-framing, be careful not to find yourself simply repeating back to people what they tell you, or only name feelings that you observe and expect that this does the trick of offering empathy.

Another possibility in expressing feelings is when a person denies them or expresses the opposite feeling from what you observe might really be going on for her. For example, a person could say that everything is fine and that she is "ok" even though she seems to be upset. Since you observed and sensed that the person's language and behavior is revealing that she might be upset, you could communicate to her that you are having a hard time trusting that what she is saying is true and that you suspect that there might be upset going on for her. It is also possible that saying *"I'm fine"* could be an indirect way for the person to take supportive space alone.

When empathizing, you need to listen, be present and attuned to the person's feelings. Evaluating other person's words and trying to tell her how to express herself is not and act of empathizing. Doing this belongs in that person's Resolution Field. As I commented earlier, avoid giving advice and direction on how one should express oneself, unless the person gives you a clear request to do so.

Just like you made sure to own your feelings when you focused on your Empathy Field, support others to own their feelings as well.

Be attentive if you find yourself emotionally resonating with the other person's distress in a "reactive" way and becoming emotionally triggered. You may get upset with the person for "causing you to feel upset". This way, not only are you letting her emotional state arouse a non-joyous feeling in you, which is disabling you from empathizing, but you are also disabling her from focusing on *her* feelings by shifting the focus onto your feelings.

Attuning to feelings can take time and not all of them can always be revealed right away. Simply trust that the other person will find a way to own her feelings without you doing it for her.

A great way to help the other person feel her feelings is to accept anything that comes up and avoid negating or pushing away things by saying things like: *"But you are stronger than that…"* or *"That's nothing important..."* Pretty much any sentence that starts with the word "but" can distract the other person from successfully attuning to her feelings.

Another distractions are attempting to cheer the person up or trying to "fix" the problem that she is having. As I discussed in Chapter 2, feeling is not about getting instant relief or fixing, it is about getting to the bottom of what's going on for a person.

Make sure to keep expanding your vocabulary of joyous and non-joyous feelings, which you can refer to in the APPENDIX ((pg. 217 and 218). This way, if you know different types of emotions that exist, you can more easily recognize them when you see them.

There are circumstances for some people, where expressing feelings could be very hard on or inappropriate due to social environment or cultural background. It can be very uncomfortable for someone to be bluntly asked how she is feeling. Consider that offering empathy is simply "being present" with another person. Instead of talking about feelings, you can use them as clues/and hints to get to the feelings and then you can be supportive non-verbally and by being attentive and receptive.

After asking how the teacher was feeling and getting an evaluation, *Lisa Listens* explored different feelings with the teacher until she mentioned some that seemed to resonate with him.

EXPRESSING FEELINGS - CLUES/HINTS

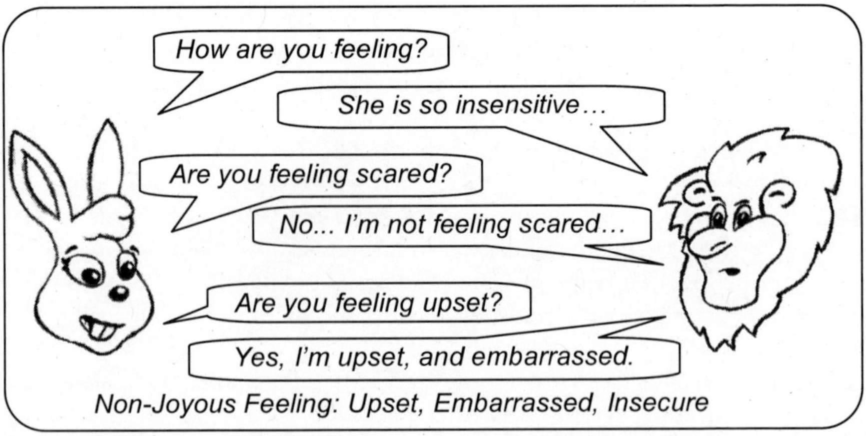

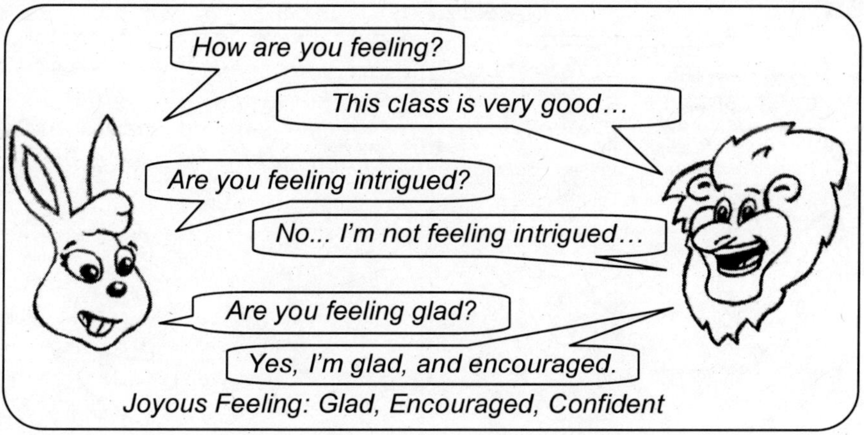

NEEDS

You can also explore different needs you think might be unmet for the other person; doing this can arouse certain feelings that are in direct connection with the identified core needs. Remember that you and the person are in a supportive space now, where this person is letting her guard down and is inviting you to support her in getting to the root of her emotions.

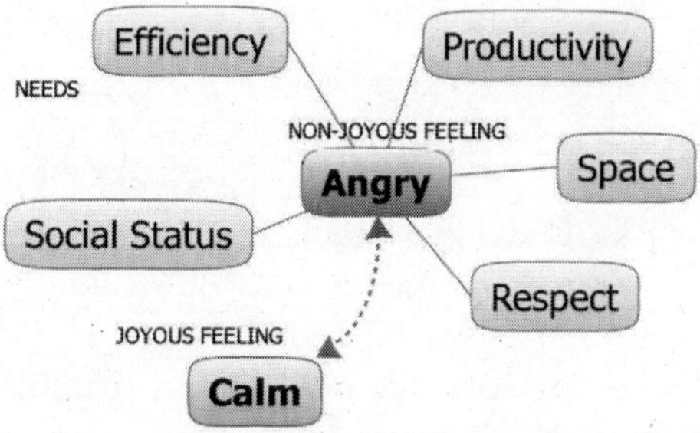

In our example, while giving support to the teacher, *Sadie Solves* explored different met and unmet needs for the teacher. The teacher didn't get respect in the way *Lisa Listens* approached him with her request, which in turn aroused feelings of anger. Since she made the request in front of other students, it got the teacher's needs for self-esteem, acceptance and dignity unmet, which brought up feelings of embarrassment too. His confidence and self-esteem would also get unmet as a result of thinking that he has to reduce his voice from then on.

At the same time, *Sadie Solves* made sure to also recognize the needs that aroused joyous feelings in the teacher. In this case, his love for teaching which got his needs for sharing, connection and participation met with the students; and ease of expression and clarity in thought he got when he raised his voice.

CLUES/HINTS - NEEDS

Constantly relying on clues and hints to get to empathize with someone can become overwhelming. You can work on building an arrangement with another person so that she would share with you her feelings and needs directly without any "clues/hints" that you would need to "decipher". You can be very clear that you are interested in hearing what is going on for her. Let her know that anything that strays from directly expressing her feelings and needs, such as thoughts, blame and criticism is something you might have a hard time connecting with. If someone insists on continuing to use harsh language and ways of talking that you have a hard time connecting to, you can pause the person and ask how exactly he would like you to support him. If the person's answer is uncertain, then you might not be able to support him at that time nor continue to feed that dynamic and take a step back and work on giving him *and* yourself some time and space.

Use caution if you find yourself telling the other person that what she is expressing is "not a feeling". If for example she says an evaluative statement like: *"I feel disrespected"*, you may respond: *"that statement is not a feeling, it's an interpretation"*. Or if she says: *"I feel the sharing"*, you may say: *"that's not a feeling, it's a need"*. Doing this may not only make the other person confused and even irritated, it can really impair your chances of connecting with her.

#2 – WELCOME THE FEELING

OWN THE FEELINGS

Having the person understand that it is her way of thinking that shapes the way she feels and that understanding this and taking responsibility for it is a very empowering place to be.

BE IN THE PRESENT

It is important to stay in the present, and welcome and attune to the emotions that are happening now. You can ask how the other person is feeling in the moment, which will help you support her in attuning to what's currently going on for her. This way you avoid having the focus on what happened in the past or what might happen in the future.

PAUSE

When people are reaching out to you in an emotionally charged way, practice developing your ability to pause instead of responding right away. If you can pause for at least a short moment when someone is reaching out to you it can make a big difference in your connection. This is essentially creating supportive space for her because it gives her time to process what she is going through right after expressing it. It also helps you gain perspective to the situation and what she might be going through.

FACILITATE ACCEPTANCE OF FUTILITY[47]

Just like you faced the futility in your own Empathy Field, which is the experience of something that you have no control over, you can support the other person in the same aspect. This can be facilitated mainly from you asserting your own supportive space. When offering empathy, while being loving and accepting, you need to make sure to stand by your values and be assertive. People's emotions can be overwhelming and their behaviors intimidating especially if you are exposing a touchy subject or naming an erroneous decision or action that she might have done.

It is easy to retreat or even attack when people become emotional. At times, it takes a lot of courage and strength to offer empathy. If you can stay present and truly listen, while making sure to keep your need for respect met, it can really help the other person face the fact that they might have no control over the situation and it could bring up many buried feelings.

In our example the teacher intimidated *Lisa Listens* as a result of having gotten emotionally overwhelmed and defensive. While giving empathy, *Lisa Listens* maintained her assertion that his loud tone of voice was and is scary for the students. This would help him face the situation, accept it and start realizing the consequences of his behavior. Connecting to this would probably bring up feelings of sadness, knowing that he cannot continue to randomly and spontaneously raise his voice and expect the students not to get affected; at least not in the current circumstances. When one accepts one's futility, sadness, disappointment and a sense of release are the underlying deep feelings that follow. Strong emotions like frustration and aggression are present when one resists accepting futility.

Having connected to the futility of his behavior and attuned to his sadness around it, the teacher attuned to his feelings of being embarrassed and also being glad and encouraged in his current dynamic with the students in an even deeper and more connected way.

Facilitate Acceptance of Futility

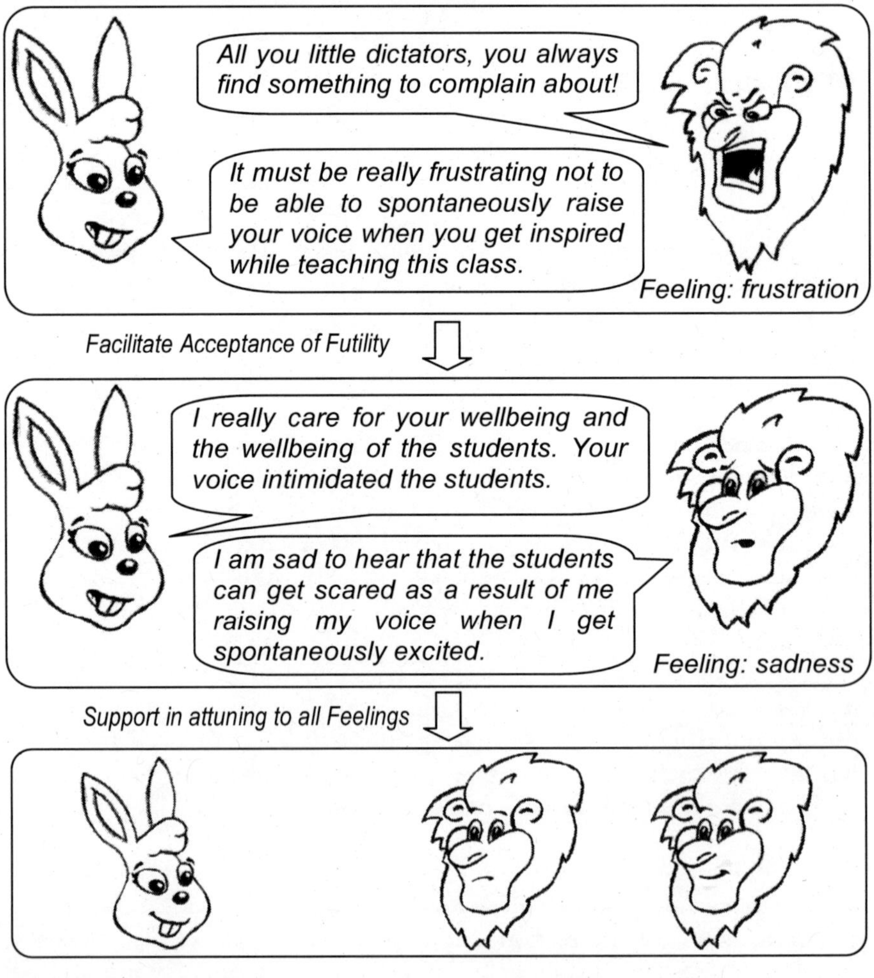

#3 –FEEL

All the previous points were mere tools to help you in supporting the other person in getting to the feeling itself. When the other person senses that she's being truly heard, and once she starts feeling, there will be an observable shift in the person. It is important to just hold space at that time. There is usually no need to talk, especially if the emotions are very strong. Just keep being fully attentive, present and loving with the other person. Sometimes the feeling might last a short time and other times it could take longer.

Note that these "quiet" moments with another person might feel unusual if you are not used to supporting others emotionally. You might feel scared about what's next, get flustered or uncomfortable and not know where to go next during moments like these. Empathizing and supporting others takes courage. Following through with these moments of discomfort can help you get in touch with yourself and really build solid connection with the other person too.

Once feelings have arisen and passed, the conversation becomes lighter and usually things naturally take their own course, the person gains more clarity, which helps her identify her unmet needs.

In our example, *Lisa Listens* stayed present and held the space for the teacher while he went through the feelings of being upset, embarrassed, and insecure.

Once non-joyous feelings passed, *Lisa Listens* also stayed present and held the space for the teacher while he went through the joyous feelings of being glad, encouraged and confident.

Lisa Listens

Empathize
- Support Another Person in identifying Needs -

Lisa Listens supported the teacher in identifying his needs:
Met needs: Connection, sharing and participation when in class and ease of expression and clarity in thought when raising voice while expressing himself.
Unmet needs: Respect, acceptance, dignity and space in his interaction with *Sadie Solves*; confidence and self-esteem when reducing his voice.

SUPPORT ANOTHER PERSON IN IDENTIFYING NEEDS

Supporting the other person in identifying her needs is the fundamental means for her to find connection with herself and others. This connection happens in the process of identifying and getting the identified needs met. If the person can identify one's core needs, those will shape her feelings in accordance to them, which will further support her in empathically connecting with herself and also help you in empathizing with her.

Questions to ask yourself in order to help another person identify her needs: *"How do I support another person around what she needs?" "How do I support another person to find what she is looking for?"*

Questions to ask the other person: "*What do you need?" "What are your needs?" "What are you looking for?"*[i]

Remember to keep asking open-ended questions (the "Six Ws").

Lets explore a collection of methods that can help *you* support another person in identifying her needs. *Lisa Listens* chose some of these to support the teacher in identifying his needs.

#1 – VOCABULARY OF NEEDS

Keep referring to the "Needs" section in the APPENDIX to maintain a good vocabulary of needs (pg. 219). This will make it easier to support others in identifying their needs.

---

[i] Note that even the process of instigating a casual conversation, or even when one is greeted in the service industry usually comes from the aim to connect to a need. (i.e. *"How may I help you")*

#2 – USE CLUES/HINTS

The way to support someone in identifying her needs is to observe her behavior, things that she says, and how she feels. You can use these as clues and hints to explore different needs that are met and unmet for the person. At times it can be more helpful to explore needs with person by guessing them until you find the right one rather than to ask the person to explore and guess the needs herself. People tend to be overwhelmed or wrapped in their heads and it might be difficult for them to explore needs as easily as it would be for you, especially if they are still emotionally overwhelmed. Simply listen to the person and based on what you observe do your best to identify her needs.

The other person might be quite in touch with her needs. In that circumstance, simply asking what her needs are could just additionally support the person in more easily identifying her needs and this step of using clues and hints might not even be very necessary.

VERBS

When others express their needs by expressing behaviors and 'wants', aim to recognize the needs underneath their words. Behaviors are direct strategies to get needs met so you can easily recognize the need associated with a specific strategy. The teacher told *Lisa Listens*: *"I need Sadie Solves to stop insulting me"*. *Lisa Listens* recognized this as a strategy and realized that what he was probably wanting to say was: *"I need respect and when Sadie Solves approached me with her request, I didn't get respect and it came across insulting"*.

She also listened for met needs once the teacher was emotionally grounded; he said that the students were very attentive, which indicated that his needs for connection, sharing and participation were met. He also said how confident he would feel when he would raise his voice, which indicated met needs in clarity of thought and ease of expression when he raises his voice.

CLUES/HINTS - VERBS

PEOPLE AND OBJECTS

Another common way to express needs is to refer to people and objects. By recognizing it, you can use these as clues and hints to identify the appropriate needs.

In our example, the teacher might have said to *Lisa Listens*: *"I don't need her…"* *Lisa Listens* guessed that he was probably wanting to say was: *"I have a need for dignity and I have a hard time getting that met if I'm around Sadie Solves"*. When expressing his met needs, he might have said something like: *"I really need this class"*. Again, *Lisa Listens* recognized that by teaching, the teacher gets his needs for sharing and participation met.

CLUES/HINTS – PEOPLE AND OBJECTS

ALIENATING LANGUAGE

Listen for various forms of criticism, evaluations or random thoughts the other person might be using and then find what needs are behind her words.

In our example, the alienating language that the teacher said to *Lisa Listens* about *Sadie Solves* after she asked him to reduce his tone of voice was: *"She is such a little dictator"*, *"She is such an insensitive person"*, *"Her words were very harsh"* or *"I don't want to deal with this"*. By scrutinizing the content of these sentences *Lisa Listens* guessed that the unmet need for the teacher was again, respect, acceptance, dignity, space etc.

As for met needs, the teacher said: *"She is an attentive students"*, which helped *Lisa Listens* recognize the need for sharing and participation.

CLUES/HINTS – ALIENATING LANGUAGE

FEELINGS

Observing any feelings that come up for the other person as you guess various needs can confirm that you identified the right need. If you word any other unrelated needs, they wouldn't stir up strong feelings. Met needs would arouse joyous feelings, while unmet needs will stir up non-joyous ones. You would need to watch for body language, behavior cues and listen for expressions that convey feelings.

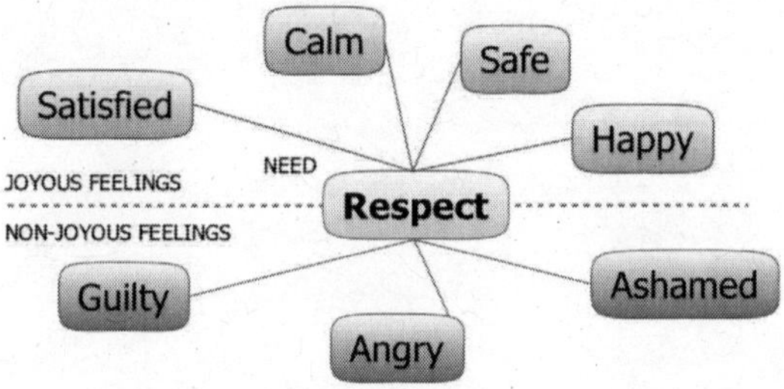

When *Lisa Listens* made a guess that the need for respect was not met for the teacher, it triggered anger, shame, guilt and other related feelings in him. This indicated that respect may be one of the unmet needs. The teacher would need to get this need met in order to feel calm, safe, etc. However, when she mentioned a random need like productivity, it didn't arouse any strong feelings in the teacher.

Similarly, *Lisa Listens* identified some met needs by observing a joyous feeling getting aroused in the teacher. When she talked about sharing and participation, she noticed joy, excitement and encouragement in the teacher's behavior and responses.

The feelings that come up for the other person can help you identify even more unmet needs. For *Lisa Listens,* anger and upset might have indicated the need for space for the teacher; guilt and sadness could have revealed acceptance, dignity, etc.

CLUES/HINTS – FEELINGS

Feelings are usually direct indicators of needs as many times they describe and quantify needs. If a person is in touch with her needs, it can be very helpful to hear about her feelings and easy to identify the appropriate needs.

#3 – IDENTIFY ALL THE NEEDS

Spend time working through and identifying different layers of needs that are present for the other person.

MET NEEDS

In our example, having attentive and interested students creates grounds for more connection, sharing and participation for the teacher. Also, when the teacher talks loudly, he gains confidence, clarity in thought and can express himself more easily.

Lisa Listens supported the teacher in identifying his met needs for connection, sharing and participation when in class; and also his met needs for ease of expression and clarity in thought when raising his voice while expressing himself.

UNMET NEEDS

The teacher's reaction revealed needs for dignity, acceptance and respect due to being exposed in front of other students and the nature of *Sadie Solve's* request. Being put on the spot could have aroused need for space. If he is used to talking loudly, he might find that not doing that could impede on his needs for self-expression and clarity in thought. As a result, his confidence, self-esteem could also diminish.

Lisa Listens supported the teacher in identifying his unmet needs for respect, acceptance, dignity and space in his interaction with *Sadie Solves.*
His needs for confidence and self-esteem would also get unmet if he were to work on reducing his tone of voice.

Find a variety of ways to explore other people's needs to avoid sounding overly mechanical. Rephrasing and having different ways of expressing oneself can keep the conversation fresh and diverse. For example, *Lisa Listens* could use a variety of different expressions to express the teacher's needs: *"Sounds like your need for respect is unmet"* or *"You don't seem to get your need for respect met", "It seem you could use more respect", "Are you looking for more respect?"* etc.

Also take extra care when attempting to tell others that what they are expressing is "not a need". If someone said: *"I need you to stop insulting me"*, it won't be very supportive to respond: *"What you said is not a need, it's a behavior";* or if one said: *"I need you to be happy"*, again avoid saying: *"Happiness is a feeling, not a need"*. Remember, unless the person asked you to assist her in correcting her language, it is a good idea to avoid focusing onto her Resolution Field. Simply aim is to empathize.

PRACTICE

EMPATHIZE

Turn to "*Empathize*" in the Practice Section on page 203. It offers different practices for empathically connecting to others.

WHERE TO GO FROM HERE?

STAY HERE

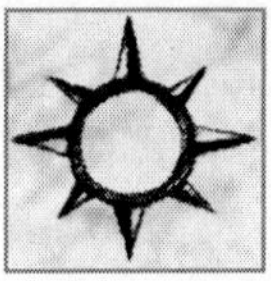

As long as the other person is emotionally overwhelmed make sure to stay focused on this Field. If you notice yourself focusing on other Fields just bring your attention back and refocus on this one. Also take extra care not to get overly caught in this Field either; doing this can set you into a "saving the other person" mentality where you could have a hard time stepping away from it and attending to the other Fields as well. To avoid this from happening, make sure to do your best to fully attend to this Field and honor your intended behaviors and agreements around it.

GO BACK

If the person you are supporting is having a hard time connecting to her feelings, she needs to find a more suitable supportive space. If the struggle persists even after having solid supportive space, make sure you are fully focused on her Empathy Field and are patient with her.

If on the other hand, *you* get triggered emotionally, you might need to request "time out" and seek supportive space in your Empathy Field. Then explore your Resolution Field to facilitate getting your needs met. Only then you can more easily refocus back to support this person in her Empathy Field. If you are well practiced and skilled in attending all the Fields, you can attempt focusing on both your Empathy and Resolution Fields and the other person's Empathy Field at the same time.

MOVE TO THE NEXT STEP

Once the other person has fully attuned to her feelings, clarity follows and both of you would be aware of what her met and unmet needs are. That person is now ready to step into her Resolution Field (Field #4) where she can facilitate and work on getting her needs met, further build resilience and create wellbeing for herself.

If the person requests help from you, you can maintain supporting her by moving your focus onto her Resolution Field.

CHAPTER FIVE

RESOLUTION FIELD FOR ANOTHER PERSON

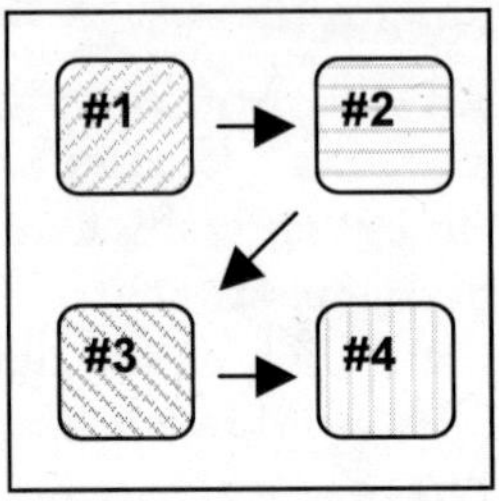

"Resolution Field for Another Person" (Field #4) is when you start focusing on another person's rational thinking, logical inference, strategizing and carrying out actions; just like *Andy Advises* would. This happens when you observe that the other person has emotionally un-flooded and seems more grounded.

Andy Advises

Andy Advises focuses onto another person's Resolution Field in every situation he is in. He first makes sure that the other person is grounded in his Empathy Field.

The purpose of the "Resolution Field for Another Person" is to support a person in maintaining the met needs identified in one's Empathy Field and pursue getting unmet needs met. Doing this sustains the person's joyous feelings, resolves non-joyous feelings, and builds resilience and wellbeing.

It is essential to make sure the other person has fully attended the Empathy Field before visiting this step. Supporting someone to find ways to get his needs met will generate weak and incomplete results without the deep learning he gains by feeling his feelings and identifying his needs. Furthermore, focusing on this step will as a result come from the aim to contribute to others and live in a nurturing community and not out of a sense of duty or some imposed responsibility.

Remember to focus onto another person's Resolution Field *only* if he seems emotionally grounded enough and *clearly* requests your support around it. Even then, only that person can really find out and know what he needs to do. What you can, and hopefully by now do know is, what that person's needs are. This can help you support the other person in together exploring what he can do, rather than to give straight up advice. Many times, the person might not even need advice. When one gets full empathy, the clarity that follows can make it quite straightforward for him to know what to do next.

When there is good connection, offering advice to one another can be very fruitful and rewarding. Unfortunately, when the other person is emotionally overwhelmed, most people first focus on this last Field #4. They put all their thoughts and energy into what another person "is" or "is not" or what he "should" or "shouldn't" be doing. Although these contributions can be very valuable in supporting the other person in meeting his needs, one's attempts usually end up being ineffective and wasted unless one does the essential work of emotionally connecting with the other person first. When people trust someone, they *do* like to seek support and advice from him.

Note that even this book largely rests it's content in offering tools toward *Mindfully Connecting*, which in itself gravitates onto this same Field #4. I would like to reaffirm that my aim is to support you in exploring what is best for you and hopefully give you some practical tools and ideas rather than tell you what you should do; and that, since you are reading this book, you are curious and open to finding new ways to nurture your connection with the people and the world around you.

Focusing onto another's Resolution Field doesn't support the idea of you just "feeling good about" or thinking you are "justified" to tell someone what to do. If you ever find yourself telling another person how to think, what he should do or should have done, trying to convince him of certain things or analyzing his behavior without an invitation to do so, you will probably have a very hard time with it and likely create more disconnection.

You might also find yourself being "tired of giving empathy". The solution in this occasion is not to offer advice instead. What this likely means is that *you* are overwhelmed and probably need supportive space and empathy.

There are also times when the other person might seem to ask for feedback, for example by saying something like: *"if you think you know better, then you tell me how it works*" or *"if you are 'so smart', why don't you address the issue"*. These kinds of statements usually come from unmet needs, where the person probably needs emotional support. Instead of asking for support, he uses language that belongs in the Resolution Field while expressing it in a very sarcastic and cynical way. By saying things like this, people usually tend to push others away and leave themselves more estranged and disconnected from the world. You can re-focus to his Empathy Field by recognizing these as clues/hints and respond with something like: "I am uncertain that you are truly able and open to listen to what I have to say, I am curious if everything is ok…" Once you've attended his feelings and needs, you can reconnect back to his Resolution Field, if needed of course.

Parenting is an example where focusing on another's Resolution Field and giving direct guidance happens naturally. As Dr. Gordon Neufeld[48] explains it, parents need to be the "Home Base" and a "Compass Point" for their children. "Home Base" (Empathy Field in essence) is being there for them emotionally, offering security and letting them know they are significant. "Compass Point" (Resolution Field in essence) is about giving direction, taking care of, looking out for and having the strength to nurture. The directions need to be simple, concise, clear and consistent.

Children inherently seek guidance from parents; the question: *"What should I do?"* is a default question in children's behavior. They seek to get proper guidance and have boundaries set in order to grow up into adulthood. Adulthood involves being able to make decisions for oneself and carry out own one's own actions. Giving directions to their children in order to nurture and protect them is inherent for parents. Neufeld points out that parents need to cultivate loving relationships with their children first in order for the children to actually want to take guidance from them. By going through the Empathy Field for yourself, you can create the "Home Base" within yourself and hence for your children too. This allows you to be fully present for your children and create solid loving relationships. This opens up doors for children to rest in your Love and grow the capacity for *Mindful Connection* of their own and then their children when they grow up.

If a relationship between a couple gets created where the dynamic and focus on Fields is out of balance or one person might be overly dependent on the other, it creates an opportunity for the couple to look within themselves and work on creating more Empathy Field ("Home Base") and Resolution Field ("Compass Points") within in order to restore the balance. Many times we subconsciously create dependent dynamics in our lives in order to offer ourselves the opportunity to learn, grow and even heal. Sometimes people need to re-create a similar dynamic many times. Every dynamic you create is an opportunity to create more nurturance and *Mindful Connection* in your life.

FOUR STEPS IN THE "EMPATHY FIELD FOR ANOTHER PERSON"

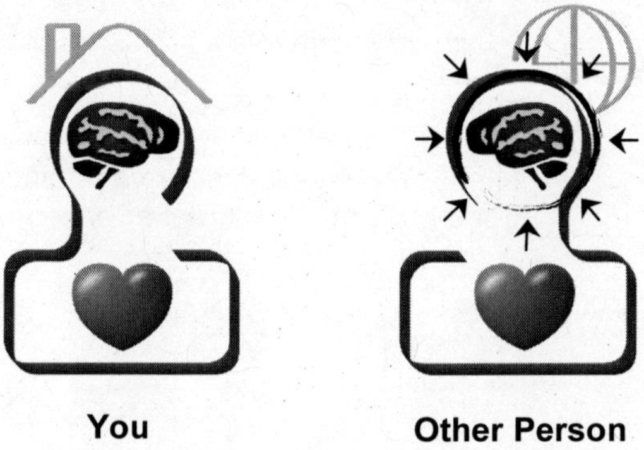

As introduced in Chapter 1, "Resolution Field for Another Person" consists of two parts: *"Support Another Person in exploring Possibilities"* and *"Support Another Person in carrying out Strategies"*.

Both these parts consist of two steps each that make a total of four steps.

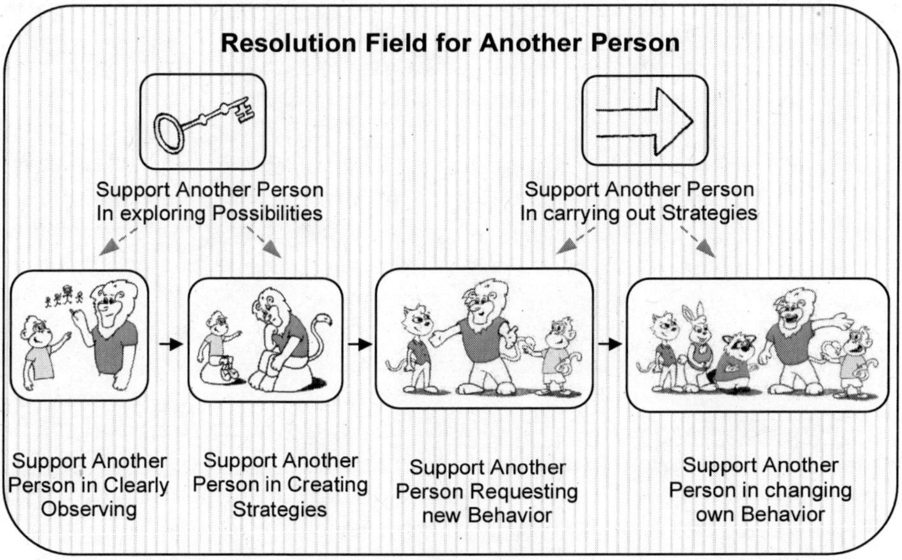

Each of these four steps has a collection of methods to carry out and you explore them all in this Chapter.

Andy Advises
Support Another Person in Exploring Possibilities

Once *Andy Advises* saw that *Lisa Listens* helped the teacher identify his needs, he asked him if he needed support in finding strategies to get them met. The teacher accepted.

SUPPORT ANOTHER PERSON IN EXPLORING POSSIBILITIES

Supporting another person in exploring possibilities is the first step in Field #4 and is the part of the journey where you support the person in exploring ways to get his needs met. You first need to support him in creating strategies before you can support him carry those out in the second step of this Field.

Imagine having successfully supported someone in going through his Empathy Field, where the person now has the ease and clarity yet is still unsure about what exactly to do around the situation. It's a good time to support him in exploring possibilities, as the person is more able and receptive to observe things clearly and create strategies.

A simple way of knowing if it's time to focus on this step is to take a deep breath, attune within yourself and check in to see if you are well grounded, emotionally stable and if you are getting clear signs that the other person is ready to get support from you and use the clarity he has to start exploring possibilities towards getting his needs met.

Some people might ask you for your feedback and advice even while aware that they are emotionally triggered. This would indicate that they are taking responsibility for what is arousing their feelings, that they trust you and in this case might want to hear the "cold-hard truth". If you suspect that another person is not displaying signs of this kind of responsibility, there a good chance that he is not ready to focus on his Resolution Field. In that case you can let him know that you believe that the time is not appropriate for you to give advice.

Note that if you were to approach another person with a request for him to see things a certain way or do something because it is affecting you and it would help you get *your* needs met, you are *not* Focusing on that person's Resolution Field; you are focusing on your own Resolution Field.

If you do give any advice, keep away from criticizing the other person's behavior. This doesn't mean that you need to refrain from disagreeing with what's being said and explored. Have an open mind and be curious.

Unsolicited input can be very hard on others. Avoid preaching your values and beliefs because *you* have decided that's the best for another person. Giving unsolicited advice can also often get people to think that you are arrogant because you keep telling them how they "should fix their behavior", as if there is something wrong with what they are doing.

Notice that this is step is about the *other person* creating clear observations and finding solutions for his own situation, *not* about exploring what strategies *you* could find. You cannot know what's best for other people, what they need to do nor make decisions for them. In this context, giving advice involves listening to people as they explore what they need to do, which involves exploring options *with* them, not *for* them.

The *only* time to ever really do this is if the person comes to you and specifically requests support or if you have checked in with the person about offering support. Even then, be mindful, as people tend to ask for help and not necessarily mean it or maybe be overly sensitive to receiving advice. When someone says: *"What should I do"*, enquire first if the person really wants input instead of just jumping into giving instructions. You can ask straight up: "Would you like me to give you some advice?" or "How would you like me to help you?"

You can also ask the other person if he would be interested in having you support him in exploring different possibilities and get consent from him before you start doing it. That's what *Andy Advises* did with the teacher.

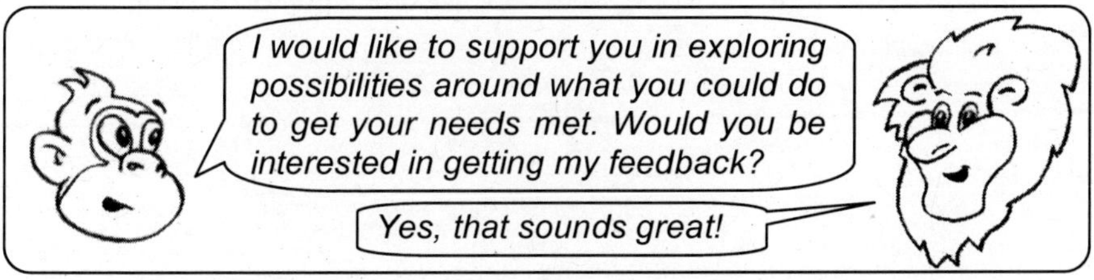

The upcoming sections explore two steps in supporting another person explore possibilities: supporting him in clearly observing behaviors in his current challenge first and then supporting him in creating strategies around these observed behaviors. The example of what *Andy Advises* did while supporting the teacher demonstrates these two steps.

Andy Advises
Supporting Another Person in Exploring Possibilities
- Supporting Another Person in Clearly Observing -

Andy Advises supported the teacher in observing both his and *Sadie Solve*'s behaviors around his met and unmet needs:
- **Met needs behaviors:** He had accepted to talk and connect with *Sadie Solves*; he had also raised his voice when teaching, which helped him gain confidence.
- **Unmet needs behaviors:** He had set weak boundaries with students when they wanted to make request; he also taught a class where he realized his loud voice was scaring students.

SUPPORT ANOTHER PERSON IN OBSERVING BEHAVIORS

You support another person in clearly observing behaviors when you have him focus on his behaviors in relation to other people's behaviors in a situation that is specific to time and circumstance. In order for him to use this observation toward getting his needs met, it is important that he primarily maintain his focus on *his* behavior rather than the behaviors of other people and to make sure that he does not get caught up in evaluating the other person's behavior. You can together use your rational thinking and logical inference, without involving either one's emotional realities or beliefs.

Questions to ask yourself in order to help another person clearly observe: *"How do I support another person in observing what he, she or the other person did/said, what happened, when it happened, who was involved, etc."*

Questions to ask the other person: *"What did you do/say?" "What happened?" "When did it happen?" "Who was involved?" "Can you give me a specific example?"*

Remember to keep asking open-ended questions (the "Six Ws").

Lets explore a collection of methods that can help *you* support another person in clearly observing. *Andy Advises* chose some of these to support the teacher in clearly observing.

#1 – OBSERVE OTHER PERSON'S BEHAVIOR FIRST

Express to the person you are supporting that you are interested in first finding what *specifically* the *other* person did in this situation. You can ask him for any specific examples that demonstrate that person's behavior. You will most probably get the other persons version of the "observation" of the challenging situation. It could be very unclear and full of mistaken conclusions, criticism and evaluations.

Even though emotionally grounded and willing to let go of criticism and examining other people's intentions, the other person could still get caught up in this criticizing and evaluative talk which would get in the way of making clear observations. Considering that he now holds emotionally uncharged clarity, and is connected to his needs, it would be much easier for him to see through these harsh judgments and misconceptions. If he *insists* with his critical way of thinking and evaluating other's intentions, you can pause the conversation. You can say that it is important for you to support him in the most authentic way you can, which is by connecting to his needs and the behaviors around those needs and that it is hard for you to clearly observe behaviors when using this language.

You need to be very attentive to what the person is saying and watch out for any false conclusions or generalizations he could make, even if he is trying not to speak that way, so that you can make it easier to uncover any verbs that describe the other person's behavior.

That's exactly what *Andy Advises* did with the teacher when the teacher insisted in staying in the evaluative language. Although the teacher had just successfully gone through the Empathy Field, his habit of thinking critically too hold again. When he started saying things like: *"She has always been a little dictator", "I don't think I talk loudly", "What do you think others would think of me", "I've never been so disrespected" and "No one else has a problem with this", Andy Advises* paused him. *Andy Advises* spoke from his heart, something that takes courage and can at times be quite an intimidating process. He said he was interested in connecting with the teacher and invited him to explore making clear observations whilst staying connected to his needs instead of getting caught in evaluative language.

A great and also very important way of clearing up these misguided assumptions and beliefs is to let the person know what the reality of the actual situation is and what other people's actual behaviors *are*. For example, *Andy Advises* asked *Sadie Solves* to let the teacher know that her aim was not to disrespect and expose him and that she wanted to connect. The teacher's response that *Sadie Solves* is *"a little dictator"* states an evaluation of what he thinks she is; it doesn't express a behavior.

By dropping the word *"dictator"* and any other evaluations, *Andy Advises* could observe *Sadie Solves's* behavior around the teacher's unmet need for respect and also met need for connection: it was her asking the teacher to reduce his voice in front of other students.

Andy Advises supported the teacher in finding another behavior that the students were doing around the teacher's unmet needs for clarity in though and confidence: their physical reaction and discomfort around his loud voice when he taught the class.

Observing the other person's behavior

#2 – OBSERVE ONE'S OWN BEHAVIOR IN RELATION TO OTHER PERSON'S BEHAVIOR

It is important to assert in supporting the person in observing the behaviors that *he* carried out that put him in a place to be exposed to this situation. You can request to do that even if he insists on focusing on the other person's behavior. He needs to recognize that he plays a part in creating these dynamics just as much as the other person.

RECALL FEELINGS AND NEEDS

Having gone through the Empathy Field, the other person will have attuned to his feelings and identified his met and unmet needs. Remember that since the event happened in the past, it is possible that he might be feeling differently now with different needs unmet, especially after having gotten empathy. Support the person in recalling his feelings and needs around this challenge.

The teacher's feelings of being glad and encouraged around connection and participation and feelings of being embarrassed and upset around respect and acceptance are associated with *Sadie Solves*'s approaching him about a concern and doing it in front of other students; whereas the feelings of confidence around getting clarity and feelings of insecurity around confidence and self-esteem are associated with the teacher raising or reducing his voice.

Recall Feelings and Needs

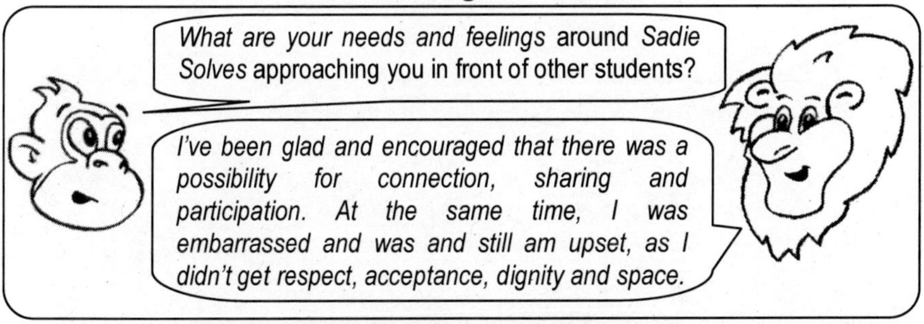

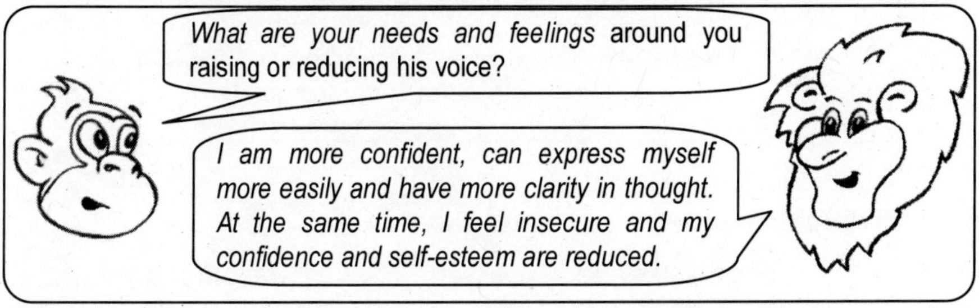

DISTINGUISH BOTH BEHAVIORS FOR MET AND UNMET NEEDS

Just like you supported the person narrow down the other person's behavior at the beginning of this section, now support him in narrowing down his own behaviors by scrutinizing his potentially evaluative language.

Find two sets of different behaviors:
- Ones that are keeping the person's met needs met and which have kept him in the dynamic that he is still in,
- And others that are keeping his unmet needs unmet, which is where the challenge arose.

Express the behaviors in terms of what the other person *did do* or *is doing* rather than the behavior that he is or was *not* doing. For example, *Andy Advises* would say:
"The teacher raised his voice" instead of *"The teacher wasn't quiet enough"* and
"The teacher set weak boundaries" instead of *"The teacher didn't set boundaries"*, etc.

Observing one's own behavior that's getting needs *met*

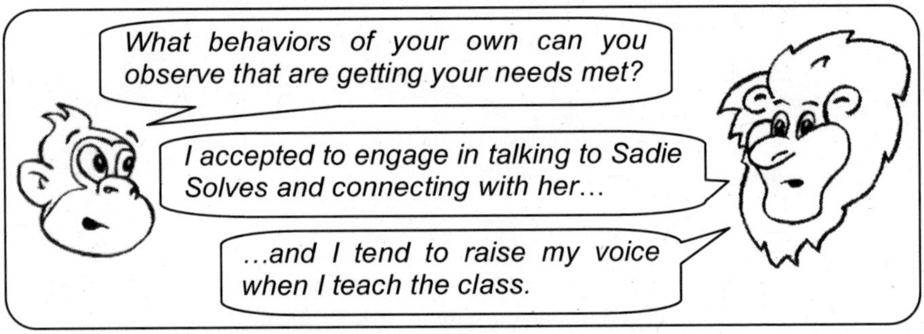

Observing one's own behavior that's getting needs *unmet*

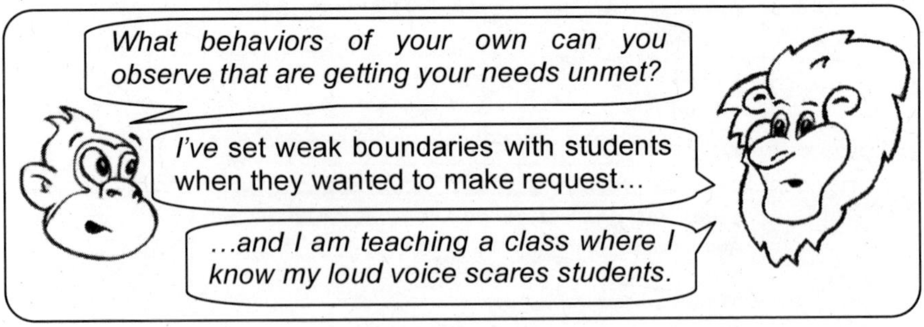

#3 – CONNECT ALL THE BEHAVIORS

This is the point where you support the other person in acknowledging that the feelings that he feels and his both met and unmet needs were brought about by the actions that *he* took in connection with the other person's behavior.

Simply support the person connect the feelings and the needs to the behavior by using the expression "because I". By doing this, he would own his actions and take responsibility for what arose his feelings. He would still express the other person's behaviors, the focus however is on his behaviors.

Connecting all behaviors around the met needs

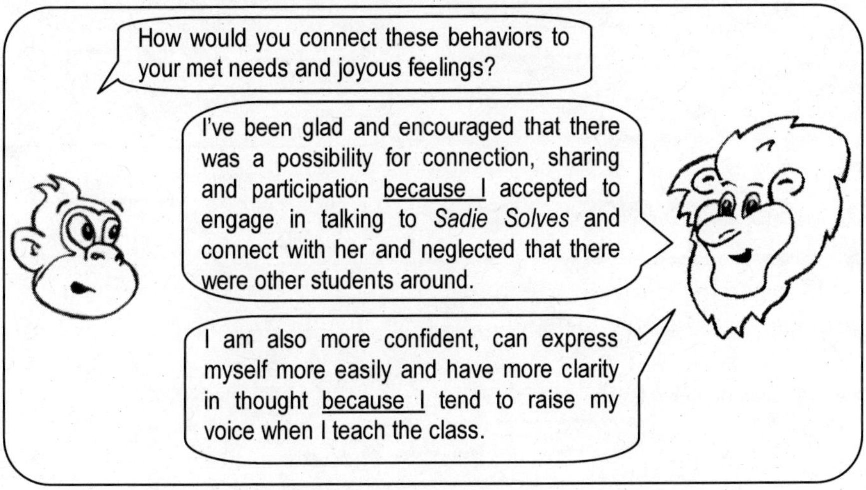

Connecting all behaviors around the unmet needs

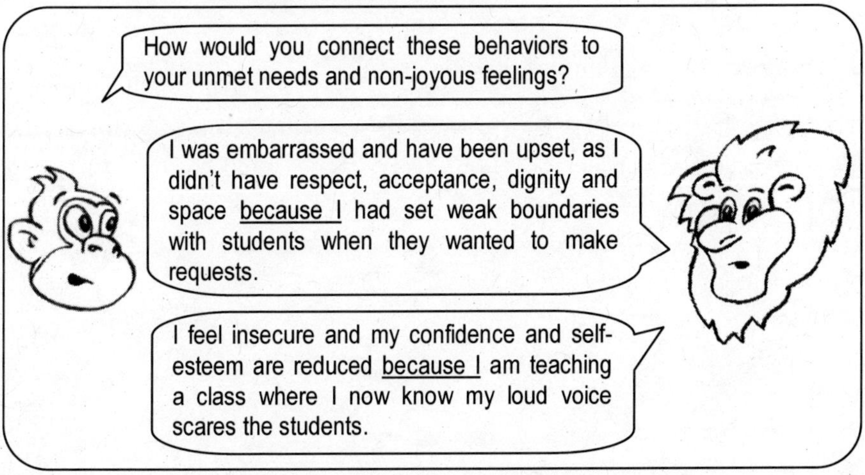

Andy Advises
Supporting Another Person in Exploring Possibilities
- Supporting Another Person in Creating Strategies -

Andy Advises supported the teacher in creating strategies toward getting his needs met either with the students or elsewhere.
Teacher's needs for connection, sharing and participation with the students were very important to him. He chose to meet them with the students. He would work on requesting from the students to be understanding and respectful if at times he subconsciously raised his voice.

SUPPORT ANOTHER PERSON IN CREATING STRATEGIES

Supporting another person in creating strategies is about exploring ideas and making plans together with that person, now that he has attuned to his feelings, identified the met and unmet needs and made clear observations.

Questions to ask yourself in order to help another person create strategies: *"How do I support another person in knowing what to do?" "How do I support another person in what strategies to plan, and how?"*

Questions to ask the other person: *"What can you do?" "What new strategies can you plan, and how?"*

Remember to keep asking open-ended questions (the "Six Ws").

Lets explore a collection of methods that can help *you* support another person in creating strategies. *Andy Advises* chose some of these to support the teacher in creating strategies.

#1 – EXPLORE WAYS TO MEET NEEDS

Having identified both the met and unmet needs, supporting the teacher in exploring the significance and priority he has around meeting either of these needs with the other person or elsewhere makes it easier for him to know how to create strategies. You can support him in this by having him reflect on the feelings that would come up if either of the needs were met or unmet depending on different explored strategies. Again, the goal of creating new strategies is to create more joyous feelings in his life, less non-joyous feelings and consequently, more wellbeing. Recall that different strategies evoke different feelings around *same* needs in people and every person can find one's own unique and different way to meet same needs.

GETTING NEEDS MET WITH THIS PERSON

The person you are supporting might find that getting needs met with the other person would overall, bring more joy than attempting to meet them elsewhere; at least in the current setting and dynamic. In that case, he could choose to strategize toward maintaining the met needs with this person and finding ways of getting the unmet needs around him met as well. With proper strategies and dedication and your support, he can increase the chances in his aim of getting all his needs met in his dynamic with that person.

With *Andy Advies's* support, the teacher might find that having connection, sharing and participation in his teaching with the students is something that could have a high priority in his life and bring more joy compared to the respect he was not getting; and that being trusted and relied on are integral parts of where he's at and weigh way more than the importance of self-expression, clarity and confidence that he gets by being loud. This option would especially be effective if he could find straightforward ways of gaining respect and finding self-expression, clarity and confidence in other areas of his life.

Getting needs met with this person

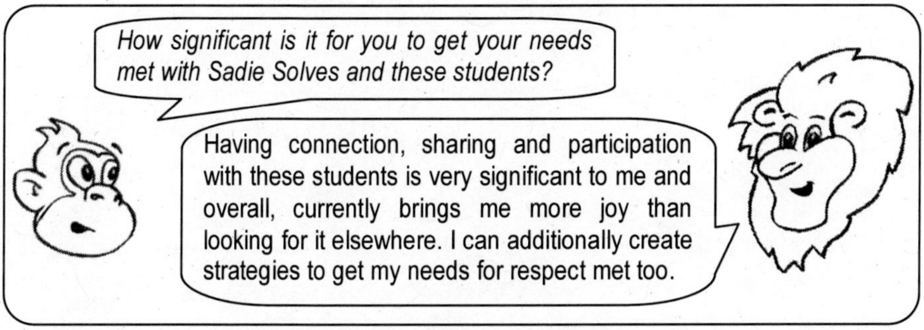

He might even find that once having gotten empathy in the Empathy Field, it wouldn't be that big of a deal to include other students in the conversation or reduce his voice a bit when teaching.

GETTING NEEDS MET ELSEWHERE

The person you are supporting might find that getting needs met elsewhere would overall bring more joy than attempting to meet them with that person. In this case, he could choose to find ways to get his unmet needs met elsewhere where he might be able to have the currently met needs met as well.

With *Andy Advies's* support, the teacher might find that the need for respect is much bigger and brings more joy than the need for participation and connection when he's approached about his loud voice in front of the students. Also he could realize that needs for self-expression, clarity and confidence he gets through talking loudly are more important than the unmet needs for being trusted and relied on if he is not.

Getting needs met elsewhere

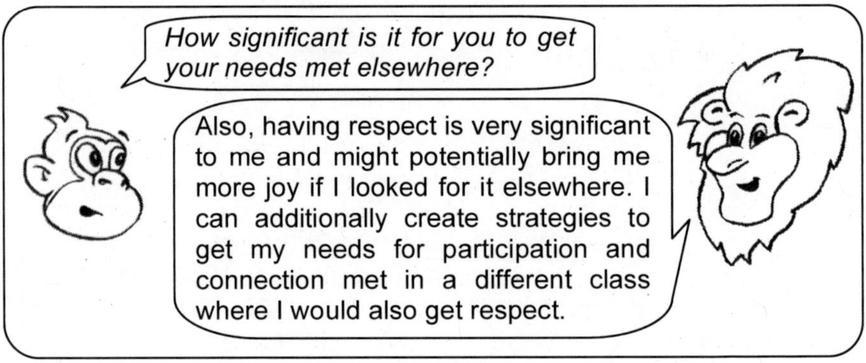

#2 – CREATE NEW STRATEGIES

When you support people in creating new strategies, it could arouse lots of resistance and irritation in them. This is due to habits and attachments that they might have developed throughout the years and are very hard to let go of. When this happens, it is important re-focus back to their Empathy Field, empathize and be present with them.

If the person has a habit of seeing things through pessimistic and negative perspectives, first thing you can do is make sure you reframe things positively. Everything that he would say he "doesn't want to do", you can ask and find out what it is that he "does want to do". This stimulates a positive outlook and way of thinking that is very helpful in creating good strategies.

If the teacher in the example were to say: *"I don't want to be put on the spot"*, he is expressing what he doesn't want to do. It is much more constructive to be clear on what he does want to do. *Andy Advises* helped him reframe this sentence into: *"I like to be approached respectfully and privately around any issues"*. He also reframed the sentence: *"I don't want to start talking quietly",* into: *"I like to express myself loudly"*.

Make sure to thoroughly examine the person's strategies as you go through them with him, find any oversights and do your best to plan them out as well as you can. You need to be honest wit the person if you believe that his strategies are faulty or not quite complete. Predicting that the person will be carrying out weak strategies and supporting him in that process without saying anything about their faultiness can be a draining process and it's a good idea to do your best to try to avoid it from happening.

STRATEGIZE TO GET UNMET NEEDS MET WITH THIS PERSON

Creating new strategies can be an emotionally charged process; you might find that the other person is very triggered in this process. If this happens, make sure to refocus to his Empathy Field right away. I he gets overly triggered and needs space, make sure to take a step back and give him time and space to work things out on his own.

In our example, the teacher got overwhelmed again with the thought of having to work things out with *Sadie Solves*, especially since he initially had such a criticizing and aggressive approach with her. Having already gone through the Empathy Field helped a lot with doing it again and easing off that way of relating and thinking. He overall had much more clarity in thought and ease around it all.

You would support the person in doing either or both of these two steps: support him in strategizing to request new behavior from the other person and also in strategizing to change his own behavior, both with the aim to get his needs met with this person. Supporting him in *carrying out* these two steps is explored in detail in the upcoming section.

- "Request new behavior" - you can support him in requesting new behavior from the other person by reaching out and requesting her to adjust or change her behavior. *Andy Advises* explored with the teacher that he could ask *Sadie Solves* and the students whether they could be understanding and respectful if at times he subconsciously raises his voice; and if they could speak to him privately if they have requests or concerns.

- "Change own behavior" - You can support him in changing his own behavior, which involves reducing the other person's behavior's impact on him, without even necessarily interacting with her. *Andy Advises* explored with the teacher that he could decide to work on reducing his voice in class, stand further away from the students, ask the students to talk to them in private later if they attempt to raise their concerns in front of others, etc.

Strategizing to get unmet needs met with this person

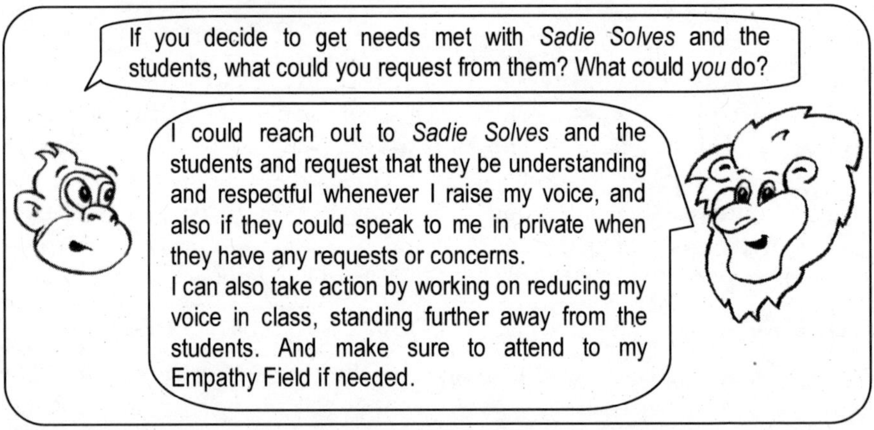

STRATEGIZE TO GET CURRENTLY MET NEEDS MET ELSEWHERE

This is about supporting the other person in exploring how he could get his needs met by creating other strategies and dynamics than the one he is currently in. This step can be even more challenging due to many unforeseen feelings that might come up. This could happen due to both the reaction of the person you are supporting *and* the other person's reaction to his attempts to get his needs met elsewhere. You need to be ready to attend his Empathy Field.

- "Request new behavior" - You can support him in requesting new behavior from the other person. *Andy Advises* supported the teacher to think about reaching out to *Sadie Solves* and the other students and ask them if they knew of other classes where students would be more at ease around his voice. He could also ask if the students would want to attend another class with a teacher they wouldn't be as threatened by.

- "Change own behavior" - You could also support the person in changing his own behavior in order to get his needs met. *Andy Advises* supported the teacher in thinking about teaching elsewhere.

Strategizing to get currently met needs elsewhere

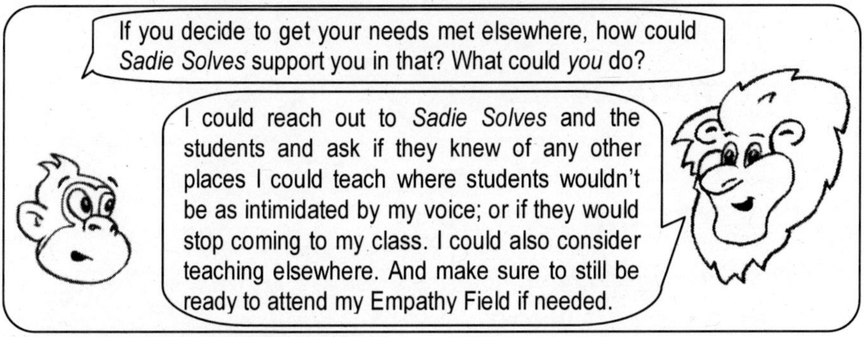

DECIDE ON ONE STRATEGY

Once you have supported the person explore all the options and create the best strategies possible, it is important for him to make a decision to commit to a strategy that he believes would be the best one for him at this time and would bring the most amount of wellbeing. He can decide this by determining which strategy holds greater importance in order to get his needs met. Clear observations and thorough strategizing helps decision-making. Be adamant about the importance of him choosing one direction and going with it instead of wanting someone else to decide for him.

This could be a challenging process for you as a supportive person, as people tend to be indecisive or not make any decisions at all. If at any point during your support the person becomes irritated by your insistence on *him* making a decision or accuses you of "mean" intentions, you can listen to him and empathize. Also remind him that your aim is to support him, that you care for his wellbeing and the reason you are doing it in the first place is because he reached out to you and agreed to have your support.

In our example, the teacher's needs for connection, sharing and participation with the students were very important to him. He decided to work on reducing his voice and also request from his students to be understanding and respectful if at times he subconsciously raises his voice.

Deciding on the strategy to get unmet needs met

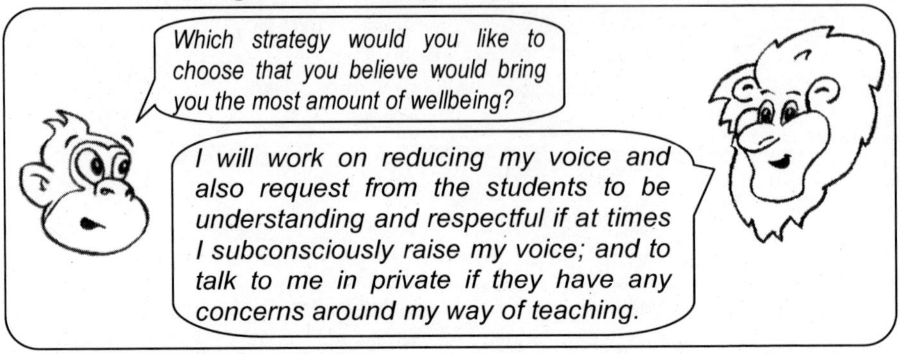

#3 – STRATEGIZE BASED ON OTHER PERSON'S RESPONSE

Based on the strategy that the person you are supporting chooses, the other person could react in three different ways. This in itself could influence what the person you are supporting could further do. You can help him plan out and prepare different alternative strategies based on these three different responses by the other person.

1 - CONNECTING (TURNING TOWARD)

Connection is what you would want the person you are supporting to inspire in the other person. Even if the other person is interested in reaching out and connecting, he still might need to do some negotiating around his strategies and open up the conversation to work together in the aims of getting everyone's needs met.

Andy Advises told the teacher that *Sadie Solves* and students might be ok with doing what he requested. Even if they were reluctant or unsure, they still might be into talking about it and working things out.

Other person connecting to the attempt to reach out

2 - ATTACKING (TURNING AGAINST)

Let the person you are supporting know that the other person might also attack his attempt to reach out. He can watch for signs of criticism, contempt and aggression in her and choose to either empathize with the person, find supportive space for himself or if the dynamic is very overbearing, entirely cease interaction with the other person.

Sadie Solves and the students might be very triggered by the request. Considering that they have already been overwhelmed by the teacher's voice, this time, they might become very attacking and insensitive. *Andy Advises* told the teacher that if this happened, the best thing to do in the moment is to empathize with the students, be caring and patient and also understand that it is not easy for many people to be subject to someone's shouting.

Of course, if students' aggression continues, the teacher can also eventually choose to move on to some other arrangements. He can try creating supportive space for himself. Sometimes it is a good idea to cease teaching these students if he has done the best he can to work things out. He might need to re-evaluate the importance of his needs again too in order to find alternative ways to pursue getting them met.

Other person attacking the attempt to reach out

3 - IGNORING (TURNING AWAY)

When the person you are supporting reaches out, the other person might ignore him or completely change the topic of conversation. This means that the other person is attempting to get her needs met by being passive and evasive. That strategy helps her avoid potential hurtful feelings to come up. You can explain to the person you are supporting that these responses are a bit harder to strategize around because there is limited amount of interaction to work with. He can wait for any cues that can help establish a connection by giving the other person some space; he can also try attempting to reach out a few times. This might delay taking care of his needs for a bit. He would still pursue with the intention of getting his needs met in the way he'd strategized.

Sadie Solves and the students might be very dismissive with the teacher's request. *Andy Advises* suggested to him that if that happened, he would need to make sure to give space to the students. He could try making the request a couple of times more and then empathize if his attempts irritated the students. Things might be uncomfortable for a while until he managed to connect, as both his and students' needs would stay unmet.

Other person ignoring the attempt to reach out

PRACTICE

SUPPORT ANOTHER PERSON IN EXPLORING POSSIBILITIES

Turn to "*Support Another Person in exploring Possibilities*" in the Practice Section on page 207. It offers different practices for supporting others in exploring possibilities.

Andy Advises

Support Another Person in Carrying out Strategies

Having supported the teacher in exploring all his possibilities and create strategies, *Andy Advises* started supporting the teacher in carrying out the strategy he decided upon.

SUPPORT ANOTHER PERSON IN CARRYING OUT STRATEGIES

This second step of Field #4 is the part of the journey where you support another person in setting off on their journey toward getting his needs met. Having supported the other person in exploring his possibilities, you can now support him in carrying out the chosen strategy, just like *Andy Advises* would. Supporting another person in carrying out strategies is when you and the other person explore ways for him to perform specific actions in order to accomplish the strategies that he created toward getting his needs met.

To actually find ways of getting their needs met and fully *Mindfully Connect* to themselves and others, people *need* to carry out their created strategies. Your support can be very important for those who struggle with getting certain tasks done. Think of what a difference it makes to have support from someone who believes in you.

Just like you needed to be careful while helping someone explore possibilities, the same applies now too. Avoid giving unsolicited directions just because you believe the other person needs to hear it. Again, the *only* time to ever do this, and do it watchfully, is if the person comes to you and *specifically* requests your support, or if you offer to give support and the person clearly and honestly accepts it.

A simple way of knowing if you can start focusing on this step is to take a deep breath, attune within yourself and check in to see if you feel grounded, emotionally stable and ready to support the other person in carrying strategies out. This process will inevitably bring up many challenges for the other person, like guilt, fear and resistance. Your presence can be of crucial significance while supporting him. By openly expressing that you believe in him and that you believe that he has the capacity to pursue these emotionally challenging tasks, you can immeasurably support him in successfully carrying out his strategies.

People might come to you with direct questions like: *"How do I do this?"* Spend time together with them exploring different ways to carry out strategies. You can trust that people will know what to do by getting support from you and you being there, rather than you directly telling them what to do. Giving straight-up instruction can work when tasks are more straightforward and require a well functioning, arranged teamwork, like being in a team where there's some kind of a leader that directs it or in a family, where there is a loving relationship between the parent and children and parents set boundaries for the children for their protection.

The teacher asked *Andy Advises* to support him in successfully carrying out his strategies. The teacher wanted to find ways to reach out to *Sadie Solves* and the students and request their understanding when he accidentally raises his voice and ask them to talk to him about any concerns in private. He also wanted to work on reducing his voice when teaching the class. If at any point the teacher would ignore or attack *Andy Advises* as he was supporting him, *Andy Advises* would check in with him in case he was overwhelmed and needed to focus on his Empathy Field and make sure he was still interested in getting his feedback.

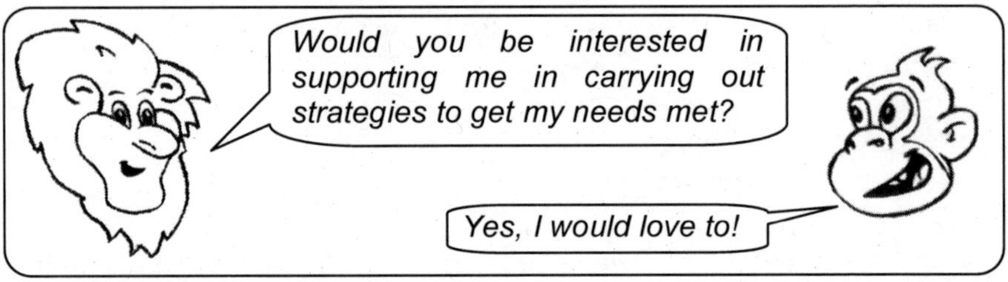

The upcoming sections explore two steps in supporting another person in carrying out strategies: supporting the person in requesting new behavior from the other person and also supporting him in changing his own behavior. The example of what *Andy Advises* did once he supported the teacher in exploring his possibilities and creating strategies demonstrates these two steps.

Andy Advises
Supporting Another Person in Carrying out Strategies
- Supporting Another Person in Requesting new Behavior-

Andy Advises supported the teacher in reaching out to *Sadie Solves* and the students to request a new behavior. He first made sure the teacher had their attention, then that he expressed his feelings and needs. The teacher then requested them to consider being understanding and respectful if he accidentally raised his voice when teaching and to talk to him in private if they had any concerns. Then he had the teacher check in if the students heard his request properly.

SUPPORT ANOTHER PERSON IN REQUESTING NEW BEHAVIOR

Supporting another person in requesting new behavior involves exploring ways of reaching out to the other person and requesting her to change or adjust her behavior so that it would help the person you are supporting get his needs met.

Questions to ask yourself in order to support another person in requesting a new behavior: *"How can I support this person in reaching out?" "How would I support the person in making a request?"*

Questions to ask the other person: *"How can you reach out?" "How would you make a request?"*

Remember to keep asking open-ended questions (the "Six Ws").

Lets explore a collection of methods that can help *you* support another person in requesting a new behavior. *Andy Advises* chose some of these to support the teacher in requesting a new behavior.

#1 – PREPARE TO REACH OUT

ROLE-PLAY THE INTERACTION

Offering to role-play the interaction with him by exploring various possible outcomes can be very helpful for him to reach out and know what to say.

CREATE CONNECTION BY NURTURING THE RELATIONSHIP

Encourage the person to build the relationship with the other person first, before making any requests. He needs to cultivate a nurturing connection with her and create a state of positive sentiment override for everyone.

BE EMOTIONALLY UN-FLOODED

You need to make sure that he is emotionally un-flooded when stating feelings. His request needs to be emotionally uncharged. If he is in any way overwhelmed, it will be hard for him to make clear request and he might need to empathically connect by refocusing back onto his Empathy Field.

HAVE THE PERSON'S ATTENTION

Remind him to make sure to get the other person's attention when attempting to connect and make the request. He would be inviting the other person to focus on his Resolution Field, which is Requirement #1 for Mindful Connection (focusing on the same Field). He can look for eye contact, a nod or a smile or make arrangements for a specific time to talk.

ACKNOWLEDGE THE REASON FOR REACHING OUT

Indicate to him that he needs to have in mind that he is still focusing on getting *his* needs met. As much as the request involves that other person to do action, this request is about *him* and getting *his* needs met. This gives him solid grounds to why he is making this request.

Connecting first when reaching out

#2 – STATE THE CURRENT BEHAVIORS

Encourage the person that you are supporting to start with expressing all the behaviors in relation to the current challenge. It is always a good idea to express these things in his own words rather than literally recite pre-made sentences. And of course when he expresses his feelings and needs, and even how his behavior contributed the creation of the difficulty, he will increase the possibility of the other person connecting easier to his request.

Stating the Behaviors

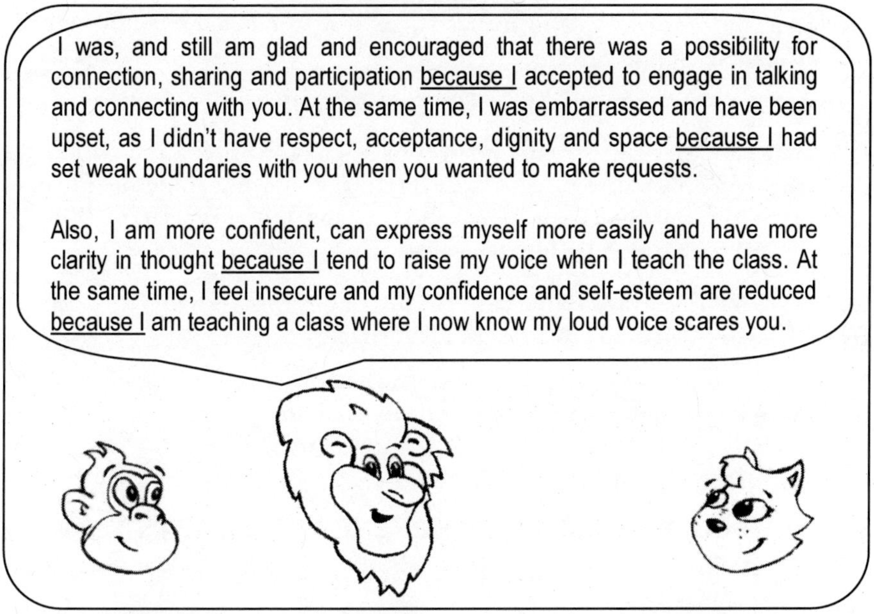

You can also clarify to the person that you are supporting that he can state the observation in much more concise and spontaneous way, unless it is a very challenging situation.

Stating the Behaviors (Alternate Shorter Version)

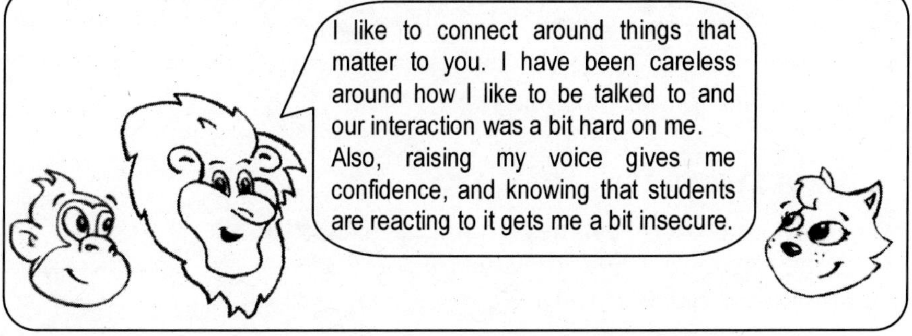

#3 – REQUEST THE NEW BEHAVIORS

SHAPE THE REQUEST POSITIVELY

You can support the person in making sure that he knows what it is that he "does want" the other person to do rather than what he "doesn't want" her to do. If he seems to only focus on what he doesn't want, spend some time exploring the positive behaviors that are related to the unwanted behaviors.

For example, *Andy Advises* and the teacher found that instead of asking *Sadie Solves* and the students not to make requests in front of others, he can ask them to talk to him in private.

EXPRESS SENTIMENTS AROUND THE REQUEST

Encourage the person you are supporting to also express appreciation for the other person's willingness to hear him out, by saying something like: *"I appreciate you taking the time to hear me out…"* and the appreciation that she would potentially consider his request by saying: *"I would really grateful for…"* He can also point out that he cares for his connection with her.

START THE REQUEST AS AN INVITATION

You can let the person you are supporting know that by giving the other person an opportunity to choose her involvement in the request, he can increase her curiosity and care for his request. He can open the request with something like *"Would you be interested in…"*

SHAPE REQUEST THROUGH DIFFERENT SENSORY SYSTEMS

Encourage him to think about which *Sensory Systems* she might respond the best to.

Andy Advises explored with the teacher whether specific students might be extra responsive in an *Auditory, Visual, Kinesthetic* or *Cognitive* way and then they shaped the request more in that direction. *Andy Advises* knew that the teacher was *Visual* so when supporting him, he was using expressions like *"look into", "see"* or *"picture"*. He also noticed that *Sadie Solves* would express her self and was receptive in conversation mainly through her *Cognitive* sensory system. He encouraged the teacher to use words like: *" think about"* and *"figure out"* when making requests to *Sadie Solves.*

REQUEST THE SPECIFIC BEHAVIOR

The request needs to be the specific behavior that the person you are supporting wants the other person to do. You supported the person to identify this behavior in the "Support Another Person in Observing Behaviors" section.

- If the person chose to get his needs met with this person, he'd request the specific behavior that gets his needs met.
- If he chose to get his needs met elsewhere, it might be unnecessary to make a request although in certain circumstances it might be appropriate when that person can do a specific behavior that would clear the space for him to be able to get his needs met.

For example, the teacher could have asked the students to take another class if he had decided to meet his needs elsewhere. He was however interested in continuing to teach this class of students.

Request the Specific Behavior

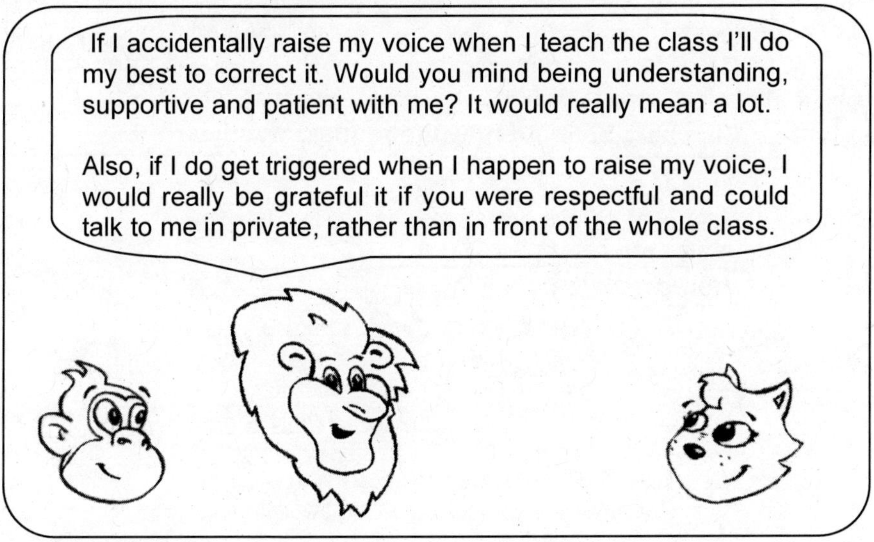

#4 – CHECK IN IF THE REQUEST WAS PROPERLY HEARD

Encourage the person you are supporting to ask for feedback from the other person around how she took his request. It is easy to make a request and think that everything is fine and everyone's on the same page, when in reality it might not be the case at all.

He can ask something like: *"How does this sound to you?" "What do you think about this?" etc.*

Sadie Solves did slightly react emotionally to the teacher's request and she ignored his attempt to connect by changing the topic of conversation; *Andy Advises* supported the teacher in focusing on her Empathy Field and reconnect. After reconnecting, the teacher could bring the conversation back to the initial request around getting his needs met.

Checking in about how the request was heard

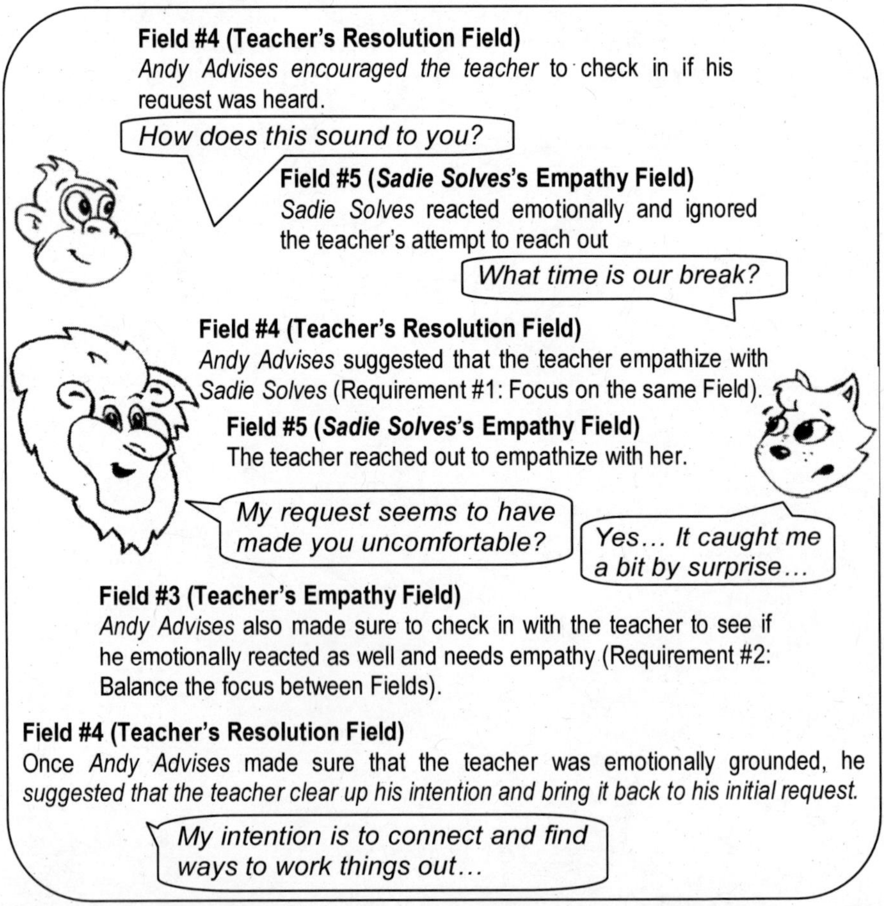

REPAIR IF ANY VERBAL HARM GETS CREATED

If the person you are supporting gets emotionally triggered as a result of the way the other person responds to his request and he slips into attacking or ignoring her, make sure to encourage him get supportive space and empathy. You can directly empathize with him too. Once he has emotionally un-flooded, encourage him to repair things with the other person. He can apologize or acknowledge his aim to work things out. He can then return to his original request with the aim to get his needs met.

The teacher already had a tendency to get upset and attacking with *Sadie Solves*. He got a bit upset and said some harsh words after which he had to take a step back and empathically connect with himself and then empathize with Sadie Solves before he could go back to his original request.

Repair if any verbal harm gets created

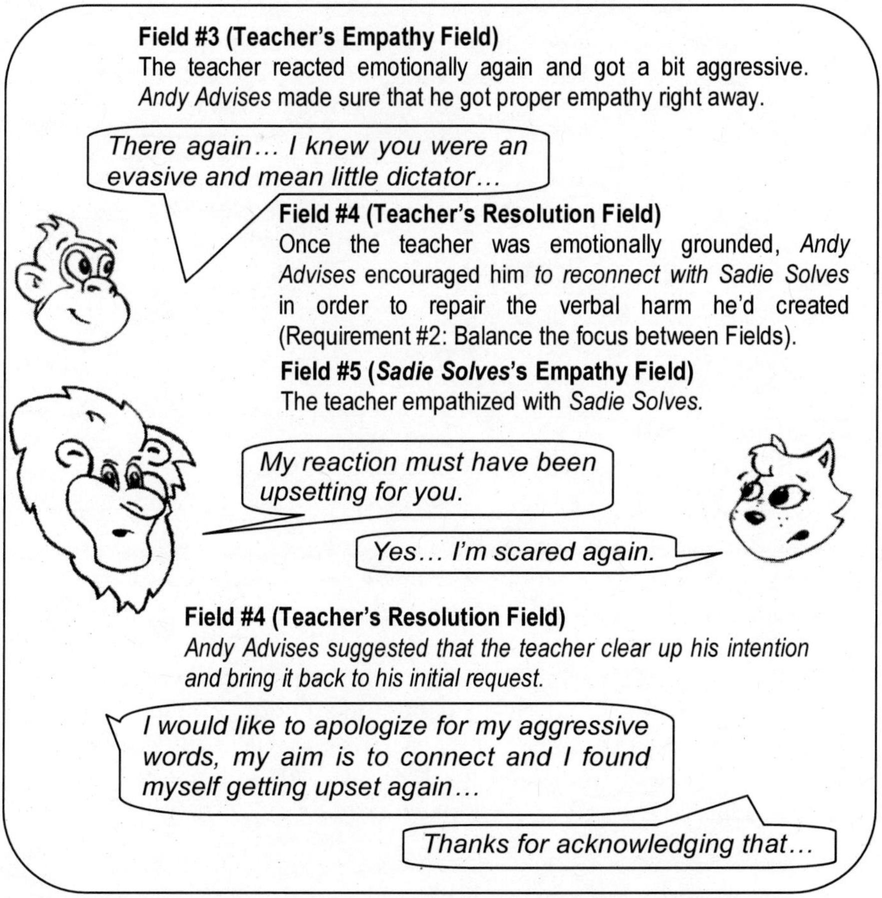

IF NEEDED, CLARIFY THE REQUEST

If the other person didn't end up hearing the request properly the first tiem, due to being overly triggered, the person you are supporting might need to repeat and clarify his request again. You can help him recognize that even if his request had been very clear at the time, it might have not come across as clearly to the other person. He can acknowledge to the other person that his request was unclear and clarify it by stating the request again.

Clarifying the Request

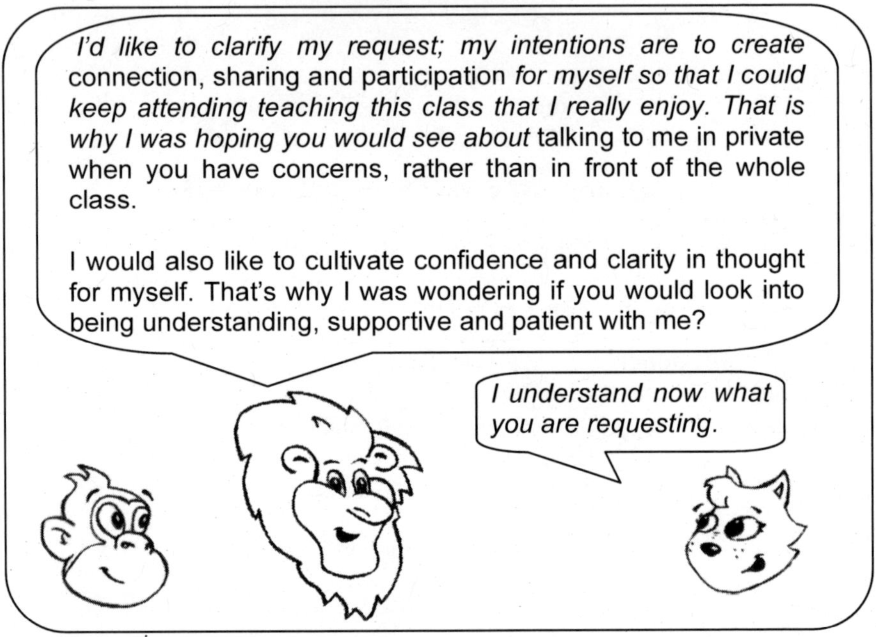

INQUIRE ABOUT PERSON'S INTENDED ACTIONS

In order for you to know how to further support the other person in carrying out his strategies, you will need to have him check in with her around what her further actions are; this could be determined by directly checking in with her, or watching her behavior and way of interacting.

Sadie Solves responded to the teacher that she would intend to be respectful, talk to him in private about his concerns and be understanding and patient while he attempts to reduce his voice. After all, they all had the same needs for connection and learning and for *Sadie Solves*, these requested behaviors were just additional strategies to help her get these needs met.

Andy Advises
Supporting Another Person in Carrying out Strategies
- Supporting Another Person in Changing own Behavior -

Andy Advises supported the teacher to also take action himself by working on reducing your voice in class, standing further away from the students, requesting them to talk to him in private if they attempt to raise their concerns in front of others.

SUPPORT ANOTHER PERSON IN CHANGING OWN BEHAVIOR

Supporting another person in changing his own behavior is when you support the person in the part of carrying out strategies that involves him adjusting or changing *his* behavior and taking action. He can think of it as if he is requesting himself to do behavior-changing actions, just like he did with the other person. Everything is planned out and in place; it just needs doing. This can involve anything from getting simple errands done, to doing huge life changing acts.

Questions to ask yourself in order to help another person change his own behavior: *"How can I support this person in taking action?" "How can I support this person in persevering?"*

Questions to ask the other person: *"How can you take action" "How do you persevere?"*

Remember to keep asking open-ended questions (the "Six Ws").

Lets explore a collection of methods that can help *you* support another person in changing his own behavior. *Andy Advises* chose some of these to support the teacher in adjusting and changing his behavior.

#1 – PREPARE TO CHANGE BEHAVIOR

POSITIVELY REINFORCE ACTIONS

If the person struggles with accomplishing tasks in general, you could explore and arrange with him some other smaller tasks that are easier to accomplish. This way he can start building a collection of successfully completed actions, which are extremely helpful in positively reinforcing getting more other tasks done.

BUILD CONFIDENCE

Remind the other person that as long as he focuses on his Empathy and Resolution Fields, always does his best and stays humble, he will gain more courage and confidence to take on all the challenges that come up.

#2 – DO IT!

When supporting the other person to take action you need to encourage him to simply *do it.* This is not a guilt-trip or an order, it is you finding a place in yourself to believe in that person and honestly support and encourage him to take on carrying out action.

Not only can you encourage him to carry out tasks but you can also keep checking in and see if he is keeping his actions consistent. Suppose the teacher decided to stop shouting when teaching, successfully did it for a few days or weeks and then totally forgot about it and continued as if no strategy had been put in place. *Andy Advises's* support would include staying in check with him about that.

#3 – RE-VISIT THE EMPATHY FIELD

Even if you encourage the other person to carry out action in an as caring way as you can, it might still arouse an emotional reaction in him. Trying to perform the action in itself can bring up many challenges. If this happens, make sure that the person focuses on his Empathy Field. You can also remind him that his actions are not who he is and that you are there to help him out bridge these difficulties and transform his undesired habits into newly strategized behaviors. Having your support will make a big difference in him carrying these tasks out.

For example, the teacher might have a very hard time thinking clearly when trying not to raise his voice in front of students and his constant focus on the volume of his voice might result in his lessons getting worse. This could bring up feelings of insecurity and anxiety, thinking that he is a poor teacher and not competent enough. He could start justifying his old habits by saying things like *"I can't do this, this is just not who I am…"* In this case, *Andy Advises* would re-focus onto the teacher's Empathy Field again for as long as needed.

RETURN TO THE RESOLUTION FIELD

Going between the Empathy and Resolution Fields helps the other person explore different strategies towards getting his needs met. It is important to explore and even change strategies and take different action until he finds the best working solution. You can be present and helpful with him in both Fields throughout this process.

#4 – BEHAVING AROUND THE OTHER PERSON

SET BOUNDARIES

If you notice that the other person is not responding to the request of the person you are supporting, is being insensitive to all his attempts to work things out toward a mutually beneficial situation for everyone and is continuing to attack or ignore his attempts to reach out, you could encourage him to "put his foot down", set his boundaries with the person and get his need for respect and space met.

You can also explain to him that assertion is not punishment. It is about respecting oneself and making sure that if others are not granting it, that one needs to provide it for himself.

By now, the person you are supporting would have done a great amount of very constructive work toward creating connection. If the other person is still having a hard time working with this and is continuing to keep her distance without connecting back, you can encourage the person you are supporting to assert his stand through words and behavior in order to create supportive space for himself. Firmness in one's self-respect, confidence and principles can be very powerful in getting the message across. He would of course do this only *in the moment* when the other person displayed insensitive behavior.

This process would help the person let go of any pending resentments, blame or accusations he is still holding against the other person. He would be able to cultivate forgiveness within himself, an action that he can get to by going through the Empathy Field where he attuned to his feelings, identified his needs and then arranged to get them met by honoring himself and setting boundaries in the Resolution Field. Once he had the opportunity to connect to the other person's feelings and needs too, the significance of being forgiving can be even more powerful.

REPAIR IF ANY BEHAVIORAL HARM WAS CREATED

Just like it was likely for the person you are supporting to say something harmful when making requests, the same could happen through his behavior when taking action. He might get aggressive and even abusive while wanting to set his own boundaries. Note that firmness and assertiveness in the process of setting boundaries while still being loving and wanting to connect is very different from slipping into attacking and aggressive behavior.

If you noticed him doing to that, have him recognize it and find supportive space where he can empathically connect to what upset him. Then you can encourage him to go back to the other person, acknowledge what he'd done, apologize if needed and through empathy repair the harm his behavior might have crated.

PRACTICE

SUPPORT ANOTHER PERSON IN CARRYING OUT STRATEGIES

Turn *to "Support Another Person in carrying Out Strategies"* in the Practice Section on page 210. It offers different practices for supporting others in carrying out their strategies.

WHERE TO GO FROM HERE?

STAY HERE

As long as you haven't helped the other person find arrangements to get his needs met, stay focused on this Field. If you notice yourself focusing on other Fields just bring your attention back and refocus on it. Also take extra care not to get overly caught in this Field either; doing this can set you into a "telling others what to do" mentality where you could have a hard time stepping away from it and attending to the other Fields as well. To avoid this from happening, make sure to do your best to fully attend to this Field and honor your intended behaviors and agreements around it.

GO BACK

Supporting another person in exploring possibilities and carrying out strategies can be hard on him and could bring up various new feelings. When that happens, the person might get emotionally overwhelmed and need to move to the Empathy Field; you need to focus on that Field (#3) with him.

If you in any way start emotionally reacting *yourself,* while you are supporting the other person, you need to make arrangements to get supportive space in "Empathy Field for Yourself" (Field #1). If you are well practiced and skilled in attending all the Fields, you can attempt focusing on both your Empathy and Resolution Fields and the other person's Empathy and Resolution Fields at the same time.

KEEP MINDFULLY CONNECTING

If the person successfully carries out all the intended actions and gets his needs met while still staying emotionally grounded, he will have created *Mindful Connection* in his life around this dynamic. It takes a lot of work and perseverance to get to this place.

Providing that you also went through your Empathy and Resolution Fields and got your needs met as well, you and the other person will probably both have an outpour of joy as a result of successfully getting all your needs met.

From here, you can keep maintaining and further nurturing this and all other connections in your life.

PRACTICE

The practice sections below contain a summarized version of the full method presented in the book. At the end of this section is an even more summarized, one-page version of the method called the "Mindful Connection Method – Quick Guide". You can use these practices around any specific challenge you might be going through, and also refer to the book itself for guidance depending on how difficult the challenge is.

The aim of this book and doing all this work is to create a life of fulfillment with abundance of nurturing *Mindful Connection*, support and loving relationships in all arenas of your life: family, friends, work and beyond. It *is* possible to achieve all that! The best way to introduce this method into your life is to live it rather than talk about it or verbally promote it. Practice it, test it and see if it works for you. There will be a balance of heartache and pleasure, play and seriousness, celebration and grief, ease and challenge, harmony and conflict, clarity and confusion and a rich overall awareness of being alive and not alone in it all!

Still the most rewarding challenge is to stay humble, keep being present with others and yourself. When in doubt, first and foremost focus on empathy rather than on resolution, thereby creating a world of emotional connections. Separate time to practice mindfulness, either through being aware, attentive and focused on every day tasks or by practicing meditation.

It is important to understand that using any technical jargon from this book can become very alienating to others. Communicate by avoiding expressions like *"I need you to focus on my Field"* or *"I'm attuning to your Empathy/Resolution Field"* and find ways to say things in your own words.

In order to gain the most out of the *Mindful Connection Method,* practice the sections one at a time. Take days or a week or more at a time with each section. This way the content integrates much better than attempting to do it all at once. Awareness gained in every Field contributes to the successful integration of the next one.

Explore all the questions in these practice sections by:
- Filling in the blank lines in the book or use a separate sheet of paper.
- Browsing through the examples and spend time thinking about it.
- Talking to someone about it by reading the examples together.
- Role-playing with a friend.
- Applying the practices directly. The best way to really integrate tools is to implement them in the real world and learn from experience.

MINDFUL CONNECTION IN YOUR COMMUNITY

Questions to ask: *"How is my connection with others?" "Where is my focus when connecting?" "How can I develop my ability to focus well and be mindful?"*

In order to become aware of what kind of balance you've kept so far in your dynamic with the other person, spend some time exploring the interaction between you and the person:
- How often do you find yourself focusing on any one of the four Fields?
- How much time and priority do you give to each Field?
- Do you seem to need more or less focus on either of the Fields?

Focusing on the **Empathy Field for Yourself (F#1)** Focus: ___%

____

____

Focusing on the **Resolution Field for Yourself (#2)** Focus: ___%

____

____

Focusing on the **Empathy Field for Another Person (#3)** Focus: ___%

____

____

Focusing on the **Resolution Field for Another Person (#4)** Focus: ___%

____

____

As you start exploring the upcoming Practice Sections, make sure to honor the two Requirements for a Mindful Connection discussed in Chapter 1
#1 - Everyone focuses on the same Field at a time (pg. 21)
#2 - Balance the focus between the Fields (pg. 23)

– Practice –

CREATE SUPPORTIVE SPACE FOR YOURSELF (FIRST PART OF FIELD #1)

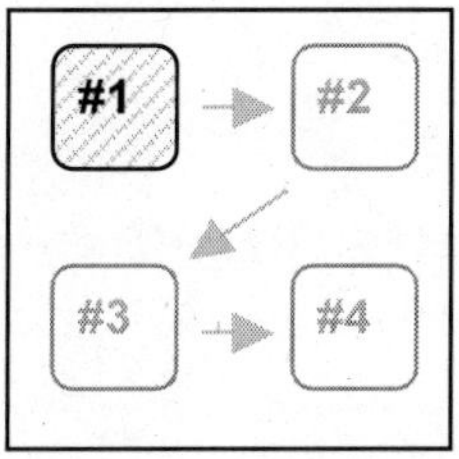

INITIATE SUPPORTIVE SPACE (pg. 38)

Questions to ask:

"How do I initiate supportive space?" "In what way do I lovingly interrupt this dynamic?"

INTIATE IT ONESELF

INTERRUPT

"BRIDGE"

FIND SUPPORTIVE SPACE (pg. 42)

Questions to ask:

"What kind of space/ support do I need?" "How can I take time away?"

ALONE

WITH ANOTHER PERSON - SUPPORTIVE PERSON OR SUPPORTIVE COMMUNITY

INITIATE SUPPORTIVE SPACE FOR YOURSELF (pg. 38)

In which way can *you* interrupt a challenging situation?

How can you find ways to "bridge" (express to the person that you want to reconnect at a later time)?

FIND SUPPORTIVE SPACE (pg. 42)

- ALONE

List a few supportive spaces you can find to be on your own where you can find solitude, quiet, safety and a peace of mind.

- WITH ANOTHER PERSON

– SUPPORTIVE PERSON

List all the people who you can think of that would be there for you through a challenge. Is there anyone you can call any time, day or night?

What kind of an arrangement can you have with the people you have in mind so that he/she can offer you the empathy and support that you need?

Explore whether it is possible or realistic to request a certain person in your life to offer you support?

– SUPPORTIVE COMMUNITY

List communities or organizations that are available to offer support?

– Practice –

EMPATHICALLY CONNECT (SECOND PART OF FIELD #1)

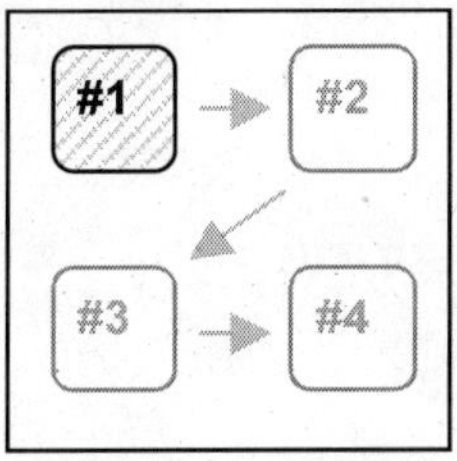

ATTUNE TO FEELINGS (pg. 47)

Questions to ask:
"How am I doing?" "How am I feeling?"

#1 – USE CLUES/HINTS

#2 – WELCOME THE FEELING

#3 – FEEL

IDENTIFY NEEDS (pg. 59)

Questions to ask:
"What do I need?" "What are my needs?" "What am I looking for?"

#1 – VOCABULARY OF NEEDS

#2 – USE CLUES/HINTS

#3 – IDENTIFY ALL THE NEEDS

ATTUNE TO FEELINGS (pg. 47)

#1 – USE CLUES/HINTS

Use the clues/hints that arise when you are in a challenging situation:

THOUGHTS (AS CLUES/HINTS)

Explore any evaluative thoughts that come to mind:

___

___

BEHAVIORS (AS CLUES/HINTS)

Explore your behavior and any observed micro-expressions:

___

EXPRESSING FEELINGS (AS CLUES/HINTS)

Explore feelings or have a supportive person give you feedback. Use joyous and non-joyous feelings in the APPENDIX as a resource (pg. 217 and 218)

___

NEEDS (AS CLUES/HINTS)

Explore both met and unmet needs:

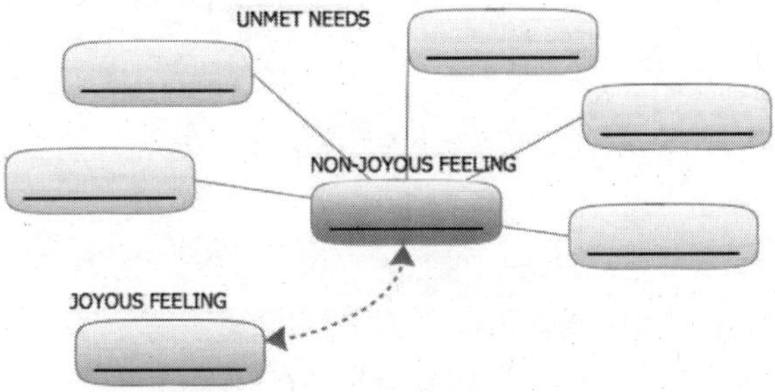

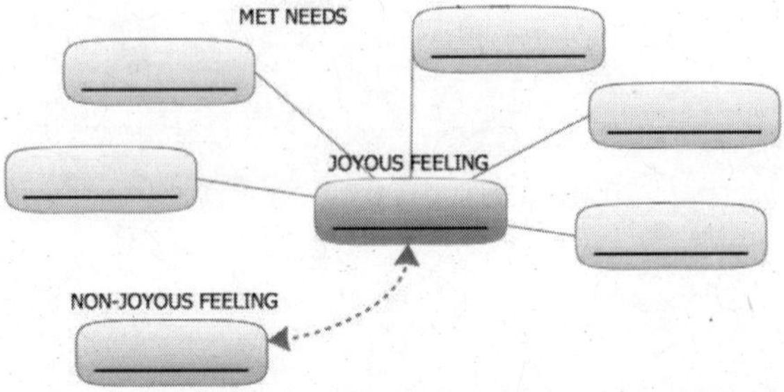

#2 – WELCOME THE FEELING

– How can you find ways to accept that it is *your* way of thinking and behaving that influences and shapes the way you are feeling?

____

– Imagine how you can *be in the present* by not focusing on what you felt in the past or how things might feel in the future, bat rather feel the feelings in this moment, right now.

____

— How can you practice p*ausing* so that you could be able to approach and accept challenging conversations and learn not to react hastily? (E.g. taking a deep breath)

____

– Explore ways to *accept futility*. First find out if there is something that you are resisting or not accepting because you have no control over it and the strategy you are using is not getting your needs met. Then move toward acceptance.

____

____

#3 – FEEL

When feelings arise, make sure to be present, loving and patient with yourself. Take as much time as needed. Notice the place in your body that the feeling is strongest.

You can write down any insights that resulted in the moment or after you have fully attuned to your feelings. Make sure to attune both joyous and non-joyous feelings.

____

____

____

Write down the best methods you have found to connect to your feelings.

____

____

____

IDENTIFY NEEDS (pg. 59)

#1 – VOCABULARY OF NEEDS

Explore the lists of needs in the APPENDIX (pg. 219).

#2 – USE CLUES/HINTS

VERBS

– Explore any "wants" and "desires" you have around your needs.

____

PEOPLE AND OBJECTS

– Explore any people or objects that come up around your needs.

____

ALIENATING LANGUAGE

– Explore criticism, interpretations, evaluations and random thoughts around your needs.

____

____

FEELINGS

– Explore feelings to confirm if a need is met or not. If the feelings are mostly joyous for a specific need, the need is met, if the feelings are non-joyous, the need is not met.

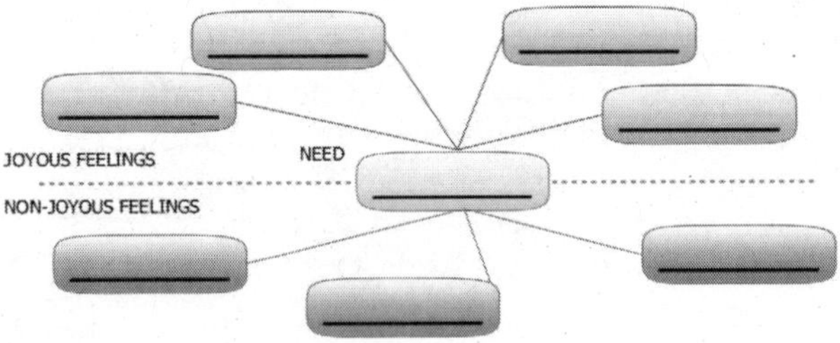

#3 – IDENTIFY ALL THE NEEDS

Identify both your met and unmet needs.

MET NEEDS: ________________________________

UNMET NEEDS: ______________________________

– Practice –

EXPLORE POSSIBILITIES
(FIRST PART OF FIELD #2)

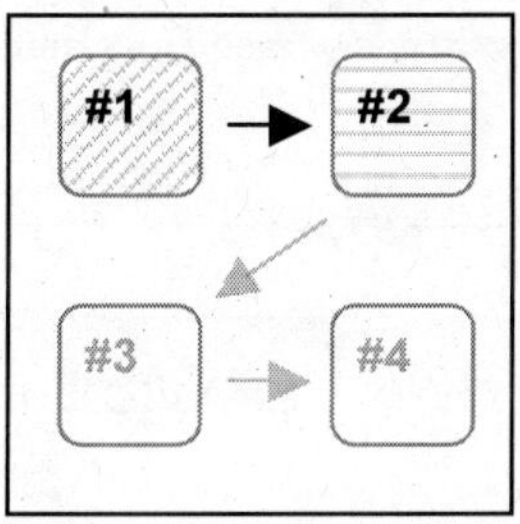

OBSERVE BEHAVIORS (pg. 72)

Questions to ask:

"What did I/he/she do?" "What happened?" "When did it happen?" "Who was involved?" "What was said?" "Do I have a specific example?"

#1 – OBSERVE THE OTHER PERSON'S BEHAVIOR FIRST

#2 – OBSERVE ONE'S OWN BEHAVIOR IN RELATION TO OTHER PERSON'S BEHAVIOR

#3 – CONNECT ALL THE BEHAVIORS

CREATE STRATEGIES (pg. 79)

Questions to ask:

"What can I do?" "What new strategies can I plan, and how?"

#1 – EXPLORE WAYS TO MEET NEEDS

#2 – CREATE NEW STRATEGIES

#3 – STRATEGIZE BASED ON THE OTHER PERSON'S RESPONSE

OBSERVE BEHAVIORS (pg. 72)

#1 – OBSERVE THE OTHER PERSON'S BEHAVIOR FIRST

Find specific behaviors the other person did that affect your current met and unmet needs.
- Remove any Evaluation/Criticism
- Have you drawn any conclusions based on incorrect information?
- Are you generalizing the other person's behavior?

____

____

#2 – OBSERVE ONE'S OWN BEHAVIOR IN RELATION TO OTHER PERSON'S BEHAVIOR

Find the existing behaviors *you* are doing that affect your current met and unmet needs.
- Express these past and current feelings and both met and unmet needs.

____

- Distinguish behaviors for both met and unmet needs
- Express your behavior in the affirmative/positive way.

Your behavior that is getting your needs met:

____

Behavior that is getting your needs unmet:

____

#3 – CONNECT ALL THE BEHAVIORS

- Assign responsibility to your behaviors in relation to the other person's behaviors by connecting your feelings and needs with your behaviors by using *"because…I"*:

I am feeling _________, _________, *with met needs:* _________, _________

because I ____

____.

At the same time,

I am feeling _________, _________, *with unmet needs:* _________, _________

because I ____________________, ____________________

____."

CREATE STRATEGIES (pg. 79)

#1 – EXPLORE WAYS TO MEET NEEDS

Looking at both your met and unmet needs, explore the priority and importance these needs have in your life.

What is significant about getting your needs met with this person?

____

What is significant about getting your needs met elsewhere?

____

#2 – CREATE NEW STRATEGIES

- Thoroughly scrutinize all the strategies as you create them and make sure that they are plausible and well planned out.
- Find what *is* possible rather than what is *not* possible.

Getting needs met with this person:
What can you request this person to do?

____

How can you change *your* behavior?

____

Getting needs met elsewhere:
What can you request from this person to do?

____

How can you change *your* behavior?

____

Decide on *one* strategy: _______________________________

#3 – STRATEGIZE BASED ON THE OTHER PERSON'S RESPONSE

Plan to reach out and request the other person to change his/her current behavior. Explore alternatives to your behavior depending on the person's response. What would you do when you attempt to reach out and:

the other person *connects* to your request?

____

the other person *attacks* your request?

____

the other person *ignores* your request?

____

– Practice –

CARRY OUT STRATEGIES (SECOND PART OF FIELD #2)

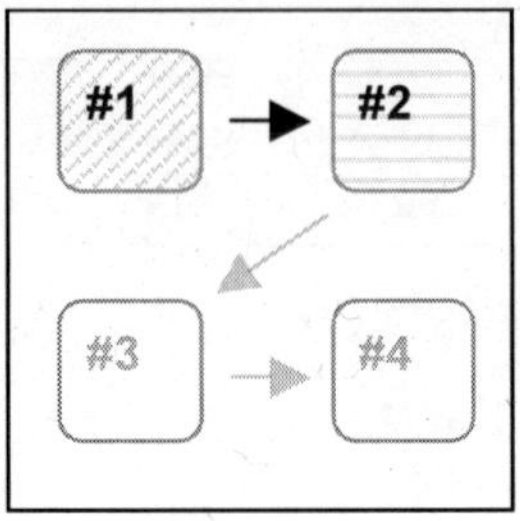

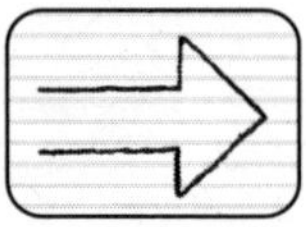

REQUEST NEW BEHAVIOR (pg. 92)

Questions to ask:

"How can I reach out" "How would I make a request?"

#1 – PREPARE TO REACH OUT

#2 – STATE THE CURRENT BEHAVIORS

#3 – REQUEST THE NEW BEHAVIORS

#4 – CHECK IN IF THE REQUEST WAS PROPERLY HEARD

CHANGE OWN BEHAVIOR (pg. 105)

Questions to ask:

"How can I take action" "How do I persevere?"

#1 – PREPARE TO CHANGE BEHAVIOR

#2 – DO IT!

#3 – RE-VISIT THE EMPATHY FIELD

#4 – BEHAVING AROUND THE OTHER PERSON

REQUEST NEW BEHAVIOR (pg. 92)

#1 – PREPARE TO REACH OUT

– Role-play the interaction with someone or on your own.
– Create connection by nurturing the relationship before giving the request.

____

– Explore ways to keep yourself emotionally un-flooded.

____

– How will you arrange and make sure to have the person's attention?

____

– Acknowledge your reason to reach out.

____

#2 – STATE THE CURRENT BEHAVIORS

– State *all* observed behaviors from the "Observe Behaviors" section.

#3 – REQUEST THE NEW BEHAVIORS

– Shape request positively: what you *"want"* instead of what you *"don't want"*.
– Express sentiments and appreciation if request is to be considered
– Find your own ways to start the request as an invitation.
– Shape the request through different *sensory systems* (Visual, Auditory, Kinesthetic, Cognitive).
– Request the specific behavior:

____

#4 – CHECK IN IF THE REQUEST WAS PROPERLY HEARD

– Ask the other person how he/she received the request? (Offer empathy)

____

– Repair any verbal harm if it was created: if you slipped into criticism, evaluative or aggressive language.

____

– If needed, clarify the request. Consider finding ways to reword the request?

____

– Ask the other person what he/she will do. Decide what you will do based on the person's response.

____

CHANGE YOUR OWN BEHAVIOR (pg. 105)

#1 – PREPARE TO CHANGE BEHAVIOR

– Positively reinforce actions by finding tasks that you know you can successfully carry out.

____

– Build confidence by finding different kinds of support to rely on when attempting to carry action out.

____

#2 – DO IT!

Simply carry out the action and see what happens. Observe if you had any difficulty with it.

____

#3 – RE-VISIT THE EMPATHY FIELD

– Did you react and do you need to visit the Empathy Field again? If reactions came up, what were your new feelings and needs?

____

– When ready, return to the Resolution Field; what are the new behaviors and strategies? Can you carry out the action now?

____

#4 – BEHAVING AROUND THE OTHER PERSON

– Find ways to *set* boundaries with the other person if he/she is being aggressive with you.

____

– Repair any behavioral harm that you might have created if *you* displayed abusive behavior.

____

– Practice –

SUPPORT ANOTHER PERSON IN CREATING SUPPORTIVE SPACE (FIRST PART OF FIELD #3)

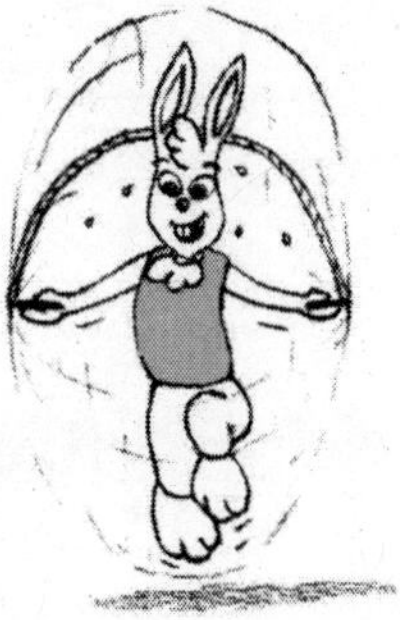

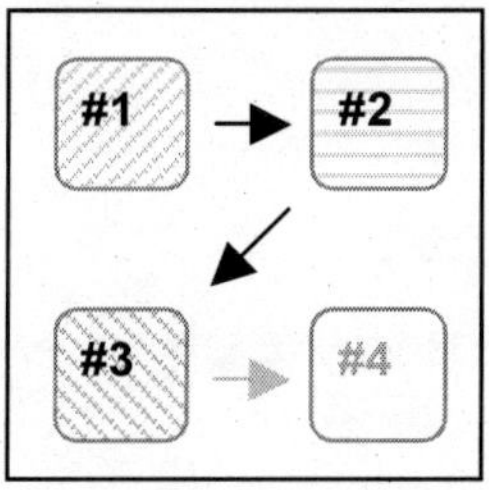

SUPPORT ANOTHER PERSON INITIATE SUPPORTIVE SPACE (pg. 122)

Questions to ask yourself:

When *you* are initiating the supportive space:

"How do I initiate supportive space for this person?"

When you are supporting the person initiate it herself:

"How do I support the other person in initiating supportive space?" "In what way do I support the other person lovingly interrupt a challenging dynamic?"

Questions to ask the other person:

When *you* are initiating the supportive space:

"What kind of space do you need?" "How would you like to take time away?"

When you are supporting the person initiate it herself:

"How would you initiate supportive space?" "In what way could you lovingly interrupt that challenging dynamic?"

INTIATE IT ONESELF

INTERRUPT

BRIDGE

SUPPORT ANOTHER PERSON FIND SUPPORTIVE SPACE (pg. 125)

Questions to ask yourself:

"How do I support the other person in finding the kind of space/ support she needs?"

"How do I support the other person in finding ways to take time away?"

Questions to ask the other person:

"What kind of space do you need?" "How would you like to take time away?"

ALONE

WITH ANOTHER PERSON - SUPPORTIVE PERSON / SUPPORTIVE COMMUNITY

SUPPORT ANOTHER PERSON IN INITIATING SUPPORTIVE SPACE (pg. 122)

How can you support this person so that he/she can find ways to interrupt a challenging situation him/herself?

How can you support him/her in finding ways to "bridge" (express to the person that he/she wants to reconnect at a later time)?

SUPPORT ANOTHER PERSON IN FINDING SUPPORTIVE SPACE (pg. 125)

- ALONE

Help him find a few supportive spaces where he/she can find solitude, quiet, safety and a peace of mind.

-WITH ANOTHER PERSON

– SUPPORTIVE PERSON

In what ways can you support him/her in finding all the people that would be there for him/her with a challenge? Is there anyone he/she can call any time, day or night?

In what ways can you support him/her in finding ways to empathically connect and get support?

Explore whether it is possible or realistic for you to offer support to him/her.

– SUPPORTIVE COMMUNITY

What kinds of communities or organizations are available to offer him/her support?

– Practice –

EMPATHIZE (SECOND PART OF FIELD #3)

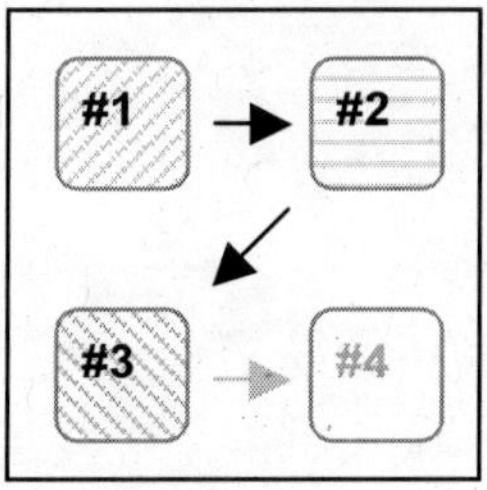

SUPPORT ANOTHER PERSON IN ATTUNING TO HIS/HER FEELINGS (pg. 130)

Questions to ask yourself:
"How do I support another person around how she is doing?" "How do I support another person around how she is feeling?"

Questions to ask the other person:
"How are you doing?" "How are you feeling?"

#1 – USE CLUES/HINTS

#2 – WELCOME THE FEELING

#3 – FEEL

SUPPORT ANOTHER PERSON IN IDENTIFYING HIS/HER NEEDS (pg. 140)

Questions to ask yourself:
"How do I support another person around what she needs?" "How do I support another person to find what she is looking for?"

Questions to ask the other person:
"What do you need?" "What are your needs?" "What are you looking for?"

#1 – VOCABULARY OF NEEDS

#2 – USE CLUES/HINTS

#3 – IDENTIFY ALL THE NEEDS

SUPPORT ANOTHER PERSON IN ATTUNING TO HIS/HER FEELINGS (pg. 130)

#1 – USE CLUES/HINTS

Use the clues/hints that arise when you are in a challenging situation:

THOUGHTS (AS CLUES/HINTS)

Listen to any evaluative thoughts that come to the other person's mind:

BEHAVIORS (AS CLUES/HINTS)

Watch the other person's behavior and any observed micro-expressions:

EXPRESSING FEELINGS (AS CLUES/HINTS)

Listen for feelings or offer feedback. Use joyous and non-joyous feelings in the APPENDIX as a resource (pg. 217and 218)

NEEDS (AS CLUES/HINTS)

Explore other person's both met and unmet needs:

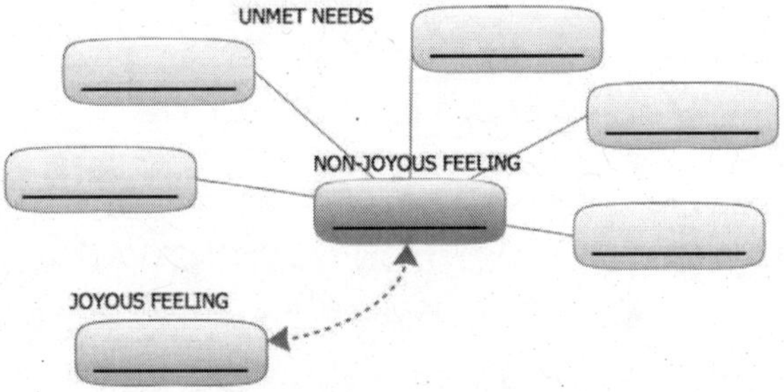

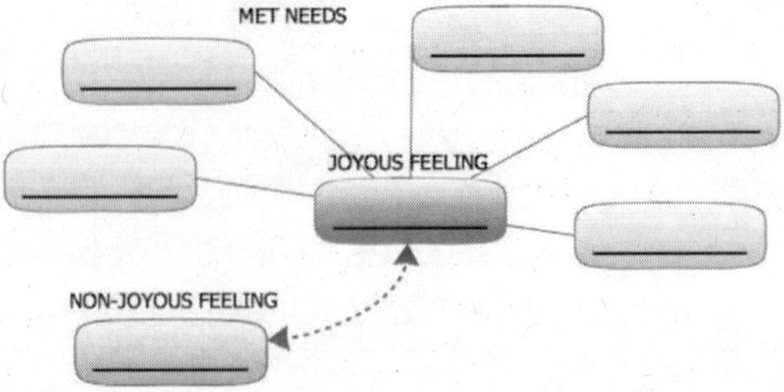

#2 – WELCOME THE FEELING

– How can you support the person in finding ways to accept that it is *his/her* way of thinking and behaving that influences and shapes the way he/she is feeling?

____

– How can you have the person explore *being in the present* by not focusing on what was felt in the past or how things might feel in the future, but rather feel the feelings in this moment?

____

– How can you get the other person to practice p*ausing* so that he/she could be able to approach and accept challenging conversations and learn not to react hastily? (E.g. taking a deep breath)

____

– Find ways to have the person explore ways to *accept futility*. First find out if there is something that he/she is resisting or not accepting because he/she has no control over it. Explore ways the strategy he/she is using is not getting his/her needs met. Then be present there for him/her so that he/she can move toward acceptance.

____

#3 – FEEL

When feelings arise for him/her, make sure to be present, loving and patient. Take as much time with him/her as needed. Ask if there are any sensations in specific areas of the body that are coming up for the person.

You can write down any insights that resulted in the moment and after the person has fully attuned to his/her feelings. Make sure that the person attunes to both joyous and non-joyous feelings.

____

____

____

Write down the best methods you have found to connect to your feelings.

____

____

____

SUPPORT ANOTHER PERSON IN IDENTIFYING HIS/HER NEEDS (pg. 140)

#1 – VOCABULARY OF NEEDS

Have the person explore the list of needs in the APPENDIX (pg. 219).

#2 – USE CLUES/HINTS

VERBS

– Explore any "wants" and "desires" the person has around his/her needs.

____

PEOPLE AND OBJECTS

– Explore any people or objects that come up around his/her needs.

____

ALIENATING LANGUAGE

– Explore criticism, interpretations, evaluations and random thoughts around the person's needs.

____

____

FEELINGS

– Explore the person's feelings to confirm if a need is met or not. If the feelings are mostly joyous for a specific need, the need is met, if the feelings are non-joyous, the need is not met.

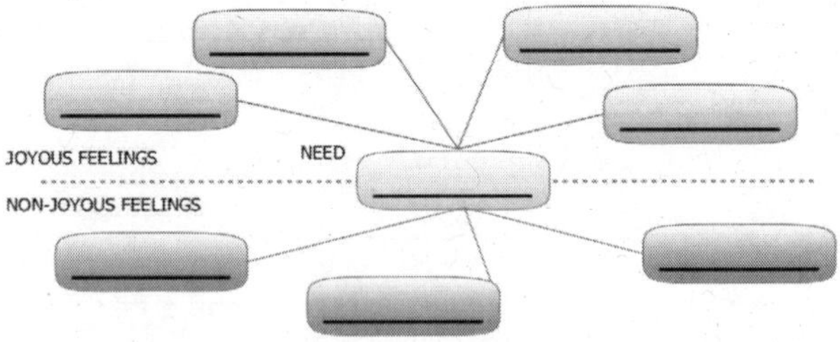

#4 – IDENTIFY ALL THE NEEDS

Identify both his/her met and unmet needs.

MET NEEDS: ______________________________

UNMET NEEDS: ______________________________

– Practice –

SUPPORT ANOTHER PERSON IN EXPLORING POSSIBILITIES (FIRST PART OF FIELD #4)

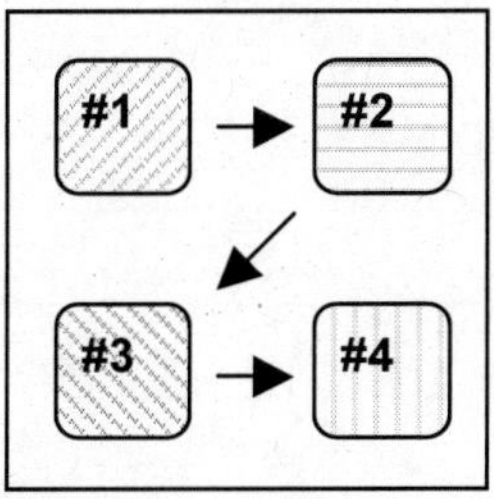

SUPPORT ANOTHER PERSON IN OBSERVING BEHAVIORS (pg. 154)

Questions to ask yourself:

"How do I support another person in observing behaviors?"

Questions to ask the other person:

"What did you do/say?" "What happened?" "When did it happen?" "Who was involved?" "Can you give me a specific example?"

#1 – OBSERVE THE OTHER PERSON'S BEHAVIOR FIRST

#2 – OBSERVE ONE'S OWN BEHAVIOR IN RELATION TO OTHER PERSON'S BEHAVIOR

#3 – CONNECT ALL THE BEHAVIORS

SUPPORT ANOTHER PERSON IN CREATING STRATEGIES (pg. 160)

Questions to ask yourself:

"How do I support another person in knowing what to do?" "How do I support another person in what strategies to plan, and how?"

Questions to ask the other person:

"What can you do?" "What new strategies can you plan, and how?"

#1 – EXPLORE THE IMPORTANCE OF MET AND UNMET NEEDS

#2 – CREATE NEW STRATEGIES

#3 – STRATEGIZE BASED ON THE OTHER PERSON'S RESPONSE

SUPPORT ANOTHER PERSON IN OBSERVING BEHAVIORS

(pg. 154)

#1 – OBSERVE THE OTHER PERSON'S BEHAVIOR FIRST

Find specific behaviors that the other person did that affect current met and unmet needs of the person you are supporting.
- Remove any Evaluation/Criticism
- Has he/she drawn any conclusions based on incorrect information?
- Is he/she generalizing the other person's behavior?

____

____

#2 – OBSERVE ONE'S OWN BEHAVIOR IN RELATION TO OTHER PERSON'S BEHAVIOR

Find the existing behaviors *the person you are supporting* is doing that affect his/her current met and unmet needs.
- What are these past and current feelings and met and unmet needs?

____

- Have the person distinguish behaviors for both met and unmet needs
- Have the person express his/her behavior in the affirmative/positive way.

The person's behavior that is getting his/her needs met:

____

The person's behavior that is getting his/her needs unmet:

____

#3 – CONNECT ALL THE BEHAVIORS

- Have the person assign responsibility to his/her behaviors in relation to the other person's behaviors by connecting his/her feelings and needs with the behaviors by using *"because…I"*:

I am feeling __________, __________, *with met needs:* __________, __________

because I ____

____.

At the same time,

I am feeling __________, __________, *with unmet needs:* __________, __________

because I ____________________, ____________________

____."

SUPPORT ANOTHER PERSON IN CREATING STRATEGIES (pg. 160)

#1 – EXPLORE WAYS TO MEET NEEDS

Looking at both his/her met and unmet needs, support the person in exploring priorities and importance these needs have in his/her life.

What is significant about getting his/her needs met with this person?

____

What is significant about getting his/her needs met elsewhere?

____

#2 – CREATE NEW STRATEGIES

- Encourage the person to thoroughly scrutinize all the strategies as he/she creates them and make sure that they are plausible and well planned out.
- Remind him/her to find what *is* possible rather than what is *not* possible.

Getting needs met with this person:
What can the person you are supporting request this person to do?

____

How can the person you are supporting change *his/her* behavior?

____

Getting needs met elsewhere:
What can the person you are supporting request this person to do?

____

How can the person you are supporting change *his/her* behavior?

____

Encourage him/her to decide on *one* strategy: ____________________

#3 – STRATEGIZE BASED ON THE OTHER PERSON'S RESPONSE

Support the person in planning to reach out and request the other person to change his/her current behavior. Explore alternatives to his/her behavior depending on the other person's response to his/her attempt to reach out:

the other person *connects* to his/her request:

____

the other person *attacks* his/her request:

____

the other person *ignores* his/her request:

____

– Practice –

SUPPORT ANOTHER PERSON IN CARRYING OUT STRATEGIES (SECOND PART OF FIELD #4)

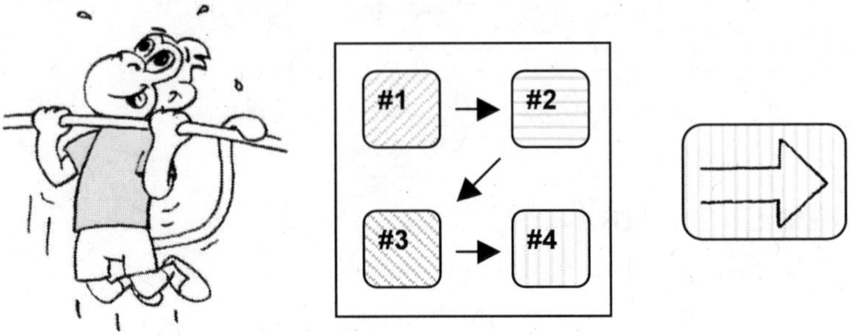

SUPPORT ANOTHER PERSON IN REQUESTING NEW BEHAVIOR (pg. 171)

Questions to ask yourself:

"How can I support this person in reaching out?" "How would I support the person in making a request?"

Questions to ask the other person:

"How can you reach out" "How would you make a request?"

#1 – PREPARE TO REACH OUT

#2 – STATE THE CURRENT BEHAVIORS

#3 – REQUEST THE NEW BEHAVIORS

#4 – CHECK IN IF THE REQUEST WAS PROPERLY HEARD

SUPPORT ANOTHER IN CHANGING OWN BEHAVIOR (pg. 179)

Questions to ask yourself:

"How can I support this person in taking action?" "How can I support this person in persevering?"

Questions to ask the other person:

"How can you take action" "How do you persevere?"

#1 – PREPARE TO CHANGE BEHAVIOR

#2 – DO IT!

#3 – RE-VISIT THE EMPATHY FIELD

#4 – BEHAVING AROUND THE OTHER PERSON

SUPPORT ANOTHER PERSON IN REQUESTING NEW BEHAVIOR (pg. 171)

#1 – PREPARE TO REACH OUT

– Offer to role-play the interaction with him/her.
– Have him/her create connection by nurturing the relationship first.

– Have him/her explore ways to keep him/herself emotionally un-flooded.

– Ask how he/she will arrange to have the person's attention?

– Encourage him/her to acknowledge his/her reasons reach out.

#2 – STATE THE CURRENT BEHAVIORS

– Have him/her state *all* observed behaviors from the earlier section.

#3 – REQUEST THE NEW BEHAVIORS

– Shape request positively: what he *"wants"* instead of what he *"doesn't want"*
– Express sentiments and appreciation if request is to be considered
– Have him/her find his/her own ways to start the request as an invitation.
– Have him/her shape request through different *sensory systems* (Visual, Auditory, Kinesthetic, Cognitive).
– Encourage him/her to request the specific behavior:

#4 – CHECK IN IF THE REQUEST WAS PROPERLY HEARD

– Ask the other person how he/she received the request? (Offer empathy)

– Repair any verbal harm if it was created: if he/she slipped into criticism, evaluative or aggressive language.

– If needed, clarify the request. Consider finding ways to reword the request?

– Have him/her ask the other person what he/she will do. Support him/her in deciding what he/she will do based on the person's response.

SUPPORT ANOTHER PERSON IN CHANGING HIS/HER OWN BEHAVIOR

(pg. 179)

#1 – PREPARE TO CHANGE BEHAVIOR

– Support the person in positively reinforcing actions by finding tasks that he/she knows he/she can successfully carry out.

____

– Support him/her in building confidence by finding different kinds of support to rely on when attempting to carry action out.

____

#2 – DO IT!

Encourage him/her to simply carry out the action and see what happens. Observe if he/she had any difficulty with it.

____

#3 – RE-VISIT THE EMPATHY FIELD

– Did he/she react and does he/she need to visit the Empathy Field again? If reactions came up, what were his/her new feelings and needs?

____

– When ready, he/she can return to the Resolution Field; what are the new behaviors and strategies? Can he/she carry out the action now?

____

#4 – BEHAVING AROUND THE OTHER PERSON

– Help him/her find ways to *set* boundaries with the other person if that person is being aggressive with him/her.

____

– Repair any behavioral harm that might have been created if he/she displayed abusive behavior.

____

MINDFUL CONNECTION METHOD – QUICK GUIDE

EMPATHY FIELD

CREATE SUPPORTIVE SPACE

Alone

Sit on a bench by myself

With Another Person

Talk to my good friend

EMPATHICALLY CONNECT

Attune to Feelings

Joyous	Non-joyous
Glad, Empowered	Scared, Nervous

Identify Needs

Met	Unmet
Learning, Connection..	Safety, Understanding

RESOLUTION FIELD

EXPLORE POSSIBILITES

Observe Behaviors

One's Own Behavior		Other Person's Behavior	
That is getting needs met	That is getting needs unmet	That is getting needs met	That is getting needs unmet
Attended the class	Exposed myself to his voice	He taught the class	He spoke with a raised voice

Create Strategies

Getting Needs met with this Person		Getting Needs met Elsewhere	
Other person changes behavior	Change behavior oneself	Other person changes behavior	Change behavior oneself
He can reduce his tone of voice	Bring earplugs to class	Ask him to stop teaching the class	Attend a class elsewhere

CARRY OUT STRATEGIES

Request new Behavior

Nurture connection, have the persons attention

State Observations: Feelings, Needs and Behaviors from above

State Request: Ask him to reduce his voice

Person Connects	Person Attacks	Person Ignores
Work it out together	Empathize, Set boundaries	Give space, Try a few times

Change own Behavior

Bring earplugs, Sit further away

MINDFUL CONNECTION METHOD – QUICK GUIDE

EMPATHY FIELD

CREATE SUPPORTIVE SPACE

Alone	With Another Person
Take time away, rest	With Lisa Listens

EMPATHICALLY CONNECT

Attune to Feelings

Joyous	Non-joyous
Encouraged, Confident	Upset, Insecure

Identify Needs

Met	Unmet
Connection, Clarity in Thought	Respect, Confidence

RESOLUTION FIELD

EXPLORE POSSIBILITES

Observe Behaviors

One's Own Behavior: That is getting needs met	One's Own Behavior: That is getting needs unmet	Other Person's Behavior: That is getting needs met	Other Person's Behavior: That is getting needs unmet
He accepted to talk	Has set weak boundaries	She connected about a concern	She requested in front of others

Create Strategies

Getting Needs met with this Person: Other person changes behavior	Getting Needs met with this Person: Change behavior oneself	Getting Needs met Elsewhere: Other person changes behavior	Getting Needs met Elsewhere: Change behavior oneself
Be understanding and respectful	Work on reducing tone of voice	Her attending another class	Teach a class elsewhere

CARRY OUT STRATEGIES

Request new Behavior

Nurture connection, have the persons attention

State Observations: Feelings, Needs and Behaviors from above

State Request: Ask her to be respectful

Person Connects	Person Attacks	Person Ignores
Work it out together	Empathize, Set boundaries	Give space, Try a few times

Change own Behavior

Work on reducing tone of voice

MINDFUL CONNECTION METHOD – QUICK GUIDE

EMPATHY FIELD

CREATE SUPPORTIVE SPACE

Alone	With Another Person

EMPATHICALLY CONNECT

Attune to Feelings		Identify Needs	
Joyous	Non-joyous	Met	Unmet

RESOLUTION FIELD

EXPLORE POSSIBILITES

Observe Behaviors

One's Own Behavior		Other Person's Behavior	
That is getting needs met	That is getting needs unmet	That is getting needs met	That is getting needs unmet

Create Strategies

Getting Needs met with this Person		Getting Needs met Elsewhere	
Other person changes behavior	Change behavior oneself	Other person changes behavior	Change behavior oneself

CARRY OUT STRATEGIES

Request new Behavior

Nurture connection, have the persons attention

State Observations: Feelings, Needs and Behaviors from above

State Request:

Person Connects	Person Attacks	Person Ignores
Work it out together	Empathize, Set boundaries	Give space, Try a few times

Change own Behavior

MINDFUL CONNECTION METHOD – QUICK GUIDE

EMPATHY FIELD

CREATE SUPPORTIVE SPACE

Alone

With Another Person

EMPATHICALLY CONNECT

Attune to Feelings

Joyous

Non-joyous

Identify Needs

Met

Unmet

RESOLUTION FIELD

EXPLORE POSSIBILITES

Observe Behaviors

One's Own Behavior

That is getting needs met

That is getting needs unmet

Other Person's Behavior

That is getting needs met

That is getting needs unmet

Create Strategies

Getting Needs met with this Person

Other person changes behavior

Change behavior oneself

Getting Needs met Elsewhere

Other person changes behavior

Change behavior oneself

CARRY OUT STRATEGIES

Request new Behavior

Nurture connection, have the persons attention

State Observations: Feelings, Needs and Behaviors from above

State Request:

Person Connects	Person Attacks	Person Ignores
Work it out together	Empathize, Set boundaries	Give space, Try a few times

Change own Behavior

APPENDIX

JOYOUS FEELINGS

Attune to joyous feelings in the Empathy Field.
Learn to recognize different feelings by exploring this chart.

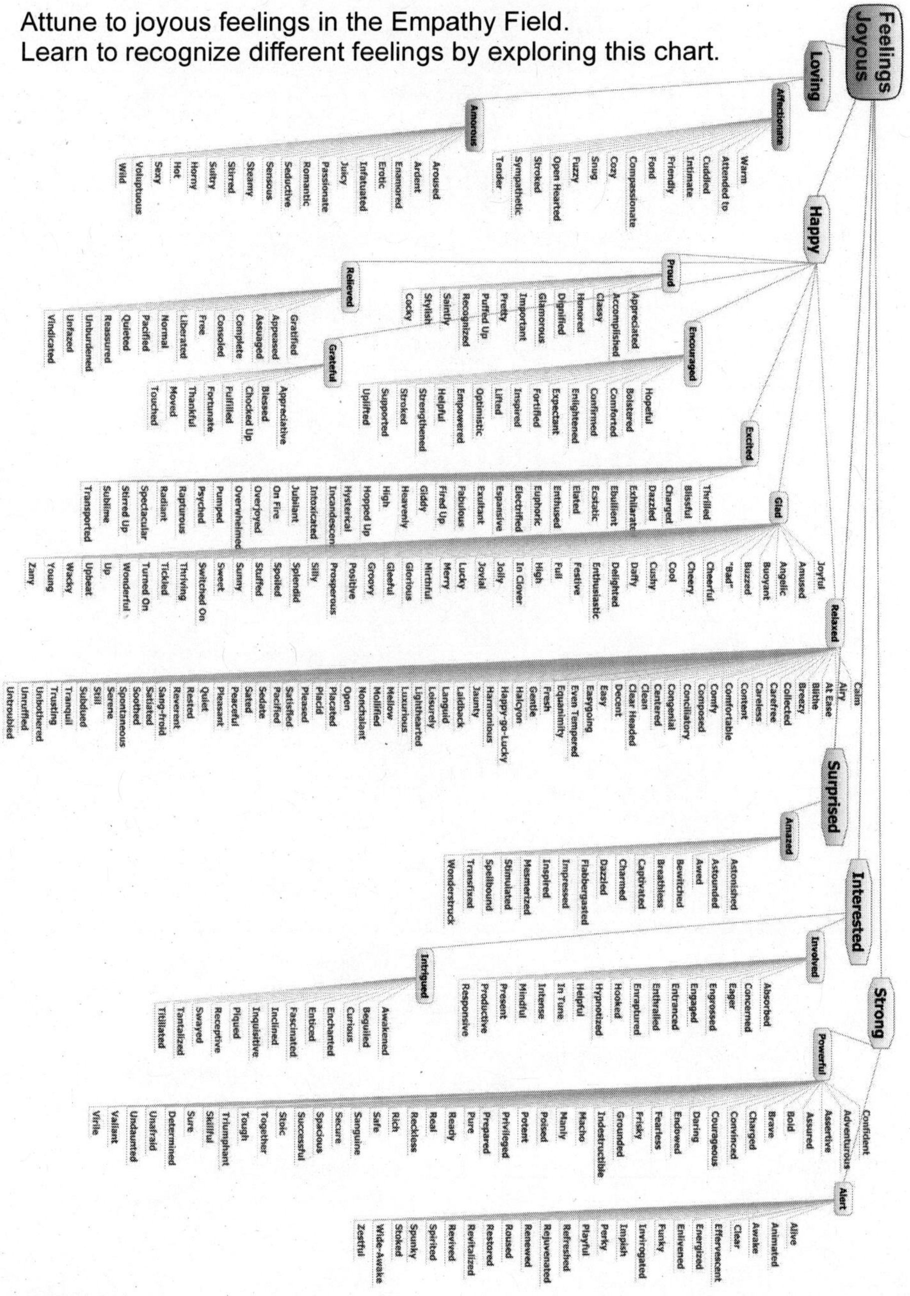

NON-JOYOUS FEELINGS

Attune to non-joyous feelings in the Empathy Field.
Learn to recognize different feelings by exploring this chart.

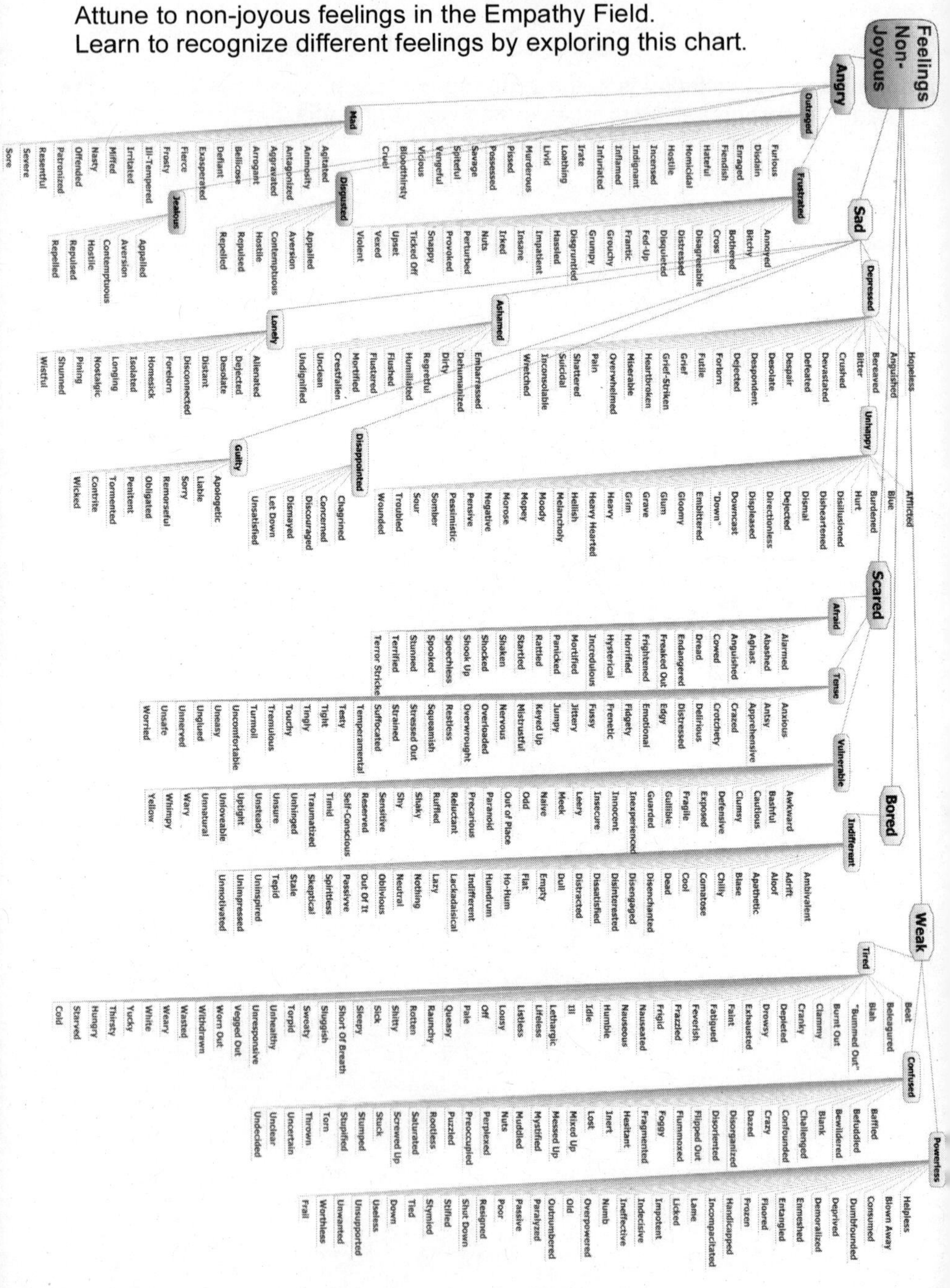

NEEDS

Identify needs in the Empathy Field.
Learn to recognize different needs by exploring this chart.

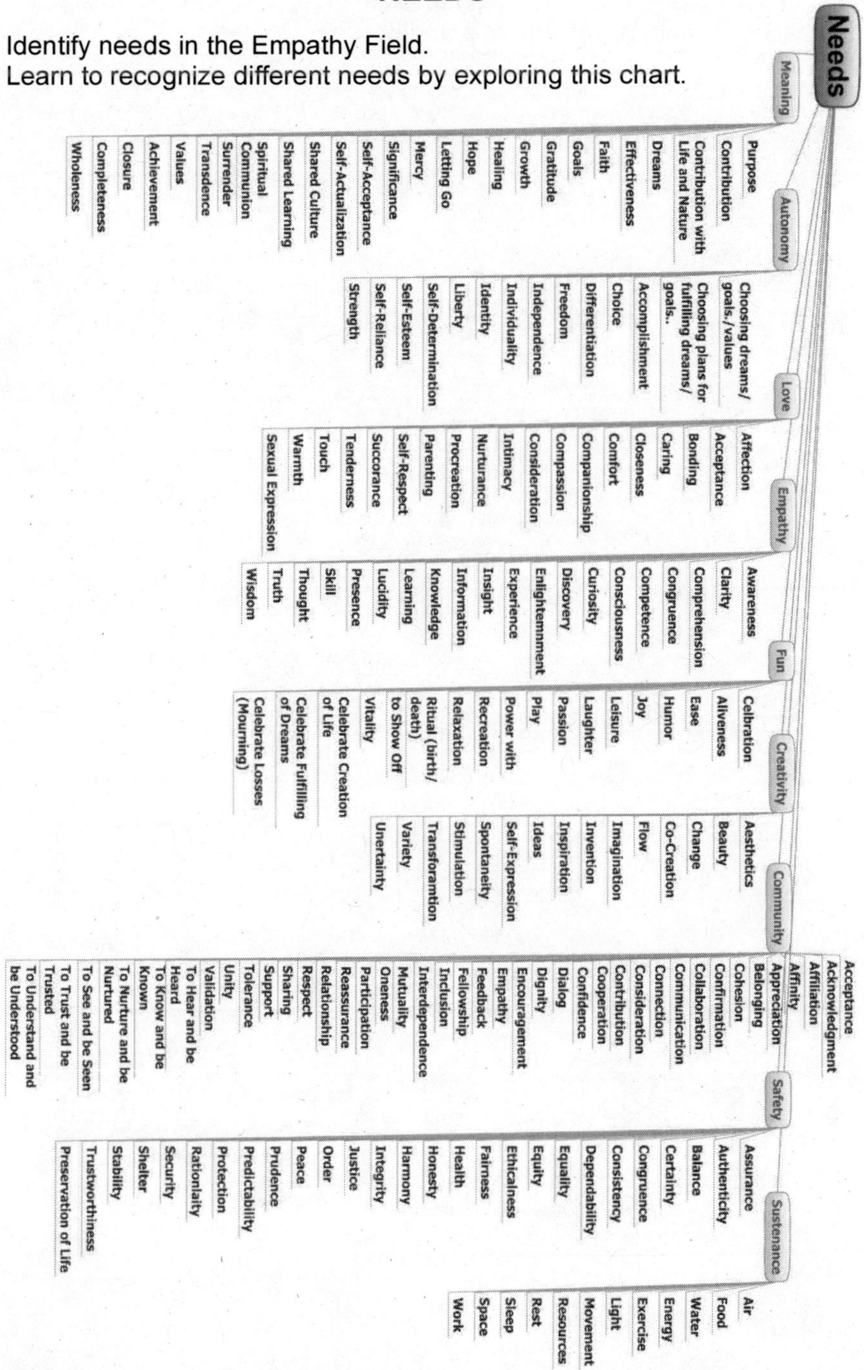

THE FEELINGS AND NEEDS CONNECTION

This chart explores the interconnection between needs and feelings and how they mutual indicate one another.

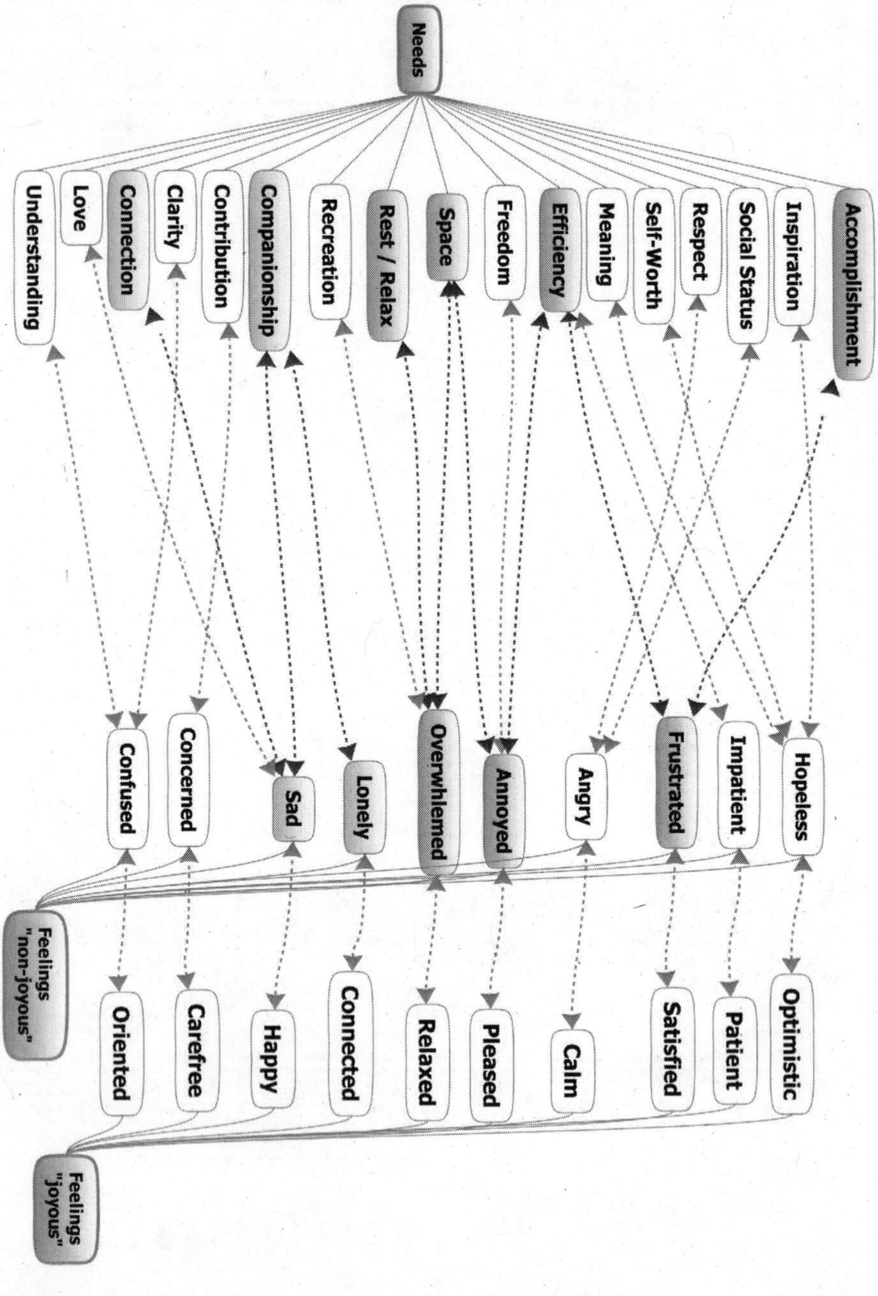

RECOGNIZING EMOTIONS AND MICRO-EXPRESSIONS

Paul Ekman[49] has made a major research contribution in psychology by demonstrating that it is possible to recognize emotions through observing subtle changes in facial expression. He discovered that what is shown on your face *is* what you feel. It's very hard to hide it. You can attune to your feelings by being attentive to your own facial expressions.

You can look for micro-expressions on other people's faces or on your own. Very fast facial movements lasting less than one-fifth of a second can reveal subtle underlying emotions.

Sadness - is one of the longer-lasting emotions
- **eyebrows'** inner corners up
- **upper eyelids** dropped
- **eyes** looking down
- **cheeks** raised as if squinting
- **lip corners** pulled down
- **mouth** dropped open (or closed)

Note: dropped eyelids also occurs in tiredness

Anger
- **eyebrows** pulled down and together (inner corners go down toward nose)
- **eyes** wide open, staring hard.
- **lips** pressed together tightly and tense – physical anger (lips may be open, in a rectangular shape – verbal anger)

Note: on their own, tight lips can reveal controlled anger, also they can be sign of determination; eyebrows also reveal controlled anger

Fear
- **eyebrows** totally raised and pulled together
- **upper eyelids** raised as high as they can go
- **eyes staring** straight ahead
- **lower eyelids** slightly tense!
- **lips** stretched horizontally back toward ears
- **jaw** dropped open

Note: lips on their own can reveal controlled fear; eyes staring on their own can also be rapt attention

Surprise – has many similarities to Fear, lets outline the differences:
- **eyebrows** pretty raised (not as high as in Fear and not pulled together)
- **upper eyelids** raised (not as high as in fear) (this could also be sign of attention or interest)
- **lower eyelids** NOT tense (like in fear)
- **jaw** dropped down

Note – Surprise is VERY short lasting

Contempt - it is only expressed towards people.
- **eyebrows** pulled down
(this is not Anger, since upper eyelids are not raised and the brows are not drawn together!)
- **eyes rolling** is a clear sign of contempt.
- **eyelid** muscles are relaxed rather than tensed
- **nose** wrinkling
- **cheeks** are raised
- **upper lip** is raised
- **one corner of lips** tightened and raised (clear contempt expression!)
- **chin** raised, as if looking down the nose at someone

Disgust - it is usually expressed towards objects/ideas. If expressed toward oneself, it can arouse a feeling of guilt.
- **eyebrows** pulled down
(this is not Anger, since upper eyelids are not raised and the brows are not drawn together!)
- **eyelid** muscles are relaxed rather than tensed
- **cheeks** are raised
- **nostril** wings are raised, with wrinkles on the sides
- **nostrils** wrinkle downward to beyond **lips corners**
(its shape forms an inverted U)
- **upper lip** is raised as high as it will go
- **lower lip** is raised, also, and is protruding slightly

Enjoyment
- **eyebrows** slightly move down
- **eye cover fold** directly below the eyebrows pulled down (impossible to do voluntarily)
- “crow's-feet” **wrinkles**
- **eyes** are narrower
- **cheeks** are higher and their contour changes
- **smile** (present in amusement, contentment, excitement, sensory pleasures, relief, wonderment…)

Any of the above facial movements can appear either on their own in an expression or in combination to convey mixed feelings.

Emotions **embarrassment**, **guilt**, **shame**, and **envy** do not seem to have clear and efficient signals of recognition.

NON-VERBAL BEHAVIOR

Here are some examples on how to observe non-verbal behavior and recognize whether people are "attacking" or "ignoring" your attempt to reach out. This is a universal language that is largely unconscious but easily observable.

- **Bodily behaviors,** such as posture, body movements and gestures.
Attacking: waving hands in the air, imposing body forward.
Ignoring: moving body away, turning head away.

- **Involuntary physiological responses**, such as quickened breathing, blushing, paleness, and pupil dilation.
Attacking: teeth grinding, sweating, shaking.
Ignoring: feeling embarrassed.

- **Space**, a person will choose how close or how far to be from another during a conversation.
Attacking: moving body closer in an aggressive manner.
Ignoring: getting further from the person.

- **Facial expressions,** eyes, lips, eyebrows, cheeks, forehead all convey different emotions (see "Recognizing Emotions and Micro-Expression" section)
Attacking: frowning, tightened lips.
Ignoring: raising eyebrows.

- **Eye behaviors,** such as eye contact, staring, eye movement.
Attacking: "stare down", eyes locked into a stare.
Ignoring: rolling eyes, looking away.

- **Voice-related behaviors,** such as tone of voice, pitch, volume, intensity, inflection, spacing of words, emphases, pauses, silences, and fluency.
Attacking: shouting
Ignoring: silence, lack of responsiveness.

ACKNOWLEDGMENTS

The journey of writing the *Mindful Connection Method* had its many ups and downs and my own community played the biggest role in bridging these un-inspiring and difficult times and transformed them into joy.

Foremost, I would like to thank my family:

My Mother, who has always offered me unconditional love and helped me shape my values and the basis of who I am; my Father, who has always believed in me and been there; my Grandmother, who played an immeasurable role in my rearing and who I hold dearly in my heart; my brother Vlad from whom I've learnt how great it is to have an older brother who was caring throughout many years of growing up and still is; and my brother Nikola whose presence is timeless and reminds me every day how special it is to have you as a brother.

Volim vas!

I would like to thank Owen Thomas for the biggest contribution you offered in the shaping of this book and its ideas; it is a result of many years of exploration and our close and sincere friendship and it would have never come together without you. Geoff Hill, many thanks for being an adventurous and trusting friend throughout the years and supporting me in persevering. Thank you Tara Newstead for your unconditional love and support and for being there during the process of writing the book. Annabelle D'Artois, you opened my life in many new ways that contributed to the ease of flow of all the new ideas in my writing. John Bews, thanks for being a great listener and a great friend. Paz Bascuñan, thank you for your everlasting inspiration. Pepe Danza, it is an honor and a pleasure to have you as a best friend and support in my life. Thank you Barb Roberts for your care and insights. Big thanks to Robyn Ross for your friendship. Michael Fraser, thanks for your energy and spontaneity. Besides having editing support from some of the people listed above, Samantha Gray did a tremendous job in the process of editing and transforming this book.

Thank you!

I Love you all!

Life brought my way so many other people and different forms of contribution that is hard to be able to list them all on one page. I would like to acknowledge and thank everyone who has been part of my journey up until now. And of course I would like to thank Life and Love for its mysteriousness and wonder, the journey we are all part of together.

ABOUT THE AUTHOR

Ivan Tucakov was born in former Yugoslavia. He spent his early childhood in southern Turkey and moved back to his hometown where he spent his teenage years. After moving to Canada he graduated an honors degree in computers and physics science at the University of British Columbia in Vancouver.

His journey then took him in the direction of composing music and managing a world fusion band called Tambura Rasa. These years also offered grounds to explore way of working with people, connect through language and music and learn various ways of communicating to create nurturing relationships with the communities around him.

Ivan Tucakov is a contemporary author that advocates a life of fulfillment, wellbeing and nurturing, loving connections. The *Mindful Connection Method* is a collective outcome of the endeavors throughout his life as a scientist, musician, artist and writer.

For upcoming events and publications, please visit his website:

www.MindfulConnectionMethod.com

REFERENCES

[1] Ken Robinson (2006) *Says schools kill creativity at TED Conference.* Retrieved from http://www.ted.com/talks/lang/eng/ken_robinson_says_schools_kill_creativit y.html

[2] Dalai Lama XIV (2001) *Ancient Wisdom, Modern World: Ethics for the New Millennium.* (1st ed.). Abacus.

[3] Marshall B. Rosenberg (2008) – *Nonviolent communication: a language of life.* (2nd ed.). A PuddleDancer Press (CA).

[4] Frans de Waal (2009) The Age of Empathy. (1st ed.). Harmony Books (NY).

[5] Daniel J. Siegel (2007) *The Mindful Brain.* (1st ed.). WW Norton.

[6] Premack, D. G. & Woodruff, G. (1978). *Does the chimpanzee have a theory of mind?* Behavioral and Brain Sciences (1st ed.).

[7] Marshall B. Rosenberg (2008) – *Nonviolent communication: a language of life.* (2nd ed.). A PuddleDancer Press (CA).

[8] Sandra Aamodt and Sam Wang (2008) *Wslcome to your Brain.* (1st ed.). Bloomsbury (NY)

[9] Carol Tavris & Elliot Aronson (2008) *Mistakes Were Made (But Not by Me): Why We Justify Foolish Beliefs, Bad Decisions, and Hurtful Acts.* Harcourt (FL).

[10] Dalai Lama XIV (2001) *Ancient Wisdom, Modern World: Ethics for the New Millennium.* (1st ed.). Abacus.

[11] Marshall B. Rosenberg (2008) – *Nonviolent communication: a language of life* (2nd ed.). A PuddleDancer Press (CA).

[12] Dr. Gordon Neufeld Relationship Matters DVD - a 2 hour presentation. [DVD] Neufled Institute (BC).

[13] George Lakoff (2006) *Thinking Points: Communicating Our American Values and Vision.* (1st ed.). Farrar, Straus and Giroux (NY).

[14] Daniel Kahneman (2010) The riddle of experience vs. memory at TED Conference. Retrieved from http://www.ted.com/talks/daniel_kahneman_the_riddl e_of_experience_vs_memory.html

[15] Robert Bolton (1986) People Skills: *How to Assert Yourself, Listen to Others, and Resolve Conflicts.* (1st ed.). Touchstone.

[16] Maggie Hyde and Michael McGuinness (1992) *Jung for Begninners*, (1st ed.) Icon Books Ltd. (GB)

[17] Erich Fromm (1962) *The Art of Loving.* (1st ed.) Harper & Row (NY).

[18] Antonio R. Damasio (1994) *Descartes' Error: Emotion, Reason, and the Human Brain,* Putnam Publishing.

[19] Daniel J. Siegel (2007) *The Mindful Brain.* (1st ed.). WW Norton.

[20] Michael Shermer (2004) *The Science of Good and Evil: Why People Cheat, Share, Gossip, and Follow the Golden Rule.* (1st. ed.). Owl.

[21] Malcolm Gladwell (2005) Blink: The Power of Thinking Without Thinking. (1st ed.). Back Bay Books, Little, Brown.

[22] John Medina (2009) *Brain Rules: 12 Principles for Surviving and Thriving at Work, Home, and School.* (1st ed.). Pear Press (WA).

[23] John Medina (2009) *Brain Rules: 12 Principles for Surviving and Thriving at Work, Home, and School.* (1st ed.). Pear Press (WA).

[24] Daniel J. Siegel (2007) *The Mindful Brain.* (1st ed.). WW Norton.

[25] Antonio R. Damasio (1999) *The Feeling of What Happens: Body, Emotions, and the making of Consciousness.* New York (NY).

[26] Gordon Neufeld and Gabor Mate (2005) *Hold on to your Kids: Why Parents need to matter more than Peers (1st. ed.). Vintage Canada*

[27] John Gottman Ph.D. (2002) *The Relationship Cure: A 5 Step Guide to Strengthening Your Marriage, Family, and Friendships.* (1st ed.). Three Rivers Press.

[28] Sandra Aamodt and Sam Wang (2008) *Wslcome to your Brain.* (1st ed.). Bloomsbury (NY)

[29] Marshall B. Rosenberg (2008) – *Nonviolent communication: a language of life.* (2nd ed.). A PuddleDancer Press (CA).

[30] Daniel J. Siegel (2007) *The Mindful Brain.* (1st ed.). WW Norton.

[31] Tara-Bennett Goleman (2002) *"Emotional Alchemy: How the Mind Can Heal the Heart*, (Reprint ed.). Three Rivers Press.

[32] Dr. Gordon Neufeld Relationship Matters DVD - a 2 hour presentation. [DVD] Neufled Institute (BC).

[33] Marshall B. Rosenberg (2008) – *Nonviolent communication: a language of life.* (2nd ed.). A PuddleDancer Press (CA).

[34] Malcolm Gladwell (2005) Blink: The Power of Thinking Without Thinking. (1st ed.). Back Bay Books, Little, Brown.

[35] Marshall B. Rosenberg (2008) – *Nonviolent communication: a language of life.* (2nd ed.). A PuddleDancer Press (CA).

[36] Okiishi et al. (2006) *Clinical Psychology: Science and Practice.* Society of Clinical Psychology.

[37] Dale Carnegie (1981) *How to Win Friends & Influence People* (Rev. ed.). Pocket Books (NY).

[38] Carlos Castaneda (1991) *Fire from Within* (1st ed.). Washington Square Press.

[39] Karen Pryor (1999) *Don't Shoot The Dog: The New Art of Teaching and Training.* (1st ed.). Bantam.

[40] A.S. Neill (1960) *Summerhill: a Radical Approach to Child Rearing.* Hart Publishing (NY).

[41] Dan Pink (2009) *Autonomy, Mastery, Purpose: The Foundations of Motivating Software Teams Speech at TED Conference.* (Retrieved from http://www.ted.com/talks/lang/eng/dan_pink_on_motivation.html).

[42] Don Miguel Ruiz (1997) *Four Agreements: A Practical Guide to Personal Freedom.* (1st ed.). Amber Allen Publishing (CA).

[43] Carol Tavris & Elliot Aronson (2008) *Mistakes Were Made (But Not by Me): Why We Justify Foolish Beliefs, Bad Decisions, and Hurtful Acts.* Harcourt (FL).

[44] Malcolm Gladwell (2008) Outliers: *The Story of Success.* (1st ed.). Little, Brown and Company.

[45] John Gottman Ph.D. (2002) *The Relationship Cure: A 5 Step Guide to Strengthening Your Marriage, Family, and Friendships.* (1st ed.). Three Rivers Press.

[46] Marshall B. Rosenberg (2008) – *Nonviolent communication: a language of life.* (2nd ed.). A PuddleDancer Press (CA).

[47] Dr. Gordon Neufeld Relationship Matters DVD - a 2 hour presentation. [DVD] Neufled Institute (BC).

[48] Dr. Gordon Neufeld Relationship Matters DVD - a 2 hour presentation. [DVD] Neufled Institute (BC).

[49] Paul Ekman (2007) *Emotions Revealed: Recognizing Faces and Feelings to Improve Communication.* (1st ed.). Owl.